The Munros

Stephen P. Smith

A walking diary following the Scottish Mountaineering
Club's list of mountains exceeding 3000 feet.

First Published 2020
SP Publishing

ISBN: 979-8-6508560-8-5

Front cover: Ben Lawers © Stephen P. Smith

By Stephen P. Smith

Fiction

The Unsound Convictions of Judge Stephen Mentall
The Veteran and The Boy

Computer Science

Thinking About Computer Programming?

Biography

The Charlie Chaplin Walk

Autobiography

The Munros

Preface - Why I did the Munros

During childhood my relationship with sporting activities was coloured by severe asthma and the humiliation it brought on the school playing fields. This was back in the 1970s when I was one of a very few diagnosed asthmatics. The condition wasn't properly understood and I was exposed to triggers such as cigarette smoke and dogs. The medical profession prescribed tablets to take during an attack, which induced immediate vomiting. At other times I was placed in a steam-filled room to try and drive my asthma out. Both approaches simply caused more breathing problems.

By the late 1980s I had graduated, had a good job and – with my asthma now under better control – was looking around for a sport I could do. So, being interested in hillwalking I spent one lunchtime sat at my desk, studying OS maps of Scotland. A colleague began to take an interest and asked me if I was off to climb Munros. I had to admit I didn't know what a Munro was. He told me they were Scottish peaks over 3000 feet and there were 277 of them in all. For some reason, about which I have never been able to fully explain, I knew instantly I was going to do them all.

That is how my road to conquering my childhood demons began. Twelve years, 1700 miles of walking, 570,000 feet of ascent later – soaked, blown over, frozen, lost and scared more times than I care to remember – I finished and became Munroist number 2599. I am sure the previous 2598 souls who broke the trail before me have just as interesting stories. But this is my account of all those wonderful views, challenges and interesting people I met along the way.

1990

The radio crackled into life, "Helicopter on its way for an uplift." Andy Glover and I glanced at each other, our expressions both saying, 'Well, we've done it now'. We looked back up the mountain, into the swirling mist. Nothing. Just the silence of the lower slopes of Carn Mor Dearg – my first Munro. Somewhere up there, maybe still around 4000 feet where the accident had happened, was the rest of our party, including Andy's brother, Ady, with a deep cut to his head.

"Cheap coat, cheap rucksack, expensive boots and they don't fit," I muttered to myself.

It was early morning, I had no idea of how the day was about to unfold and I was disillusioned. This was my first determined crack at a Munro and I was struggling. Struggling beyond what I'd ever imagined. The pull up the main Ben Nevis path was far harder than I'd envisaged, the pain in the front of my upper legs was fighting my body's wish to immobilise itself. My calf muscles ached and the blood was thumping against my skull. And I was at the back. At the back again, just like when I was at school – the last time I did any regular, fitness contributing, exercise.

Through the thick mist, with the wind flapping my hood in my face, I could just make out the others. The rest of the party were fitter and all had at least one Munro under their belts – conquered on a holiday the previous year to Loch Mullardoch in Glen Cannich. I had failed due to my asthma. Today I was determined; whatever the pain, I wanted a Munro.

At the junction in the path, which can either take one on to Ben Nevis or round past Lochain Meall an t-Suidhe, the others were waiting for me. A fellow walker, descending, passed us.

"What's it like up there?" I asked.

"Very windy, didn't make it to the top." And with that he was gone.

I studied the map. "We could go past this small loch and try and do Carn Mor Dearg instead."

I really wanted a Munro today.

I half expected the others to pooh-pooh the idea but it got nods of agreement.

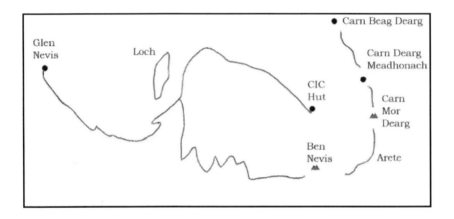

The walk past the loch gave me some relief, lochs by nature being flat. A drop down into the glen preceded the real climb and my introduction to Munro bagging: no paths and just under 2000 feet of ascent in about a mile.

The climb was painful; my upper legs ached with each step and I needed to pause every few paces to catch my breath. At the age of twenty-four – such were the restrictions in my windpipe – my air intake was that of a seventy-year-old man. My toes and heels were sore and I was feeling damp. Every time I sought sustenance from food, I wrestled with my rucksack. Financial worries had turned me to the cheap end of the outdoor equipment market and I was now paying for it: a jacket made of thin material, not up to the ravages of the Scottish weather, and a rucksack best undone in laboratory conditions. But then there were the new boots, purchased two days ago and at the top end of the market. But I'd gone for one size too small and my feet were in a fair mood for rubbing in the mistake.

The others waited for me before the final pull to the minor top of Carn Beag Dearg, apart from David George, noted for never conforming, who was so far out in front we had to use whistles to rendezvous with him. Then we hit winter, late for May the 7th.

The wind whipped snow up into our faces. I felt miserable, cold and annoyed that I still couldn't keep up. Taking up the rear I used the footprints left in the snow by the others to reassure myself I was on track. Over the summit of Carn Dearg Meadhonach we continued along the bleak snow-swept ridge where, in appalling visibility, we reached the Munro summit of Carn Mor Dearg. The celebration was no more than a miserable photograph in a blizzard.

Carn Mor Dearg and Ben Nevis

From the summit three alternative routes beckoned and there was duly a three-way split in opinion. I wanted to go back the way we came, Andy and Ady Glover wanted to go on to do Ben Nevis, the others wanted to take the route to the CIC hut in the glen below. We compromised on the option of the CIC hut; going on to do Ben Nevis, even with my dogged determination, didn't look viable.

The drop from the top of Carn Mor Dearg towards the CIC hut was very steep and we had to negotiate rough and rocky terrain intermixed with snow and boulder fields. We found a good stretch of snow and had fun sliding on it. Ady took this a stage beyond caution and went for a deliberate bum slide. My memory is of him hurtling past me, in the half-light of the blowing snow, just to hear a loud crash a few seconds later. He landed standing upright between two large boulders, blood pouring from a head wound. At first it looked very bad but, upon reaching him, we were offered some degree of relief as it appeared all his limbs were okay and it was just his head to worry about, in more than one sense.

While Ady was tended to by the others, Andy and I took a straight line off the mountain to the CIC mountain rescue hut where a wind powered radio put us in touch with the police in Fort William. After they sent a patrol car out, to get a better signal, we managed to convince them it was a head and not a hand injury.

The fear of the RAF helicopter crew landing and wanting us to take them to the accident site was now daunting. Could we navigate our way back up? Was I strong enough to re-ascend? I felt drained, weak and exhausted. The rush off the mountains to make the call to the rescue services caught up with me. I slumped down with my back to the hut and gazed back up the mountain.

"Voices," said Andy.

"Are you sure?" I replied, looking up.

"Yep, they're coming off."

A few minutes later the voices became dim figures emerging from the cloud line to the open glen. Ady was moving under his own steam with dried blood caked about his head. Andy and I were relieved we didn't have to deal with the helicopter crew ourselves. After an exchange of stories we all sat and, after a tense wait, we made out the distant buzzing of a helicopter. A minute or so later it appeared as a distant pinprick through the mist. Gradually its shape grew bigger and did justice to the mechanical noise that preceded it.

The helicopter did a circuit over us and dropped a flare on the only suitable landing spot, just across a stream from the hut. On the second time round the pilot skilfully lowered his machine amongst the rocks while Ady was guided to it. With the rotor still spinning, poised for a quick getaway before the mist closed in, a crew member leapt out and examined Ady, gave us the thumbs up and helped him aboard. Seconds later the craft was airborne, disappearing back into the mist. We were left in silence, the drama over – returned to nature with a three-hour energy sapping walk ahead of us.

Taxi for Glover

The long walk back gave me plenty of time to think. I had set myself a personal challenge of doing the Munros before even setting one foot on them. But now – with Ady injured, the poor summit weather and experience of the sheer physical effort required to climb a Munro – I was reviewing my ambition.

Since graduating I'd tried a mixture of sports: squash, badminton and running. I really wanted to find a sport I could do on my own terms, but my asthma continued to frustrate. I had hoped doing the Munros might be it, but it felt as if asthma would, once again, take the upper hand. Now I was downcast.

Back in Glen Nevis the police met us next to our minibus. I sensed the sage-like glances of an older policeman, probably mirroring the other's annoyance, of having to deal with a bunch of youngsters who had overstretched themselves. He viewed our kit; it looked passable to his eyes. Perhaps not my jacket, but my boots spared me criticism. If only he knew they were too small and both my big toe nails were poised to come away. I sensed he wanted to give us a ticking off but we were reasonably, if not perfectly, kitted out. And we knew exactly where we'd been when the accident had taken place despite Ady incorrectly telling them, "It happened somewhere on the Ben Nevis Arete."

The policeman was quoted as saying, "I wouldn't walk down the high street in those Doc Martens he had on."

Munro Count: 1

"Shall we zigzag?" I asked.

Andy looked back at me, quizzically.

"All the best paths zigzag up mountains," I responded. We were well beyond territory a path would care to grace.

"Okay."

We turned sharp right and traversed for about a hundred yards, rising gently before doubling back to a point thirty feet above our conversation.

"Is that better?" he asked.

I nodded, but paused for breath and to allow the tops of my legs to catch up with the pain.

We were on the last stretch of our approach to An Socach, about six hours into the day and with 2000 feet of remaining ascent over a slope averaging a one in seven gradient.

I was glad to be walking with Andy, fitter and stronger than me but more than willing to travel at my pace. With me, Andy, Ady and David staying in a cottage in Kyle of Lochalsh, we had drawn lots for this walk: two of us would walk from Killilan through to the dam near Benula Lodge on Loch Mullardoch while the other two would drive the car round to the dam and do it in reverse. The hope was that we would meet somewhere in the middle of the twenty-one mile route that takes in four Munros. I had drawn Andy and to start from Killilan.

My legs were killing me, blood was thumping round my head and again I was wondering, 'Why am I doing this?' With not even one Munro of the four done I was struggling well beyond the bounds of a hobby.

Slowly we made progress and reached the summit in just under nine hours. There was then a demoralising drop followed by the painful ascent of An Riabhachan. Summiting shortly before

19:00 it was already very late in the day; we were barely half way to the dam at the head of Loch Mullardoch.

"We could drop down to the shore of the loch," I suggested.

Andy's reply was slow in coming; it meant missing the last two Munros. "Do you think the other two are too much for you, Steve?"

I nodded.

"Okay," he replied. I cringed at the disappointment in his voice but knew he'd accept it in his usual gentlemanly manner.

A few moments later we were off, cutting down to the shores of Loch Mullardoch to a cottage only accessible on foot or by motorboat.

"Looks like the cottage is inhabited," I said.

"Yep," replied Andy, nodding.

"We could ask if they'd give us a lift up the loch," I replied.

"Do you think they would?"

"We could offer to pay," I suggested.

"What time does it get dark?"

"It's July the tenth today?"

Andy nodded. "Just past midsummer's, quite late then."

We both paused.

"I'll pay if you ask," I offered hopefully.

"I haven't got the bottle," said Andy.

"Nor me, that's why I'm offering to pay."

Shyness got the better of us and instead we opted for the tough five mile walk along the vague path of the shore.

The route was very wearing with no real opportunity to pick up a brisk even pace. We tried walking hard for a few minutes at a time but were quickly thwarted by undulating terrain, pain in our legs and difficult tributaries to negotiate.

I played games in my head of trying to judge the remaining distance against our pace and came up with estimated times of arrival between 23:00 and 02:00.

For the last two hours I was able to flash my pathetic torch and get a response from Ady and David flashing the headlights on the car, confirming our suspicions they hadn't done the walk in the opposite direction.

I felt the walk would never end and knew I'd overdone it. With darkness also came exhaustion. I tried to put it from my mind by concentrating on placing one foot in front of the other but the necessity of frequent rests gave me too much opportunity to dwell on our situation.

I cursed myself for the stupidity of taking on this walk; this had been my big idea, too ambitious. I had fallen into this trap before. For example I couldn't keep the final year project on my degree simple and instead designed and built something that took every spare moment I had for six months. Before that, when I was sixteen, I scraped all the money I had together and bought a new bicycle. The next day I took it for a 150 mile test ride. Setting off at 06:30 and arriving home after 22:00 – barely able to pedal and so exhausted I couldn't speak – I just managed to point out on the map where I'd been to my shocked mother as she prepared me soup. Soup I could only just manage to pass through my lips before a night of hallucinations and a racing heart.

I was overcome with a sense of relief when the dark shape of the dam at the head of the loch became more focussed, our haven where David and Ady waited for us in the car.

Within a quarter of a mile of the end I had to lay down in the heather with exhaustion.

Andy stood over me and spoke, "You need to get up, Steve, keep going."

"I can't," I replied, "I feel so weak."

"We are nearly there."

"My heart's racing, go and tell the others."

Andy peered down at me through the half-light, "Okay, try and rest. I'll go and tell the others."

Lying alone, half-drunk with tiredness, with the heather scratching the back of my neck, I realised how much I'd overdone it. I tried to move my legs but they were just dead appendages. My heart was working in overdrive and I was unable to regulate my breathing. I just laid back, accepting I was now reliant on David and Ady finding me. A dreamy twenty minutes passed with hallucinations flirting with lucidity. Slowly my strength started to return and I came to my senses and managed to struggle to the car. I fell in through one of the back doors and found Andy half asleep. David and Ady soon appeared from their aborted attempt to find me. They must have passed within a few yards of me, calling out and I never heard them.

On the trip back to our holiday cottage, in Kyle of Lochalsh, we got stopped by the police. It was very late and some IRA prisoners had just escaped from Brixton Prison and this was a recognised route for them to escape back to Ireland.

Back at the cottage, and after an early hour feast, I slept until 11:45 the following morning.

Years later Ady told me they had waited for about five hours for us at the dam and, with only one cassette tape, they now knew the words to all the Abba tracks by heart.

We felt we wasted much of the holiday with no further Munros to add to an earlier failed attempt at the Five Sisters of Kintail.

We only made it over to Skye, the classic destination from Kyle of Lochalsh, on the last day of the holiday. We also crashed the hired Ford Sierra twice: the first was where David reversed into a picnic table (causing about £1000 of damage to the car and about £5 worth of damage to the picnic table), and the second was where

Ady did a time trial from Cannich to Loch Mullardoch and – while passing over a wet wooden bridge with me saying, "The wood will be wet Ady" – slammed the brakes on as hard as he could. This caused us to slide all over the place, hitting the side runners of the bridge, denting the wheel and losing its trim.

Going Solo

During 1991 my company based me in Glasgow to continue working on a computerised 999 call-taking project for Strathclyde Police. The proximity to the Highlands added nine new Munros to my list. This may sound like a good start, given I achieved none on my first attempt in 1989 and only one in 1990, but I always felt I could have made more of an effort.

The project infiltrated my life and at a very young age I took on the massive technical responsibility of delivering a 1.5 million pound bespoke computer system. The project was late, became very political and those of us working in Glasgow came under a lot of pressure – I was regularly doing in excess of eighty hours a week. However, the strife and the common cause bonded us with the customer to make the project a success.

I made friends with one of the police officers on the project, Willy Newlands. Willy soon discovered I was an apprentice Munro bagger and, on the May bank holiday, took me up the popular Ben Lomond, the most southerly of the Munros.

After the Kyle of Lochalsh holiday, I increased my Munro tally by six. For the first of these I thought I'd be brave and on Saturday August the 10th I took the train from Glasgow Queen Street to Tyndrum Lower arriving in time to start walking at 11:00. I almost didn't make it because the guard failed to call the stop and my carriage wasn't lined up with the platform. By pure chance I happened to glance out of the window and caught sight of the tail end of the platform. Leaping to my feet I made a mad dash to alight before the train set off again.

On the platform I had my usual panic of making sure I'd collected everything together and nothing was left on the train. The sudden rush of adrenalin did nothing for my mental state of venturing onto the cloud-covered hills, alone.

I found the going tough but was thankful I could rest whenever the notion took my fancy. I was soon into the cloud and the rain. With my map case letting in water and my gloves becoming a squelching mass, I made progress.

After the worry of solo navigating, with the continual unease of leaving the security of the railway station behind, I reached the summit of Beinn Dubhchraig, the first Munro of the day, at 15:00. I then set off for Ben Oss and reached its summit in a further hour. At this point a crowd of walkers turned up and one called out, "Here's another one." I wondered just how many they were doing – my pride in having just soloed two was relegated to mere inner satisfaction.

It had rained all day and by this time I was very wet. The poor visibility also made things miserable. I cut down via Coire Buidhe and was relieved when Tyndrum came into view through the heaviness of the mist and rain.

The Little Chef restaurant in Tyndrum, a beacon for the holidaymaker motoring north, proved to be my sanctuary. I ordered myself a massive feast, a reward for my efforts, and once devoured I spent a long time in the loos drying myself off with the hand dryer. I then sat at a table hoping the staff would let me stay, out of the rain. Fortunately I was left in peace and when it was time to leave I ventured back to the station and waited for the welcome sight of the train.

Working at the Police Headquarters in Glasgow meant we were in frequent meetings and informal discussions with the police. Willy Newlands often stopped by my desk for a technical discussion about an issue or a brief social chat. He also brought up the subject of further Munros. That evening, sat in my hotel room, I studied the only map I had with me – the one with Ben Dubhchraig and Ben Oss on it. The next morning Willy dropped by my desk again and broached the subject of a further Munro-bagging expedition during a weekend. I was keen and we talked about which Munros to do. He mentioned a few names and I knowledgeably chipped in a few for good measure. After a while Willy tipped his head back and roared with laughter as he said, "Steve, we can't be just doing the Munros on your map." He should have been a detective.

On Sunday August the 25th Willy picked up me and Mike Linnett, a contractor working on the project, to do Ben More and Stob Binnein. I perched in the back of Willy's Ford Fiesta and soon found my nose running and my breathing tightening. I then noticed dog hairs. "Willy, do you ever have dogs in the back of your car?" I asked.

"Aye," he replied, glancing at me in the rear view mirror.

Mike and I swapped seats and I was able to travel in more comfort with the window slightly down.

The two Munros of the day were near to the village of Crianlarich and we parked in a lay-by at the foot of Ben More, setting off walking at 10:15. I found the climb tough going, with Mike and Willy frequently way ahead. They would wait for me but as soon as I caught up they took it as an immediate cue to move on. After a few occurrences of this I asked them to wait so I could catch my breath. They did, but the slightest twitch from me and they were off again.

This evoked painful memories of childhood cycle rides when the exact same thing happened.

We reached the peak of Ben More in less than three hours and went on to claim Stob Binnein in just under an hour. There were reasonable views on the way up but both summits became covered in cloud between the arrival of Mike and Willy, then, me some twenty minutes later, my breathing problems denying me a view from the tops.

By now I was thoroughly demoralised trailing behind Mike and Willy. I decided there were definite advantages to solo walking: finding my own pace, not worrying about dropping back behind other people, being able to rest and savour the view when it was there.

Finally for the year, Sunday September the 22nd, me, Willy, Mike and a chap nicknamed Snigger tackled An Caisteal and Beinn a'Chroin from the road south of Crianlarich. We set off on the six-hour round trip in good weather, which held until I approached the first summit. With the others already waiting for me, cloud descended as wind and rain whipped in. This led me to get a reputation for attracting bad weather.

I commented at the top of Beinn a'Chroin I had now done ten Munros and only had 267 to go. A fellow walker then *kindly* told me a Corbett (peaks between 2500 and 3000 feet) had just been reclassified as a Munro so I still had 268 to go! I realised at this stage the sheer enormity of the task that lay before me; I had elected to participate in a somewhat gruelling hobby.

Subsequently the information supplied by the walker, about the promoted Munro, proved incorrect and, for the time being, the total Munros still stood at 277.

Munro Count: 10

1992

A Winter's Walk

In 1992 I bagged fifteen more Munros in three separate trips. Although this more than doubled my total to date, in real terms it was still only scratching the surface.

The first was Ben Wyvis, the only Munro I walked in the winter equinox – in Scottish mountaineering the term 'winter' is more often lent to describe the conditions rather than the time of year. Starting at 10:00 I made steady progress, a change in medication making things a bit easier. Just over two and a half hours later I was walking the very windy summit ridge.

In May I caught the train to Glasgow, hired a car and drove on up to Drumnadrochit to stay in a holiday cottage I'd taken for a week. The cottage was a bit too modern for my taste but comfortable nonetheless.

On Sunday May the 24th I took in Toll Creagach and Tom a'Choinich, starting from Glen Affric at 10:45. I found the going very tough and, on the approach to the first Munro, Toll Creagach, I became disorientated and unsure of the route ahead. I really wanted to press on but it was fast becoming a reality that I might need to abandon all the hard climbing done so far, and return to the car.

In exasperation I pleaded to the god I have never believed in to clear the clouds so I could see the peak. My prayers were answered and the cloud blew off the summit for no more than fifteen seconds – enough time to get a fix and proceed. I imagined a committee of white-haired old men in the sky raising their eyebrows at my request and passing on a message to the weather god, "Let him have fifteen seconds then close up again, the rest is down to him."

During those few seconds, when the clouds swept down off the mountains and performed a striptease with the sky, I thought how easy it would have been for people in ancient times to believe the mountains were mystical and produced the weather – which, of course, in a sense they do. The Inca tribes of Peru believed in mountain gods who had to be pacified into providing good weather, going as far as making child sacrifices in pacification. It's very easy to scorn this behaviour but putting myself in their shoes, with the limited scientific knowledge available to them, it would be very easy to think a storm raging down off a mountain was because the mountain gods were angry with you.

I reached the top of Toll Creagach in just over three hours whereupon the weather cleared (evidently I was in favour with the weather gods) to reveal fantastic views down to one of my favourite places, Loch Mullardoch. I then took an hour and a half to walk to Tom a'Choinich, completing the Munros I'd abandoned on a walk in 1989, before the descent back to the car to complete the seven-hour round trip.

The following day I was due to meet Willy Newlands but I was unable to get through to confirm the arrangements. I travelled down to the tentative meeting place but he did not arrive. Therefore I was in Glen Coe and decided to do the two peaks of Beinn a'Bheithir: Sgorr Dhearg and Sgorr Dhonuill.

I started in perfect weather at 11:30 from South Ballachulish and, after missing my way and ending up on a very scary steep bit, reached the first Munro in just under four hours. Although the weather was perfect, with fantastic views, I was struggling with my fitness and debated going on for the second summit. I decided to give it a go and reached it an hour and a half hour later. A thunderstorm then closed in with forks of lightning dancing off the peaks about me. When I decided it was getting a bit too close for comfort I headed down. It was a fantastic sight and one that will live with me forever. The power and beauty of nature had combined to give a magnificent spectacle.

Beinn a'Bheithir: Sgorr Dhearg and Sgorr Dhonuill

Next – deciding my Munro tally was a bit low – I contrived to make the numbers more respectable by taking in the Glen Shiel ridge with its seven Munros that can be bagged in a day. So at 08:10 on May the 28th I set out from the Cluanie Inn on the A87 and reached the first Munro of Creag a'Mhaim at 11:05. Then Druim Shionnach at 11:55, Aonach Air Chrith at 12:52, Maol Chinn-dearg at 14:19, Sgurr an Doire Leathain at 15:25, Sgurr an Lochain at 16:10 and Creag nan Damh at 17:55.

By the fourth Munro, Maol Chinn-dearg, I began to sense that something was wrong with one of my knees. Considering the situation and being at the point of no return – the easiest way off being to complete the ridge – I continued. By the fifth Munro the mild ache had turned to a pain which I controlled, to some degree, by binding my scarf around my knee. By the sixth Munro the pain had become excruciating, and by the seventh I was hopping along with a crutch fabricated from a broken trekking pole I'd found. I was the last person on the ridge; fellow walkers had long since streamed passed me. And although I'm shy and don't like a fuss, I would have asked for help.

Creag a'Mhaim – a pile of rocks for my efforts!

It took two hours to make my way down the lonely steep descent. Only by twisting my body on each step could I keep my body weight on my good leg. Thanking the weather gods for clear and sunny spells, with just the odd rain shower from a wandering cloud, I appreciated the deep meaning of the old adage, 'adversity introduces a man to himself'.

I got back to the A87 at 20:00 where, nauseous with pain, I realised the seven-mile walk back to the car wasn't possible. My inner soul had got me off the mountain and plonked me down on the verge in a place of relative safety. So, for the first time in my life, I stuck out my thumb and relegated myself to the once noble pursuit of hitchhiking which now, post-Thatcher, is regarded as an occupation for the great unwashed.

Druim Shionnach

A number of cars passed, nobody stopped. I started to hobble along, crippled in agony. I didn't want this, I couldn't do this. Then I happened upon a lay-by and discovered the real art of hitchhiking. Backtracking a hundred yards I allowed my potential saviours the chance to view me before making a decision to stop in the lay-by. It worked; within a minute I was safely ensconced in the back of a car being co-driven by two Italian girls who had as much grasp of English as I did of Italian. The drive felt like it took ages and underlined the extent of the day's walk. On one occasion I tried to tell them I'd walked across the tops of the hills we were now passing. But they misinterpreted tops as 'stop' and I had to explain, by way of hand signals and facial expressions, "No, I really want this lift!"

Back at the cottage the pain in my right knee made it

apparent there were to be no more mountains this week.

August Bank Holiday

My final trip to Scotland of the year was with Ady Glover and we chose the August bank holiday weekend as a convenient time. We hired a car for the weekend and drove up from Wiltshire, stopped off in Glasgow then headed for the Highlands. We planned to walk for at least two of the days but in the event we made our only walk of the weekend on Saturday August the 29th. We started from Arrochar (Succoth) at 10:25 and reached the summit of Beinn Narnain in just under three hours.

Unfortunately my knee complaint was still with me and it became very painful on the descent. I struggled up the second Munro of the day, Beinn Ime, summiting two hours later. By this time I was in a lot of discomfort and had had enough. However, Ady wasn't hearing me and I got talked into going up Ben Vane, a day trip in its own right. We got there at 18:35 – a very long way from the car. I felt ill with the pain and I seethed with frustration towards Ady. Ultimately I should have refused Ady's persistence in going for the third summit but I had not. At the time I blamed Ady but largely managed to keep my feelings to myself. In retrospect I blame myself for being too weak willed to say no.

It was only when we neared the summit that Ady realised the agony I was in. We swapped rucksacks as mine, with all the emergency gear, was much heavier than his. Yet it is amazing how one's perception of events can vary. Years later Ady claimed, "I had to carry you up Ben Vane." My recollection was that I was very slow and that we swapped rucksacks for only the last few minutes of the ascent. His idea of "carrying me" was to keep about 100 yards ahead of me and occasionally wait for me to catch up!

At the top I realised the extent of my exhaustion and our

predicament: 18:35 is very late in the day for being on the summit of a mountain. After a struggle down the hill with my knee feeling like a pin jabbing tribe of pygmies had settled behind it we got to the hamlet of Inveruglas (on the A82) at 21:30, miles away from our car and with no accommodation booked. The prospect of a ten-mile walk along the dark road was daunting especially as the previous clear weather had now yielded to drizzle and rain. To add to the despair, the only phone box was accepting nothing but operator and 999 calls. I felt extremely low, exhausted and angry. I got Ady to beg with the operator to give us free phone calls to the Arrochar Hotel and a taxi firm. Very luckily both of these businesses answered first time and came up trumps.

I learnt a big lesson on this walk: to trust my own instinct so I only have myself to blame. I should have said no to Ady and, if he hadn't accepted that, just turned around and headed back.

It rained heavily the next day so we abandoned any further Munros and just drove about visiting a few places. As we had a hire car Ady wanted to drive it as fast as possible in contrast to me who gets freaked out by hell-for-leather driving. At one stage we were heading down a steep hill in pouring rain. As we approached the bottom I was yelling at Ady to slow down. He was doing 110mph. I was concerned there would be standing water at the bottom of the hill, fortunately we survived which gave me the opportunity to yell at Ady some more. Thinking back to this event, the walk the previous day, the car crash we had on the bridge in Glen Cannich in 1991 and Ady's bum sliding activities that resulted in him being helicopter-rescued off Carn Mor Dearg in 1990 leads me to the conclusion the part of the brain that allows one to sense danger had malfunctioned in him.

Munro Count: 25

1993

Alone in Glasgow

In December 1992 my partner, Gisella, and I moved from our rented house in Great Bedwyn into an old property in Marlborough we had bought to do up. This meant I changed doctors and during an introductory appointment I mentioned the problems with my knees. The doctor examined them before asking, "When does it occur?"

"Oh, after five to six hours of walking up mountains," I replied.

She gave me a desperate look and I sensed she wanted to shout, 'Next'.

I resolved to plod on; the need to do the Munros was real and powerful. Not much would stop me.

In the May, with a short spell between jobs, I decided to bag a few more Munros. The day before leaving I confided in Gisella I was nervous about the drive. Just the length of it I guessed.

I set off at 06:30 on May 29th, and soon discovered I was very tired. I stopped at various service stations and bought food I didn't really need just so I could have a rest. I felt myself lose concentration a couple of times so I stopped and dozed for a few minutes. I couldn't get it out of my head I was unhappy with this journey. I pressed on and the day passed by with the miles.

As the M6 ended and Scotland began so did the A74. It was undergoing a major upgrade with some bits up to motorway standard and other bits still the old dual carriageway, interspersed with road works. Consequently the traffic was pulsing between fast and slow sections. Still feeling tired I stopped in a lay-by. As I came to rest another car pulled in and just clipped my wing mirror. A very minor incident, with no damage done, but it added to my state of worry.

Once suitably rested I continued with the journey. Soon, in my rear view mirror, I could see an MG Midget. I am very fond of the MG marque so slowed down to let it pass enabling me to get a better look at it. The Midget nipped by and was soon lost in the distance. I remained in the inside lane and, as I approached an ever so slight incline, a black cloud of smoke suddenly mushroomed high in the air with a column of similar smoke propping it up like a nuclear explosion. It didn't look good at all. Within a few seconds I pulled up. A car angled towards the central reservation was a complete fireball and another car to the left had its front on fire.

I killed my engine and, for some unknown reason, grabbed my wallet and sprung out of the car. The fire in the first car had engulfed it to such a degree that barely any metal was visible. Thick black acrid smoke pumped out of what had become a roaring furnace.

A woman with smouldering hair was standing to the left, bent forward and bringing her arms up and down while screaming, "Help me, help me, my bairns."

A man to the right of the car was picking up some tool debris that had strewn out when the cars collided. He picked up what looked to me like a hammer and was shouting, "I'm going to kill you, you bastard."

I looked to my left and realised his rage was directed toward the driver of the other car who was standing by his fire-bound vehicle. The first man started to run towards the other with the hammer raised. I diverted my path and blocked him and with my arms raised said, "It's no use, it's no use."

I went to see what could be done. Nothing. The car was so alight that to get anywhere near it'd have been certain death.

The screaming woman and the man I'd blocked, had

managed to get out of their car but were unable to rescue their two daughters who were sat in the back. Myself and a rapidly expanding group of other motorists stood and watched, our eyes slowly becoming accustomed to the darkness. I kept thinking the kids would suddenly emerge from the car unscathed. My mind didn't want to accept the reality as an option. They were dead.

The second driver began removing articles from his car. As the front was on fire, from the impact, I suggested he and everybody else should move away from it. He said it was a diesel so it wouldn't explode. Not being one to hang around discussing the flash point of diesel I retreated and left him to it.

Both directions of the dual carriage way were blocked and we were about seven miles north of Lockerbie, of all places. We had to stand through each of the four tyres exploding in turn sending out a punch of flame with it. The driver of the second car joined a group of us and asked if anybody had a light for a cigarette. He asked quite a few people, unaware of the tragic connotations of his request. During this time the father of the two children had moved to a bank opposite, where he shouted abuse at the driver of the second car.

"You're dead, pal."

"I'm going to find you, you fucking bastard."

"Do you know where we have been today, you fucking bastard."

"Do you know?"

"To see the kids Granny, she is dying in hospital."

"You bastard. You're dead, you fucking bastard."

And so the language and the abuse grew and with it the horror and the futility of the situation. I could sense the "C" word coming, it was almost a relief when it did. A woman was praying "Lord have mercy on him, he doesn't know what he is saying."

The driver of the second car said, "You cannot blame him."

This was a statement I was questioned in detail on in the ensuing court case.

Eventually the emergency services arrived, unfortunately the fire brigade last. Perhaps it was fortunate, if they'd arrived first then the parents of the dead children might have tried to reach them in the tortured metal remains of their car instead of being sedated by the ambulance crew.

I gave a statement to the police, for what it was worth. I think most of the witnesses were in shock, we all spent about three hours at the scene. The practical approach of the emergency services struck home the cruel reality of the situation. Some people complained about the waste of their afternoon. Some late arrivals, not fully aware of, or not suitably shocked by, the situation took photographs. There was no sign of the little MG Midget I slowed down to see. If it had never been there I'd have kept up my speed and perhaps never known this had happened.

Once the road was cleared I carried on my journey to Glasgow, shaking and barely able to drive. When I worked in Glasgow there was a joke about Duncan's hotel which was around the corner from ours. It always looked very seedy and the line was if you were naughty you'd have to stay there.

I stayed there twice the previous year while passing through Glasgow on the way north. It was grim and run down but cheap. This time I was destined for it again. The grimness of the hotel was no longer amusing, it was now depressing.

As I sorted out my kit, the reality of the day hit me. I found myself bringing my right arm, with fist clenched, up and down in utter despair. I thought about my role in it all. I had pulled up in my car, had run towards danger but danger had raised her hands and backed away from me and then stared me in the eyes and told me to advance at my peril. I had possibly stopped the children's father from attempting to murder the driver who'd run into the back of them. Other than that I felt so totally useless.

I went for a walk. When I worked in Glasgow it was the European City of Culture, there were always friends about, people to go for a pint with after work, a buzz, a good time. I now noticed the dirty buildings not the ones that had been cleaned. Where before there were friends there was nobody. I crossed at a crossing and two lads in their van revved the engine and jeered as they succeeded in making me jump.

Suddenly I was alone in Glasgow.

I'd arranged to visit Janet Casey, and her husband Gary for the evening – they'd met on the Strathclyde Police Project and married a short time after it'd finished.

I phoned first to say I wouldn't be in the best of moods, but they convinced me to still get the bus over. I stopped at a bar first and had a stiff drink.

Gary and Janet met me at the bus stop and we walked quietly to her parents' house – Mr and Mrs McAlinden.

I was unprepared for the evening. Mrs McAlinden, an A&E nurse, met me at the door and told me she sees tragedies like that on a daily basis. I remained quiet, somehow I doubted she watched children burn to death on a daily basis.

I was offered a seat in the lounge and was surprised to see quite a crowd. Mr McAlinden sat next to me and bent my ear about everything he considered to be England's oppression of Scotland. I just sat there, took it and wished I was anywhere but there.

After some three hours Gary, a man from the Republic of Ireland, broke in and told Mr McAlinden, "Steve has had a bad day."

As the evening was breaking up an older woman, who'd sat chatting to her friends all evening, got up, walked towards me, pointed into my lap and told me, "All English are snobs."

32

A taxi was called for me. I was glad to leave and vowed never to return.

During the war my grandparents and father were briefly stationed in Glasgow. Despite having a common enemy they received a great deal of hassle for being English. On one occasion my grandmother and my father (as a babe in arms) were refused entrance to a shelter during an air raid.

Fifty years later I'd walked right back into it.

Half-Hearted Munroing

I spent a miserable few days in Glasgow, not setting north until Tuesday June the 1st to join Willy Newlands to do Meall nan Tarmachan and its famous ridge.

Willy brought his two dogs along which he claimed, in his usual dry style, he got to keep after losing a long, and bitter, custody battle with his wife. It was cloud and mist all day and I found it a bit of a struggle. The ridge, with no view and no further Munros, was against my better judgement. When Willy and I parted company I felt sad and alone.

I looked around for accommodation and felt the world was conspiring against me as all that was available was quite expensive. After about an hour of trying I saw a sign for a B&B on the road between Tyndrum and Crianlarich. I turned into the drive in a hesitant mood. I often find the proprietors of these establishments feel they have adopted you for the evening. Any painful rule they can think of, on the spot, will be relayed to you with the same glee they get from knowing it is restricting you, as much as running a B&B is restricting them.

This was to be no exception. On arrival the chap running the place said they only had a double room left. I said I'd leave it before he offered to split the difference between the price of a single and the price of a double. Then followed the house rules as he directed me to my room. After about ten minutes of interrogation, I just wanted my own space, and was glad when he left me to it in my room. However, he called by every few minutes by way of a sharp heart-jumping knock on the door. Initially it was the extra rubbish he'd forgotten to tell me on the previous monologue but on the antepenultimate visit he complained about my wet boots soaking the newspaper I'd put beneath them. The penultimate visit included an observation on the odour of the Deep Heat I'd put on my aching knee, "You're honking man."

By this time I was getting fed up and I think the annoyance showed on my face. The final visit was all too much to bear, I opened the door to see him standing there in his clan Marks and Spencer kilt informing me I'd better hurry if I wanted an evening meal. This time I failed to retain the mirth, he was clearly put out by my seeing his dress sense as humorous and left me to myself for the rest of the evening. Years later I relayed this account to a friend who thought perhaps he was gay and was trying to seduce me. Perhaps so, I was only twenty-seven at the time and still had a bit of a baby face.

I rested on June the 2nd and was re-joined by Willy on the 3rd along with Mike Linnett. We attempted Meall Glas and Sgiath Chuil, with an initial hiccup of a farmer being unhappy with Willy taking his dogs onto the hills in the lambing season. After kennelling was negotiated we started the ascent. Soon we found ourselves in deep mist and deep conversation about odd jobs we'd done in our adolescence, e.g. paper rounds, cleaning shops etc. Each trying to win the mantle of 'biggest mug' we failed to keep an eye on the map.

"Where are we?" asked Willy.

Mike and I looked gormless.

"You're the oldest Willy?" I added.

"What the fuck's that got to do with it, Steve?"

"And you're a policeman," chipped in Mike, backing me up, "if lost you should always ask a policeman."

"So, what you are saying," said Willy, drawing out his words slowly, "is that because I am an Officer of Her Majesty's law and older than you two you are blaming me for the fact we haven't a fucking clue where we are?"

Mike and I nodded in defeat.

I was all for trying to carry on and bag the two Munros but Willy and Mike could see what a fruitless exercise it'd be.

Willy had to work the following day so Mike and I, staying for one more night, found a hotel – the same hotel, and the same room, I'd checked out of in the morning, having moved on from the Gay Gordon's B&B.

On June the 4th we tackled Beinn Dorain and Beinn an Dothaidh. Starting from Bridge of Orchy at 11:05 we reached the summit of the first Munro two and a half hours later and the second in a bit over four hours into the day. There was a good view on the way up but the summits were hit by cloud and gales. The top of Beinn an Dothaidh was so atrocious we could barely stand as the rain bullied us all the way.

Once the two soggy 'mountaineers' reached their cars we headed for the Little Chef at Tyndrum for refreshment and a chance to get dry. This brought back memories of my first solo Munro-bagging expedition where I'd got the train up from Glasgow, got soaked and spent ages drying myself off in the toilets.

After Mike left to go back home to his parents in Edinburgh, I struggled to make up my mind whether to go home or stay and attempt another Munro the next day. It was Friday, I felt alone, and I had to get back home sometime over the weekend. I set off with a half-hearted attempt to look for a hotel. In the event

I ended up driving all the way back to Marlborough, arriving at just after seven in the morning.

Munro Count: 28

1994

Braemar

After three years, the time felt right to arrange another holiday with David George, Andy and Ady Glover. I met David at his flat near Paddington Station then, after taking the tube to Kings Cross and then changing trains in Edinburgh, rendezvoused with Andy and Ady in Perth. We then did a big food shop and drove in Andy's heavily laden Ford Fiesta to Braemar. The poor car was only a 950CC and struggled on the hills while David and I sat wedged in the back amongst luggage and bags of food.

We arrived at our cottage, the 'Knock' near Braemar, and found it a very up market place, very well done out. Unfortunately it had a television which, throughout the week, was a tough job to drag the Glover brothers away from.

Our first walk was as a foursome on Sunday May the 1st and took in Beinn Bhrotain and Monadh Mor. We started off by wondering whether we should walk down the private road, from the Linn of Dee, or chance it and drive.

"Andy, I think we should park here and not drive," I suggested.

"Do you reckon, Steve?"

"Nah, the gate's open let's go," replied Ady, slapping his thigh.

"But there is a loose chain and padlock," I added.

"Who's going to come and lock it on a Sunday?" retorted David condescendingly.

"Nobody else is driving down," I replied.

"Go for it, Andy," added Ady.

"I'm not sure," responded Andy.

"It'll save us hours," chipped in David.

Andy, always a sucker for the lazy option, stuffed the Fiesta into first gear and we bounced our way onto the track with no guarantee the gate would be unlocked on our return. After a mile or so a Land Rover in the fields to our left diverted its course towards the track. I immediately thought 'we are in trouble' and wasn't surprised when the Land Rover blocked our path and the driver, clothed in deerstalker and tweed, jumped out of his vehicle and headed for us. Andy wound down the window as I sank as low as I could into the car's upholstery.

I felt myself cringe as the estate worker explained the bleeding obvious. "You can no be bringing your car down the track, it's private."

"The gate was open," added Andy with all the defence of a child handing a broken ornament to a parent.

"You'll have to be turning around, it was lucky I caught you otherwise you'd have had your car locked in."

So back we turned and, with the humiliation of other walkers strolling past, drove back to the public road where we parked up. By now I was keen to get going and I felt agitated towards the others as they procrastinated over donning walking boots and coats.

We set off at 10:30 and, after crossing a few snow slopes that caused my head to hurt from the glare of the sun, reached the summit of Beinn Bhrotain in just under five hours.

David had a pair of CB radios so we had fun spreading out then holding daft conversations. Andy and Ady now turned back as they'd arranged to meet two friends at the cottage. David and I pressed on for Monadh Mor. We reached it at 16:40, good going but alas a long way back to base.

In places the snow was quite deep and I felt miserable as it tipped over my boots freezing my feet with meltwater. Cutting back to the glen, for the outward retreat, we took in some very deep patches, giving David and I the opportunity to revert to our degree days when, as flatmates, we used to have snowball fights on the back streets of Brighton. Like Inspector Clouseau and Kato each promise of a truce was about as sincere as a used car salesman.

The walk back was long and arduous and we ran out of food for the last few hours. Reaching the Linn of Dee at 22:30 still left us with a long walk back to the cottage – Andy's Fiesta having long since conveyed the brothers back. This is where David is so useful because he'd no hesitation in flagging down a car and asking for a lift. I admired his confidence just as I admired the way the couple who stopped, to avoid running him over as he stood arms outstretched in the road, didn't put up any resistance as we piled into the back of their car.

Back at the cottage we found the entire place locked up with no sign of a key or Andy and Ady. So, tired, starved and fed up we sat on the doorstep for about an hour until they returned.

After a rest day, full of the news of the death of Ayrton Senna, Ady and I tackled the three Munros readily accessible from the Glenn Shee ski area. Andy, with his feet badly blistered from the previous walk, took the day off. David chose to spend some time by himself, before keeping Andy company.

After winching Ady out of bed we started walking shortly after midday. Navigating between the ski lifts we reached the summit of The Cairnwell in under an hour and a half. On the way up we found four pound coins and a fifty pence in change on the ground. The coins were very grey and the newest was dated 1985. We could only guess they fell out of some skiers pocket many years ago and we promptly renamed our affectionate term for this pursuit, 'Munny Bagging' to 'money bagging'!

These three Munros are some of the easiest to do as the starting point is so high, however this doesn't mean the summits are any lower and are therefore positioned to receive the full wrath of the Scottish weather. Today was no exception. On the way to Carn a'Gheoidh we made reasonable progress but we found navigation difficult in the lashing rain and strong wind. I felt many moments of misery as I tried to keep up with Ady. With the tops of my legs aching, the weather didn't allow us to spend any recovery time at the summit, arriving and leaving at 15:45 before pressing on to Carn Aosda which we reached in just over six hours from the start of the day.

The wind on the summit of Carn Aosda made conversation almost impossible but we just managed to use the CB to radio back to Andy and David we were at the top of the last Munro. They had gone off for the day and arranged to pick us up from the ski lift car park. As we descended we kept in contact and when the ski area came into view, a murky grey picture in the driving rain, we asked Andy to flash his headlights so we could see him. He did so and it was a welcome sight to head towards. Although we could see them, it apparently took a long time before they could make out the two grey silhouettes descending the mountain.

After another rest day, May the 5th arrived and David and I decided to do Derry Cairngorm and perhaps another if time allowed. We did a long tough walk on the track from Inverey then via the Linn of Dee and Derry Lodge. This is a formidable building set against Scots Pine with the Southern Cairngorms as a backdrop. Derry Lodge is long abandoned but some attempt has been made to protect it by boarding the windows. Parts of the roof had fallen in and it is sadly going to decay unless the estate does some emergency repairs.

The approach to Derry Cairngorm was in poor weather and intricate with many cairns on route. Iron in the rocks threw the compasses and, given each cairn felt like the summit (visibility was so poor it was impossible to see if we were on top), we were reliant on David's excellent navigation and his 1:25000 scale map showing each cairn. We reached the summit at 16:20. Even though I'd really struggled I wanted to press on for Ben Macdui but David, quite rightly, talked me out of it. We arrived back in the Linn of Dee very late and David flagged down another vehicle for a free ride back to the cottage.

Throughout the week Ady's late starts became a source of frustration for us all. On one occasion we didn't get out of the cottage until 15:00 after Ady had taken his time getting up. The day of leaving was no exception with a reasonable start required for David and I to catch our train from Perth. Ady's procrastination meant we missed our train and had a fairly long wait for the next one. Completely oblivious he, in what he viewed as a noble gesture, volunteered to wait with us.

Unfortunately Perth railway station had been the victim of some vandalism to the extent the gent's toilets were only accessible by borrowing a key from the ticket office. With all of us succumbing to the call of nature David obtained the key and we went and relieved ourselves. As we left an old chap was walking in, oblivious to the toilets being normally locked. David, despite protests from Andy and me, locked him in. After the poor old chap had relieved himself he could be heard banging on the door. As Andy and I shook our heads in utter embarrassment, Ady and David were falling about laughing. If they hadn't just relieved themselves I think they'd have wet themselves.

"David, what if there's a fire?" I asked.

"There won't be a fire," replied David dismissively.

After about half a minute he went over to the door and called through, "Are you locked in?"

"Aye," came the reply.

David called back, "I'll see if I can get a key."

41

With that David came and sat with us for a minute or so and then went and unlocked the door. Andy and I were very embarrassed but it is one of those things where David's gift of carrying something through came off as the old guy was pathetically grateful to him for having "gone and got the key" especially to free him.

David's ability to get us into trouble is endless. When we were students, and flatmates, he wandered into my room one evening and announced, "There's a disused military base just down the coast, do you fancy going to visit it?"

It was a sunny evening and we'd just taken our final exams. "Okay," I replied. Having travelled around Northern France with him, visiting disused military structures, I knew this to be a hobby.

"Are you sure about this?" I asked as we met with a barbed wire fence.

"Yeah, we can soon climb it."

With growing unease I followed him over then ascended a short, well-kept, grassy slope.

Peering over the top of the bank we looked down upon a fully operational military barracks complete with armed patrols and dogs.

"I thought you said—" I began. But it was futile, David was hurtling down the bank. I caught up with him at the fence, "I thought you said it was disused?"

"Let's get out of here."

"Bloody understatement," I hissed back.

As we drove off, passing a police car coming in the other direction, I reiterated, "I thought you said it was disused."

"It looked like it on the map."

"Looked like it on the map!" I hissed. "How could you bleeding well tell that?"

"Well there were no red danger signs on it."

"No red danger signs! I was expecting you to say it had 'disused military base' stamped on the map. Jesus Christ, David, how would we have explained that one away? 'Oh sorry officer we just mistook this barbed wire fence and well-kept grassy bank to be an error along with the missing red danger signs on the map'."

"Well there's no need to be sarcastic," he replied.

For a second, just a second, I felt sorry for him.

David and I arrived back at London's Kings Cross Station in the late evening. I needed to make a dash across London to meet the last train to Great Bedwyn where Gisella was due to pick me up. We got on the tube at Kings Cross and were about to pull away when the carriage filled with smoke. Passengers were pouring out of the next carriage where it appeared the problem was. We took no time in joining in the spontaneous evacuation and as we were moving up the tunnels the public address system announced the emergency evacuation and closure of the station. I literally felt the hairs rise on the back of my neck.

Kings Cross was the site of one of the worst fires in recent history and many passengers were wary and commenting about this. An old chap started to talk to David and said, "They had a big fire here a few years ago, scores of people killed."

David in an all-time understatement replied, "You'd better get out then."

I gave David a sharp glance. "Count yourself lucky this isn't Perth Station and you hadn't just locked somebody in the loos."

Once we surfaced the air was filled with the howls of fire engine sirens as the London Fire Brigade were throwing as many appliances as they could muster in the direction of Kings Cross. David and I didn't fancy becoming part of the crowd scene so we hastened down to Euston and got the tube to Paddington. We arrived three minutes before my train was due to leave. I dumped my rucksack with David and sprinted to the ticket office, got the ticket, sprinted back and made the train with seconds to spare.

This fire, on the tube, was the third of four different fires I was to be involved in over a five-year period.

August Bank Holiday

The next foray into the hills was a weekend break where I flew to Glasgow on Friday August the 26th and met with Kevin Enright in a hotel near Queens Park. I was worried Kevin would want to stay in the bar all evening but I managed to get out of a massive drinking session and instead had a good night's sleep before we were collected by our mutual friend, Mike Linnett.

All three of us had worked on the infamous Strathclyde Police Command and Control Project, therefore meeting in Glasgow was a convenient point. After our brief reunion, in the hotel lobby, Mike drove the three of us to Crianlarich where we looked for accommodation. We tried a couple of places first and ended up settling on a B&B where the guy decided it was our divine right to be constantly talked to. His opinions always stood and anything to the contrary was greeted with a scowl.

However, he did offer us some 'useful' advice on the best route to tackle Beinn Tulaichean which turned out to be fundamentally flawed when we discovered a wide, heavily flowing river barring our path. We forded it, getting very wet, before the long haul to the top, taking about five hours. The weather was quite good on the way up but the top was in mist. Kevin found the walk a struggle, I did as well but I think it was tougher on him. We pressed on and after another hour reached Cruach Ardrain (which you could rearrange as Curac Hard Rain) from where we descended back to the car.

Mike and Kevin

When we started in the morning a bull had got itself stuck across a gate in our path. It looked as if he'd tried to charge it and broken the top two rails, leaving him straddled across the debris. As we passed him on the way back he barely gave us a look having long resigned himself to the fate of having the humiliation of the farmer setting him free.

Back at the guesthouse the proprietor, with all his expertise, came into action again. Our enquiries of the drying facilities he'd promised us were met with, "Leave your boots on the pavement boys as otherwise it will make my house wet."

"They won't dry out on the pavement," I retorted, "and they might get stolen."

"I don't know what you mean," he said, glaring at me.

"Well my boots are new," I explained, "and they night prove tempting to somebody."

He glared at me some more, taking it as a complete insult to every Scotsman who'd ever graced the planet. In the end I found myself apologising and conceding the most likely source of crime in the Highlands would be English holidaymakers. It grated with me, especially as that kind of person is so used to going through life unchallenged he manages to get his way. Anyhow after a swift bit of renegotiating he took the boots in and dried them for us.

When we'd first enquired about vacancies his dog had greeted us at the door. With my asthma I'd began to say we'd look elsewhere but, given his reassurances the dog wasn't allowed upstairs, we took the rooms. When we got upstairs after our walk his cat was freely roaming around.

On Sunday August the 28th Mike and I dropped Kevin at a pub near Ardlui and set off to bag Ben Vorlich (Loch Lomond).

We started at 10:45 and reached the summit in just under four and a half hours. The weather was very wet, even my Gore-Tex jacket let in water. Mike wanted to return by going down the south side toward the Ben Vane and Loch Sloy area. I wanted to go back the way we'd come but Mike felt the longer route was safer. I felt at the time this was a mistake but as Mike was determined we did his route, compliance was a better option. He was genuinely worried about going back the way we'd come – there were some quite exposed places and the weather was very poor. My fear was Mike's route would involve a long walk up the A82 where, with no pavement, vehicles would pass dangerously close to us in the pouring rain.

My fears were correct, once on the A82 I was genuinely scared of being hit. This was the same 'A' road that Ady and I avoided by swift use of a taxi when bagging Ben Vane.

Graham Disselduff, another Strathclyde Police Command and Control Project veteran, was due to meet us at Crianlarich for the evening and I was hoping he'd drive past while we were doing the route march up the road. He did, but not until we'd got within a hundred yards of Mike's car. Graham said he recognised my stoop from a long way off.

We collected Kevin from the pub. Mike and I'd speculated on how many pints of beer he'd have consumed and we weren't surprised when Kevin greeted us with a sloppy lashed up grin.

"Six pints," he exclaimed with pride.

"Just the one Munro for us," I added mournfully.

"I've had a great day," added Kevin.

Neither Mike nor I could retort with any hint we'd had a great day. In fact we'd had a fairly dire day. Exhausted, wet and miserable we just wanted back to the guesthouse for a shower. Kevin dutifully piled into Mike's car sensing, through his beer-filled view on the world, further beverages would have to be delayed.

Once washed and feeling human again the four of us had an enjoyable evening before departing the following morning for Glasgow to kill some time before my flight home. We parked on the edge of the centre, strolled in and went to the cinema and watched *Four Weddings and a Funeral.*

We then strolled about a bit and it started to rain heavily. I suggested getting a taxi back to the car to avoid a twenty-minute walk. Kevin and Mike were non-committal. I said, "I'll pay for it." I got no response for they were already in the middle of the road flagging one down. From there Mike and Kevin dropped me at Glasgow Airport for the flight back to Heathrow.

On the flight up a very attractive lady, I guess about the age of thirty-five, had sat next to me in the departure lounge and struck up conversation. I am pretty hopeless at picking up signals but this did feel like flirting. By chance she was in the departure lounge for the return trip from Glasgow to Heathrow. She came across to me and I sensed an interest from her. We were in separate seats so on arrival at Heathrow I made for the baggage collection point alone. I knew she had only hand luggage and thought it was best to try and avoid what could become a tricky situation. While waiting for my baggage to appear on the carousel the public address system announced, on more than one occasion, "Would Stephen Smith, recently arrived from Glasgow, please report to the customer services desk where there is somebody waiting to meet him." I grabbed my bag and legged it. Now why did that never happen when I was single?

Munro Count: 37

1995

The Big Ben

Ben Nevis is the highest mountain in Britain and being in Scotland is therefore the highest of all the Munros. Because Ben Nevis is special I intended to leave it to be my last Munro but during the run up to my thirtieth birthday, June the 27th 1995, I was looking for something memorable to do so decided Ben Nevis would be the thing.

I also wanted to celebrate with my partner, Gisella, so we agreed on a holiday together in Scotland during my birthday week. Gisella and I never spent much holiday together, this was to be only our third holiday in five years, mainly due to differences in interest. Touring around sunny cities was never for me and climbing Scottish mountains was never for her. While we discussed the holiday I was trying to find common ground so we could both enjoy the week. I said I was happy to just do the one Munro, Ben Nevis and she said she'd be happy to have a crack at it. I was also concerned about money as we were currently in the expensive phase of doing up an old house and it was hard for Gisella to manage on her local government salary. Therefore I raised the possibility of camping for a few nights. Gisella gave me one of her quick 'you must be kidding' glances and promptly informed me her idea of camping was a bed and breakfast without ensuite. I relented and agreed to pay for hotels.

In the event, after swimming in a freezing rock pool at the start of the week, my birthday was spent in a Drumnadrochit hotel, bedridden with flu. Therefore we tackled Ben Nevis on Friday June the 30th.

Gisella started the walk, from a point near Glen Nevis Youth Hostel, with me but soon struggled with a major fear of falling and troublesome knees. It took me a while to persuade her to turn back; she was hanging on to tufts of grass for fear of falling on a slope I regarded as an easy grade. She was determined to go on but I was very unhappy and I was glad when, after an hour, she conceded defeat and I was able to watch her walk back to her car.

Having started the walk shortly after 07:30 I followed the zigzag stone path all the way in a hot sunny haze. I reached the summit at midday to be met with excellent views of the surrounding mountains, lochs and back towards Fort William. A ruined Victorian meteorological hut and a series of memorials were very interesting and made it more of a pilgrimage than a mountain climb.

A German couple approached me and asked, "Is it always this cloudy on top?"

"No," I replied. I then attempted to explain how lucky they were to climb it without much cloud – they were actually asking if the few wisps of cloud on view had any right to be there.

I then looked north-east towards Carn Mor Dearg, my first Munro more than five years ago, and recalled the miserable conditions and Ady Glover's helicopter rescue. With Ben Nevis my thirty-eighth Munro I reflected on the journey so far.

I spent the best part of an hour taking in the glorious views from the top before starting the descent back into Glen Nevis. With the zigzag path tough on my knees and feet I had to keep my pace in check.

About an hour and a half into the return trip I met a couple ascending in the heat. He was about seventy, open-necked shirt, which wouldn't look out of place in an office, shorts and a white hat. She looked about ten years his junior, slim but out of condition. They might both have just walked off a bowling green.

"Much further to go?" he enquired.

"Err, a fair way," I replied thinking by the look of them

they'd at least seven hours ahead of them.

"We only set out at one o'clock, a bit of a late start."

"Got much water?" I asked.

"One bottle."

I was beginning to get concerned about them. His face was red and covered in sweat, their footwear was average and the one rucksack was of no size to carry anything close to the right equipment.

"What about food?" I added.

"We had a big lunch, and have a few provisions. How long to the top do you think?"

I was beginning to think they'd perish on route. By the look on my face they read my thoughts.

"Perhaps we'll have a wander on for a bit," said the man.

And that's how we left it, presumably they continued for a while to save the awkwardness in turning back with me.

I reached Glen Nevis at 15:25 and took a further hour walking to Fort William meeting Gisella at the Grand Hotel where we were staying. In total I spent about eight hours up and back, the record for running the ascent and descent is about an hour and a half. I have spent much time trying to make sense of how somebody can be that fit – it defies all belief to me.

August Bank Holiday

During the May 1994 trip to Braemar, David George and I both felt we hadn't done enough walking in the Cairngorms. We therefore planned an August bank holiday trip to bag some more Munros. As time was tight I drove to his house, near Hampton Court, on Friday August the 25th from where we took his Land Rover to Heathrow and caught a flight to Inverness.

Without any spare footwear with me, I sat in the departure

lounge wearing heavy leather boots and full Gore-Tex gaiters.

A voice spoke from somewhere in front of me. "Afraid of flying over water are you?"

I looked up to see the face of a typical self-assured, know-it-all, lump of a man, sitting opposite.

"No," I replied while secretly wishing I'd the courage to tell him to fuck off.

"You look an idiot in those boots, it's summer now."

"I don't want to carry spare footwear," I explained, "so it's easier just to wear them."

With that he folded his arms, sat back and smiled while looking around at other passengers, trying to jolly them into a communal ridicule of me. I seethed, while recalling I'd come across a few too many people like him.

On the flight David and I got separated and I ended up sat next to a RAF Tornado pilot. It was an interesting chat although he was taking full advantage of the free drinks on offer.

We arrived very late at Inverness and, with no chance of getting a train or a bus, we took a taxi via Aviemore to just below the ski centre. Here we gave the taxi driver his well-earned £40 and pitched David's tent.

David assembled his stove, pouring in petrol from a metal canister.

Until this point I hadn't really thought about camping stoves. "David," I said, "did you bring that bottle of petrol with you on the plane?"

"Yes," he replied defensively.

"Is that allowed?" I asked.

"Well," he protested, "their planes are stuffed full of aviation fuel, a bottle of petrol isn't going to make any difference."

I let the subject drop.

The tent was a new experience and I found it hard to sleep.

We started walking with our heavy packs at just after 08:00, thinking we were losing civilisation for a few days. However, after two hours of trudging along in the wet we reached the café at the top of the ski lift area. Amazingly it was open despite the horrible weather. It was too good an opportunity to miss so we delayed the 'getting away from it all' feeling and stuffed ourselves with drinking chocolate and cake.

From the café we had an hour of easier walking to the summit of Cairn Gorm. From there we continued in the miserable rain and, with me struggling with my full backpack, reached Ben Macdui at 15:00. Ben Macdui is the highest mountain in the Cairngorm region and overall the second highest Munro. For many years it was thought to be the highest mountain in Scotland and there is a story, on discovery of Ben Nevis being taller, there were moves to raise its height.

We pressed on from Ben Macdui and decided to look for a suitable place to camp. At just after 17:00 we strategically erected our tent, to the south-east of Loch Etchachan, to maximise the full impact of the gale force winds that were to blow through during the night. I only managed to get about three hours sleep due to the violent wind buffeting the tent and causing the material to flap wildly about my head. We both had hooded sleeping bags and at one point I woke to see David, now a hooded figure, sat up in the very dim light. "Fuck me it's the grim reaper," I yelled. We had picked the wind tunnel from hell.

In the morning we decided to leave our stuff in the tent and climb Beinn Mheadhoin with the least amount of kit as possible. We set off at 08:30 and on route we discussed our options.

"You're very slow with the pack," remarked David.

"Well my breath intake is about 15% below the average a person of my age, height, gender and weight should get."

"I guess that tips the balance when it comes to carrying a

full pack," he replied.

"At least my knees are behaving themselves," I added. "The exercises the doctor gave are working."

We did have ambitions of walking Beinn Bhreac, North Top and Ben Avon but realised it'd required one or two extra days. Therefore we decided to just walk Beinn Mheadhoin and leave the other three for a later date.

We staggered on through poor weather, reaching the rocky outcrop of a summit in an hour and a quarter. With high wind rendering a proper rest impractical, we descended a bit, to another outcrop, and sat eating the rations we'd carried in our pockets. After a few minutes we were joined by two chaps who were making their ascent. We briefly shared our plans and experiences before they set off back down.

"David," I said slowly.

"Yes," he replied, familiar with my tone of voice that builds up to something.

"You don't suppose those chaps just mistook us sitting here for the summit do you?"

Adding to the understatement he offered, "You could just be right, Steve, just be right."

"Should we go after them?"

"No," he replied, "they'll never know." And I suppose they never will, unless they happen to read this account and remember they 'climbed' Beinn Mheadhoin early on Sunday August 27th 1995.

We got back to the tent at 10:45 and I was very glad the weather remained poor as I was able to snuggle deeply into my sleeping bag and listen to the Belgian Grand Prix. However, at 13:30, and lap 28, there was a break in the weather and David wanted to get going. I was reluctant, but despite my protests, we set off with my radio stuffed inside the hood of my jacket.

With the rain eased, and the wind still strong, my clothing managed to dry out a bit. We pitched the tent alongside the Fords of Avon Refuge Hut – open to those who wished to sleep in it. However, it looked depressingly uninviting so we opted for the tent instead. Life was much better at this point and we managed to get some rest.

We set off at 09:20, leaving our kit in the tent, and reached the summit of Beinn a'Chaorainn an hour and a half later. There was no visibility at the top so it was nice when we dropped out of the cloud and could see the tent from the distance. A chap was wandering near to it, we speculated on what he was up to and were relieved when, after some twenty minutes, he went on his way.

We got back to the tent at about midday and rested for about an hour and a half before packing up and setting off for the three-hour trek to the northerly access point of Bynack More. By this time David had more than taken pity on me and was carrying the entire tent and stove by himself.

Barns of Bynack

At the foot of Bynack More we hid the kit amongst some rocks and free-walked this Munro. It was such a relief to be free of the pack it really lifted my spirits. The weather had eased by now and the views to the east were superb and I enthused about them in contrast to the miserable weather we'd had until now. Bynack More is an interesting Munro with the Barns of Bynack situated as a wild isolated outcrop of rocks to the south-east.

After descending we reclaimed our kit and carried on along the path, heading north and camping on high ground above Bynack Stable.

The following morning was a relatively short walk, via the Glenmore Forest Park, then a bus ride back to civilisation in Aviemore where we had a slap-up meal in a café.

David has a well-honed knack of putting his foot in it. While queuing for our meal he spoke to a smartly dressed older chap, stood in front of him. Overlooking the black tie he asked, "Going somewhere nice?"

The guy gesticulated towards a lady sitting at a table and in hushed tones replied, "The wife's brother's funeral."

David sat opposite me and said, "How was I supposed to know?"

I shook my head in despair.

From Aviemore we took the train to Inverness where we took the bus back to the airport.

Despite my struggles, and the bad weather, I did enjoy my first experience of camping in Scotland. I learnt a few lessons including, (i) tinned food and packets of crisps were, due to their size and weight, inefficient and (ii) it is worth camping above the line at which the dreaded Scottish midge can survive.

Shortly before this trip I'd phoned my parents. My mum was out so I was able to have a longer chat with my dad. I told him of our plans; he roughly knew the area we were going to as we'd once been to the Cairngorms on a family holiday. Later in the conversation we got on to one of our usual topics – cars. He asked how mine was running and I said it was fine, having just got to 125,000 miles. He then mentioned something I was vaguely aware of – in his first car he'd got through three engines and had clocked 100,000 miles in five years.

"Hang on a second," I said, "you averaged 20,000 miles a year when you actually lived where you worked."

He then told me the things he used to get up to in it. Apparently it was nothing for him and some fellow young police officers to finish a shift in the early hours and then shoot up to the Lakes, in his car, and bag Helvellyn. I never knew that, perhaps the love of mountaineering could be inherited. If it is then it is like malaria, once in the blood it is hard to get rid of.

Later in the evening he phoned me back to say, "You know you've done Cairngorm before."

"Really?" I replied.

"Yes, I've got a photo in my hand with you on the top of it."

This was a surprise to me as I'd no recollection of this trip, which apparently took place on a family holiday in 1978. I think the chair lift got involved somewhere along the line so I won't claim it as a genuine 'bag'. Although I could extend the length of time it took me to stand on top of them all by twelve years.

Munro Count: 43

1996

The M74 and Youth Hostels Revisited

On Thursday May the 2nd I set off to Scotland by car for the first time in three years. The car crash I witnessed in 1993 had left me nervous of long journeys, and instead I'd been making trips by train or plane. However, I was now beginning to feel more comfortable about driving again, putting some of the ghosts to rest.

Prior to the accident I'd invested in a 1965 MG Midget. 'Invested' being euphemism for a hobby better known to require the emptying of one's wallet, on a regular basis, into the said machine. Knowing I'd the courage to now drive to Scotland I got the MG Midget and my 1986 Toyota Corolla out on the drive and eyed them up. 'What a trip all the way to Scotland in a thirty-one-year-old car, with the top down and the wind rushing through my hair, stories to tell and experiences to look back on. I would only need to take out the passenger seat to make room for my luggage', I thought.

Gisella wandered out to join me on the drive and gave me a quizzical look. "You're deep in thought, what you up to?"

"Just thinking which car to take."

"You're kidding!"

"Well—"

"Doesn't it rain a lot in Scotland?" she asked, clearly trying to outfox me.

"Yeah," I replied.

"And you told me a month or so back you were thinking of selling the Midget because of its unreliability."

"Yeah," I replied. "I was thinking it'd be a good selling point if I said it had just made it to Scotland and back."

"What happened when we last went out in it?"

"It broke down, only a wire off under the dashboard."

"And the time before?"

"We just ran out of petrol."

"And why was that?" she added.

"Because the petrol gauge is broken."

"Have you mended the lights yet?"

"Well, sort of," I replied, sensing myself losing. "I tightened the wires up a bit."

"And can you manage to put the hood up without me helping you now?"

"Just about, as long as I don't have to do it in a hurry."

"And putting the hood up in a Scottish downpour wouldn't be regarded as a hurry?"

So I made it to just south of the Scottish border and pulled up, in the Toyota, for a night at Dufton Youth Hostel before continuing on to Inverarnan, south of Crianlarich on the A82.

I set off walking, following the Ben Glas Burn for three and a half hours before breaking off to the north-east to bag Beinn Chabhair. Just before the main ascent I came across three girls sitting by the loch Lochan Beinn Chabhair. I briefly said hello as I passed by. A few seconds later one of them called out, "I don't suppose you have any plasters have you?"

One of the girls was wearing new boots and had developed bad blisters on her heals. Given they were a long way from their car, and having had painful blisters myself, I let her have two proper second skin plasters. I applied the first myself to show her how they worked. Apologising for having to man handle her I left her to do the second in case she thought I'd some type of foot fetish.

Foot fetish or not she called me a "hero" and a "life saver" which boosted my ego somewhat.

The day was a nice start to this Munro-bagging trip with

clear weather and just a bit of snow falling. It was a chance to try out my latest purchase, a Global Positioning System (GPS). It proved a useful backup to conventional navigation techniques but, with accuracy only to about 100m, it was only an aid, not the solution to my poor navigation.

Saturday May the 4th saw me take in Ben Vorlich and its neighbour Stuc a'Chroin from the starting point of Ardvorlich. I made a relatively early start from Killin Youth Hostel and got walking at just before 08:30, pausing to read some notices stating you should only venture onto the mountains if you had an ice axe and crampons. As I'd neither I was very wary. The dilemma stalled me for a while but, given the clear day, I thought I could see a path up through the distant snow and ice.

Stuc a'Chroin

I found the climb a struggle and after a few of hours people were streaming past me who'd set off two hours after me. I muttered under my breath as my restricted windpipe held me back.

I reached the summit at 12:30 from where I set off to Stuc a'Chroin, necessitating a frightening climb over an exposed boulder ridden rock face. Regulating my breathing I managed to keep my nerve and composure before reaching the summit some two hours later. Here I was confronted by a fell race with runners streaming up the other side as though it were a jog to the local shop and back.

In the evening I went for a walk from Killin Youth Hostel, taking in the town. As I was returning to the hostel I was propositioned by three young ladies. All three of them had been drinking and two of them were swigging from lager cans.

"Are you no coming to watch me in the Miss Wet T-shirt competition?" asked one.

At this point I recalled the poster I'd seen earlier in the day advertising the event at one of the local pubs, in aid of some charity.

Now I had a dilemma. This girl was quite up-front, in both senses of the phrase, and I must admit her offer did have certain tempting elements. However, the thought of her exposing her breasts in front of a bar filled with jeering drunken men was somewhat off putting so I politely declined the offer.

I later reflected I'd peaks of another variety on my mind while considering if this is quite how society should be going. When I was their age such a thing as a 'Miss Wet T-shirt' competition was unheard of, and even if anybody had heard of it daring to host such an event in early 1980s Chippenham would have met with a barrage of objections. Considering quiet backwaters in Scotland are probably more behind the times than the quiet backwaters of Southern England one can begin to comprehend the massive social changes Britain has experienced in the last fifteen years. It could be at my mere thirty years of age I'm showing a greater capacity for middle-age than is healthy but I did go on to wonder how the girl's parents or grandparents viewed this. On my grandparent's mantelpiece is a photograph of me at my graduation ceremony, what if I visited the girl's grannie's house?

"Is this your granddaughter then?" I'd enquire looking towards the mantelpiece.

"Aye, that's when she won Miss Wet 'T' Shirt Killin 1996. She's come out well, don't you think."

Mountain Bunnies

I took the Sunday off then tackled Ben Chonzie on Monday May the 6th. I set off from Invergeldie at 09:00 and reached the summit just under three hours later. The views from the top were so superb I rested for half an hour, taking it all in. Only a bit of hail and rain whipping in got me moving. A half an hour rest on the summit may sound a short period but it is never a good idea to hang about at the top as you can get quite cold.

On the descent, still amongst some hail and rain, I witnessed a large number of mountain hares playing in the upper slopes of the Munro. I reflected they should be called 'mounting hares' as opposed to 'mountain hares' as there did appear to be rather an excessive number of them. I got back to the car at 14:00.

Sunday's day of rest clearly did me good as the time taken to make it to the summit was just under the upper estimate in the guidebook. My effort on the Saturday was a full three and a half hours over the upper estimate. This was possibly something to do with the difference in the amount of ascent between the two walks: I am okay on the flat and can make a good pace but when it comes to climbing I really slow down as I can never make a consistent pace and normally have to rest every few steps.

On May the 7th I planned to climb Ben Lui and its neighbour, however it was far too snowy and cloudy so I headed north to do Beinn Mhanach in the Bridge of Orchy range via a much more sociable south face. At this time of the year there is still an appreciable amount of snow about so it always pays to try hills from southerly approaches.

I parked on the edge of the road, opposite where the West Highland Railway crosses a viaduct, and set off at 08:40. I soon passed under the viaduct and continued on fairly flat ground for three hours before climbing for a further two hours to reach the summit. It was a lonely day, I only saw one other person during the entire time but I managed to have a quick chat with him.

Infuriatingly it rained for the last fifteen minutes of the eight and a half hour walk. Wet and bedraggled I piled into my car wishing the last fifteen minutes had been dry and windy.

From there I went to stay at Crianlarich Youth Hostel which I found a soulless place. I missed the friendlier atmosphere of Killin Hostel where I'd got friendly with the warden, Paul, to the point we'd tried to fix the heating together.

I took the Wednesday off, firstly to rest my legs and secondly because I'd spent the night being tortured with sleep deprivation through being billeted with the snorer from hell. The following day I managed to move rooms but I was later apprehended by the snorer, asking why I was no longer in the same dormitory.

I decided not to spare his feelings and said, "Sorry but it was your snoring."

I had a nice day taking the train on the superbly scenic West Highland line between Crianlarich and Fort William. I find Fort William a bit of a soulless place and wandered aimlessly around the Nevis Sport outdoor gear shop. I had a go on their heart beat monitor – I came out with a rate of fifty-seven which is apparently athletic. So either their machine is faulty or underneath I am quite fit.

On the train ride back I continued to read a book I'd picked up in a charity shop, *Carve Her Name With Pride*. It was uncanny to read the central character, Violette Szabo – a British wartime spy murdered by the Nazis while held as a POW – had taken this very train ride during her training in the early 1940s.

At 09:20 on Thursday May the 9th I set off for Beinn Bhuidhe from a starting point on the A83. The first part of the walk was a tedious three hours via a private road. Only then did I start to climb, reaching the fallen trig point, marking the summit, at just after 14:00. All trig points are redundant now, relics of a time where the servants of the Ordnance Survey actually climbed these hills to map them.

It was a lovely day and there were fantastic views with Ben Nevis many miles to the north. On the descent I paddled in the gorgeous water fall fed pools of the stream feeding the River Fyne while contemplating the route march back along the private road.

On approaching the private road I stopped to chat to a shepherd unloading a trailer of sheep and lambs.

"Have you been up on the hills?" he asked.

"Yes, it has been a lovely day," I said, while all the time thinking 'go on offer me a lift – please, please'.

"Did you do Beinn Bhuidhe?"

"Aye," I replied in a desperate attempt to not sound like a hated English holidaymaker.

"It has been a lovely day," he added.

"Aye," I added while thinking 'go on say it, offer me a lift. Oh please, I'll even support Scotland against England in Euro 96 if you like'. I was just giving up hope and getting ready for the three-hour walk back when, as he climbed into his Land Rover, he said as a casual after thought, "Can I give you a lift?"

Brilliant, a lift and I could still support England in Euro 96.

Friday May the 10th brought in Beinn Achaladair and Beinn a'Chreachain. Beinn Achaladair was to be my fiftieth Munro and, by way of a small reward, I'd booked to stay in the Grand Hotel in Fort William for the night with the plan to head north the following day to meet friends for a week's holiday.

I started at just before 08:30 from Achallader Farm where an interesting ruined turret stands in its ground. I reached the summit some four hours later. From there I did the two-hour ridge walk to Beinn a'Chreachain taking in the minor peaks on route. From this second Munro, while day dreaming of the hotel room, I set off down the wrong side. The first hint of trouble was when I found myself staring at a loch not on my map. To add to my problems my right knee had been playing up. I got out the GPS to navigate myself back on course and set off. Immediately my knee stopped hurting and once I was back on course, a good hour later, it started to play up again. I got back to the car at just after 18:00 and set off for Fort William.

The bedroom in the Grand Hotel had an ensuite bath and loo – yes! A bit more luxurious than the youth hostels but it was nice to have tried youth hostelling again after a seven-year break. I had been concerned I was now too old for them, but the word 'Youth' is a misnomer as I was still one of the youngest there.

Mullardoch Revisited

It is amazing how one particular place can draw you. When in Scotland I often find myself experiencing the peace and tranquillity of Glen Cannich up which lies Loch Mullardoch. I first came here in 1989 with a large group of friends and hired Mullardoch

Cottage. I always fancied a repeat performance so this time I hired the same place for a week and roped in two original members of the 1989 party in the form of Andy and Ady Glover and managed to add Chris Howard and Mark Neale with Robin Bacon and his girlfriend, Kelly, staying for just the first night.

The cottage was still owned by the same people, Carl and Ninon Lawaetz, although they now let it privately instead of via an agency. They are quite an amusing couple from Denmark with Ninon doing most of the talking as Carl's English isn't so good.

Some months previously I was driving to work and listening to the *Today* programme on Radio 4 when they started to discuss a love retreat that had hit the news. The broadcast went something like the following:

"... now this love retreat is in the wilds of Scotland and only reachable by boat across Loch Mullardoch and a few moments ago I spoke with the owner, Carl Lawaetz:"

"Hello, Mr Lawaetz?"

"Yah."

"This is the *Today* programme, Radio 4 here."

"Yah."

"I believe you own what the papers are describing as the most remote love nest in Britain."

"Yah."

"Only reachable by boat we believe."

"Yah."

"Do you get many couples staying there?"

"Yah, zome."

"And is it a romantic paradise?"

"It only haz the bunk beds."

"Ah so not so comfortable then, Mr Lawaetz."

"No."

"Do you take your wife there often, Mr Lawaetz?"

"Yah, once a week."

"For romance, Mr Lawaetz?"

"No, I take her there once a week to clean it."

At this stage I had to pull over as the tears of laughter were pouring down my face and I was in no fit state to be in control of a motor vehicle. Maybe you have to know Carl to appreciate the story so I shall pester you with no further details and instead carry on with the tale of my 1996 visit to Mullardoch Cottage.

I arrived on Saturday May the 11th and, with other people arriving throughout the day, I had to wait until the Sunday to set out for the hills. Leaving the cottage at about 10:00, a good start considering the Glover brothers were built into the equation, we got to the summit of Carn nan Gobhar shortly before 13:30 after a walk most of us found hard going. The summit of Sgurr na Lapaich was reached at 15:45 and we rested for a while, chatting, familiarising with each other. Kelly was quite a character and, while emanating the most outrageous farts, announced, in her broad Australian accent, "Better out than in, boys."

Ady while looking west, pointed to the horizon and asked, "Is that Skye over there?" It was quite an obvious one to walk into as we all started on, "And that's a mountain, and that's a rock, oh look a bird."

Rob told us a great story about a walk he'd done with a group of people. On the ascent they had relentlessly teased a chap about the enormous rucksack he'd brought for a day hike. At the top all was revealed, along with the last laugh, as he unpacked his paraglider, leapt off and was back in comfort within a few minutes.

Our walk back was very tiring especially along the shores of Loch Mullardoch, reminding me of the walk Andy and I did during July 1991. Kelly kept our spirits up with some anecdotes of her travels including the bizarre acts of inmates at a nursing home in the USA. Kelly also made reference to a particular, and rarely executed, sexual act.

Me on Sgurr na Lapaich

Andy sidled up to me and quietly said, "That's the second woman to mention that in this glen."

I thought for a second or so and realised he was absolutely correct for, in 1989, Alison Read had mentioned the same unusual (but always welcome) act in the self-same glen. This is a typical example of Andy's dry humour, he is able to connect things up in a very funny way, spotting humour I never knew was there – as if women making references to sexual acts in Scottish glens was a normal thing to keep tabs of.

Later in the week we were packing in preparation for a

walk. Ady was chucking some food into his rucksack for both him and Andy. He called across to his brother, "Andy, Penguin?"

At this point Andy rocked his buttocks on the chair and said, "No just painful piles."

On the Monday we hired a motor boat from the Glen Affric Hotel and motored down to the end of Loch Mullardoch and came up with the idea of a repeat performance for the Tuesday as a launching point for tackling the three very remote Munros of Beinn Fhionnlaidh, Carn Eige and Mam Sodhail.

We had problems getting the boat for a second day as the hotel owner, who by strange coincidence was a friend of a chap working on Gisella's and my house, had no spare fuel. We were discussing this in the hotel bar when a customer piped up, "You can borrow my engine, it's just in the shed half a mile from where you're staying."

Over mechanisation, industrialisation, urbanisation takes many things away from the spirit of humanity. Trust being one of them – thankfully the Highland folk are still there to reaffirm what we've lost and to show what we could get back.

We cast off at just after 09:30 and got to the end of the loch an hour and twenty minutes later. We reached the summit of Beinn Fhionnlaidh, taking just under a further three hours in good weather in a party consisting of Andy, Ady, Chris and Mark. From there we set off for Carn Eige and Mam Sodhail which took a further one and a half hours then just over one hour respectively.

The weather at the top of Carn Eige was very poor with wind and mist. The conditions on the approach to Mam Sodhail were so windy, snowy and bleak that Chris and Mark dropped out and waited back for us. With my hands now very cold, I questioned myself whether I should press on. However, with Andy and Ady willing to go on and my desire to bag all the Munros, I decided to risk it. When we reached the summit we gingerly took photographs, sat and shivered while contemplating the return in the gale.

Mark, Chris, Andy and Ady on Carn Eige

The descent was long and Andy started to develop a pain in one of his knees. Fortunately I'd a spare, but rather damp, knee sock and a tube of Deep Heat. We plastered his knee in the embrocation and held it in with the sock. It improved things a bit but not as much if the knee sock had been dry.

As we descended we speculated whether the boat would still be there – we'd have been a bit stuck without it. Fortunately it was and we launched it into the loch with a sense of relief the final leg of the day was about to be embarked upon.

Time dragged on the boat ride back, we were cold by now and the fun of taking the boat out for two days in a row had now lost its appeal.

Loch Mullardoch is a flooded loch because of the hydroelectric dam. Apparently when the water is low you can see the chimneys of the buildings lost when the loch was expanded on completion of the dam. A horrible, chilling, thought came into my head as we chugged back – what if I fell out of the boat and dropped down one of the chimneys?

The following day, with the others unwilling to venture into the hills, we toured around a bit, visiting this and that. Only on Thursday May the 16th did I dare to mention the Munro word again. I had to use my powers of persuasion to get everybody to buy into the idea and then only by selecting a straightforward single Munro. Therefore we selected a drive north to take in Fionn Bheinn.

We started shortly after 11:30 and reached the summit just before 14:30 and got back to the cars in just over an hour. We nearly climbed the wrong hill on the way up and had to use the GPS to confirm which the right one was. The weather was good at the top but there was a bit of snowfall on the way back down and a peak opposite, clear on the way up, was now covered in snow.

In all we had a good holiday. However, it did convince me large group holidays have lost their appeal. It had worked much better in the past. Although this was good, it was noticeable people become less flexible in their early thirties and trying to organise things to keep everybody content was, at times, trying. However, I got a lot out of staying in Glen Cannich again as it is a place I really love. We had a nice meal in the Mullardoch House Hotel on the last night – the owner told us the dam had been slipping down the glen and over the last few years they have had to pin it with metal rods lowered from a helicopter.

I have given some thought as to why I keep returning to Mullardoch. During the time of doing the Munros (1989 to 2001) I visited it in 1989, 1991, 1992, 1994, 1995, 1996, 1997 and 1998. Maybe all these visits were because I'd such a good time in the glen in 1989 but the potential for more was never quite fulfilled.

Therefore I often go back there, alone, in search of it. When I get there only three of the four dimensions I require are present, the fourth, time, is when we hired the cottage. I should just make the decision never to go back but something draws me and I often find my car nosing its way along the rugged beauty of this glen. It's like I'm searching out some form of happiness that cannot exist in reality, the happiness of dreams. Where we play cards all night and all enjoy it, where we walk all day and love it. Cook huge meals and sit round telling tales of the mountains, experiences from the past and sharing jokes. I have done all these things in the Mullardoch Cottage holidays, but never in a roll. My mind yearns for the roll, a week of non-stop laughs, entertainment and exercise.

Ben Lui Again

As the others packed their bags at the end of the Mullardoch holiday I was busy arranging things in my rucksack for a trip over the Sgurr Fhuar-thuill – Sgurr na Ruaidhe ridge.

"Good luck with the Munros," said Mark.

Chris eyed my rucksack as I practised swinging it onto my back. "I'd hate to be stuck with having to do the Munros."

We finished saying our goodbyes and I headed north to drive round to Strathconon, my elected starting point requiring at least one night of camping. Before the turn into Strathconon, at Marybank, there is a phone box from which I phoned Gisella to say what my plans were in the event of any problems. As I was walking away from the phone box it rang, I went back and answered it in case it was Gisella calling me back with a sudden thought.

"Is Kevin there?" asked a voice on the end of the phone. Not Kevin Enright, I thought? I know Kevin via four different independent sources. Was this a fifth, tracked down to a phone box in the middle of nowhere?

Alas it was not.

I'd felt unease about this camping trip and when I was parking up in Strathconon I started to feel a bit ill and also had an eerie feeling what I was about to do would be a mistake. I therefore followed the route of caution and blew it out and instead drove south and stayed in a hotel in Tyndrum so I could tackle Beinn a'Chleibh and Ben Lui on Sunday May the 19th.

I'd a restless night through some Karaoke party taking place in the hotel bar and my mood wasn't improved over breakfast as the waitress got into a stand-up argument with one of the other guests. The only common ground they could find was their total agreement they had both, "Never been spoken to like that in their life before."

Once in my car I felt a bit better and, after I'd parked up, I started from the same approach I'd looked at some weeks previous when there was far more snow about. It took me just over two hours to reach the summit of Beinn a'Chleibh from where an hour and a half of extra walking brought in Ben Lui. The entire high ground was extremely windy and, on taking my rucksack off, I had to hold it down with rocks to stop it blowing away.

On the descent from the summit of Ben Lui I chatted with a chap who worked for IBM in Edinburgh. He knew a chap called Alan Robertson who provided consultancy to us on the Strathclyde Police Command and Control Project – it's a small world at times. Further on during my descent I listened to the Monaco Grand Prix on my pocket radio, all was going well until Damon Hill's engine blew while he was in the lead. I got back to the car just before 15:30 and a relatively short journey for a one-night stay at Killin Youth Hostel.

I reflected how my mood had improved during the day; exercise is a great stress reliever. I can start a day feeling uptight but after a few hours of walking the endorphins are flowing around my body and I'm feeling on a high, harmonious, good about the world and my breathing feels easier. I think this is a reason why life is getting more stressful, the days of walking or cycling to work have long gone for many people. If we all did a bit more exercise then there might not be so many problems in the world. I feel very sorry for elderly or disabled people who cannot exercise, if I were in this situation I'd become very frustrated, agitated and temperamental.

May the 20th brought in Meall Ghaordaidh, best approached from a starting point of Tullich in Glen Lochay. During the four-hour walk I experienced knee problems so this was definitely the last Munro of this trip. It was very cold and misty and wet all day and I remember feeling a sense of being lonely and very cold at the summit. At the end of the walk I had to cut through a field where, in the distance, a guy with a Land Rover was waiting by my car. 'Here goes, I've done something wrong,' I thought. As I approached my stress levels rose and I prepared myself for confrontation. 'Three, two, one', I counted myself down to within earshot.

"I saw you way up on the hill there and I hung on for you as there is a red squirrel moving her young into that tree there. I thought you'd like to see it."

What a sad person I am, there was me thinking I was in trouble and all the time he was waiting to share an experience with me.

This Munro was quite a quick one taking about four hours in all so I was back at the car for just after 12:30 and drove straight back to Marlborough.

With three years having passed since last seeing Willy Newlands, we arranged to meet up with Mike Linnett for some Munro bagging.

    With Mike kipping in my spare room I woke at 04:30 on Saturday September the 7th and, not wishing to disturb him, lay in until 07:30. With a subsequent rendezvous on the landing it turned out he woke at 04:30 too. If we'd known we could have got a three-hour head start. Either way we arrived at the Clachaig Inn in Glen Coe on time.

    In our triple cabin Mike and I emptied out our rucksacks, sprawled out on our beds and generally made ourselves comfortable.

    Willy arrived a few hours later, bursting into the room he'd booked, and surveyed the scene. "For fucks sake you didn't waste a moment trashing this place."

    Willy hadn't changed.

    "Aye," he said, continuing to glance around, "I'd have probably taken the best beds too."

    These were his first words to us in over three years.

    Mike and I took a bet on how long it'd be before he took the mick out of the GPS system I'd bought – eleven minutes forty-eight seconds. He then appeared disappointed that Mike and I were too tired to spend the entire evening in the bar.

On the Sunday we made the very long and arduous walk to Sourlies Bothy via Glen Dessarry. I carried a full pack and the heat was just blistering so I really struggled during the nine-mile trek. The weight of the pack was too much for me even on this relatively level ground and all the time I was thinking about how I'd cope the following day when I'd have to carry this pack over the mountains.

During part of the walk I took my mind off the pain by listening to the Italian Grand Prix but came to the conclusion, given Damon Hill crashed early on in the race, I am a jinx on him when I listen to Grand Prix on the radio while out walking.

The approach to Sourlies Bothy was a welcome sight. The Bothy is on the shore of a sea loch and surrounded by dramatic mountain scenery. The evening sun glinted on the calm waters of the loch and the place had an overwhelming sense of peace and tranquillity. From the point of first seeing the bothy and actually getting there was some three quarters of an hour – this is often the case in Scotland as the sheer vastness of the place makes distance deceptive. As I approached I had to tread carefully as there were many tiny frogs, no bigger than a thumbnail, in amongst the moist grass.

Willy's hot tip for bothy life is to get there first and lay out your sleeping bag. The reasoning being at any moment a horde of people could turn up and take all the best places. When I arrived only Willy and Mike were there so I'd no such worries.

Later in the evening two chaps arrived, father and son, by canoe from Mallaig. We had a fantastic evening relaxing first by gathering drift wood and then by burning it on a beach fire while failing to ignite a railway sleeper which, judging by the state of it, many an eager bothy inhabitant had tried to seek comfort from.

We all sat round chatting and admiring the most beautiful star-lit night I'd ever seen. Because we were so far from civilisation there was no ambient light to ruin the display. The Milky Way was absolutely fantastic and the event was set off by shooting stars and moving satellites.

Mike and I both have scientific backgrounds so we got into a discussion about Einstein's theory of relativity.

Willy was aghast. "Never did I think I'd live to see the day when we'd sit far out in the wilderness discussing Einstein's bloody theory of relativity."

Arts graduates, typical!

Mike and Willy have developed banter between themselves I can only ever be a witness to. Towards the end of the Strathclyde Police Command and Control Project we went out for a meal to celebrate and we all had a great deal to drink. Alcohol changes people in different ways and with Mike he just sits there smiling a lot. Willy just gets louder and more outrageous than normal. Willy took it on himself to start hurling humorous insults at Mike. Mike was unable to defend himself, in fact he could barely speak. Willy picked up on this and started hurling the abuse thick and fast. Never have I seen a spectacle where a man has had to take so much abuse, it was a very funny moment. We were all cracked up as Mike desperately tried to defend himself and only ever got as far as saying, "Well Willy," before the next barrage hit him.

While staying at Sourlies another example of this banter displayed itself. Mike and I retired to our sleeping bags first whereas Willy stayed up to enjoy more of the night sky. In the morning Willy said he'd heard a rutting stag from across the loch. Now a rutting stag has a distinctive sound, something like a cow with a sore throat.

Mike said, "Are you sure it wasn't a cow, Willy?"

The reply was a classic Willy line. "I suppose if it bounded across a mountain, forded streams climbed near vertical slopes, made its way along the shore of a loch and shagged three deer then yes it could have been a cow."

Bothies are extremely basic accommodation. They are normally no more than re-roofed ruined cottages. The floors and walls are bare, they have no electricity, water or loo. There is no charge for staying in them, the idea being you can just turn up for a night of shelter. Any improvement in facilities could be a mistake as then people would start to use them as alternative holiday accommodation, which isn't what they are intended for.

On waking at Sourlies I lay in my sleeping bag and looked around the grim-looking single roomed bothy. I started to reflect on what life might have been like here when it was actually a family home. It must have been tough, especially in the cruel Scottish winters. Trying to imagine it with the modern world in mind is hard to conceive. I imagined having a family there with the trappings of modern day life just twenty miles away: television, electricity, central heating and opportunity. It wouldn't work, the grass would be greener on the other side of the loch. Life back then must have been tough but perhaps, given everybody had the same, it'd have been free of envy and jealousy.

I carried these thoughts outside and looked up to the head of the loch where there were many other ruins, hinting at the community that once lived there. I then remembered a conversation I'd had with my grandparents some six years before in which they were describing life to me just after the war. They were living in a rented house and things were very tight. My gramp was saying all the things they didn't have, what they had to go without.

My gran then turned to him and said, "But we didn't know we were missing out, nobody else had anything either, we didn't have the stress the youngsters do today."

Sadly the people who once occupied these homes, now dejected shells of hopes and dreams, probably did suffer extreme stress on the day of their departure. The depopulation of the Highlands was driven by the clearances where land owners, wishing to convert their land to more profitable pursuits, evicted the communities of crofters in a genocidal act of violence in which houses were burnt to the ground and the peoples left to fend for themselves. Many moved to Canada, where, in complete irony, they built a better, less class-ridden country.

We set off for Sgurr na Ciche at 08:00 on Monday September the 9th and I lost sight of Willy and Mike within forty-five minutes. They reached the summit at 11:00, I arrived at 13:35 frustrated and exhausted, having abandoned my rucksack in the heat. They said it was the best day they'd ever had on the hills – the bastards.

For most of the way I could barely put one foot in front of the other, the combination of the weight of my pack, the gradient, my asthma and the temperature rendered me virtually stationary.

Sgurr na Ciche and Garbh Chioch Mhor

From the summit we returned to the saddle between Sgurr na Ciche and Garbh Chioch Mhor where Willy kindly shot off and collected my rucksack for me. I then left the rucksack between the two Munros while we scaled Garbh Chioch Mhor, getting there at about 15:30.

The original plan was to have also done Sgurr nan Coireachan and Sgurr Mor and stay at Kinbreack bothy. I wasn't up to it and offered to bivi the night in the hills while Mike and Willy went on. They would hear nothing of it and insisted they stayed with me so we made an alternative plan of heading to A' Chuil bothy which is about half way between Sourlies and where we'd parked the cars. Once this plan was made, such that we could remain together, we set off and in no time I lost sight of Mike and Willy as I again struggled with my rucksack.

In all it took me another four and a half hours to get to A' Chuil. Mike dropped back to walk with me for the last hour. Willy had gone ahead and we saw him collecting wood in the distance. I was still struggling and the last few miles were very difficult as we had the bothy in sight but the ground was very peaty and difficult to cross. Many times we had to backtrack as we painted ourselves into a corner. As we approached the final few hundred metres Mike said, "You know they say after a tough day of travelling whatever standard the accommodation is it looks appealing."

I was poised to agree when Mike added, "Fuck that little theory."

I could see what he meant as it did look a grim run down ramshackle place. I stepped through the door at 20:00 but once inside the relief of being able to rest and not have to wrestle with my rucksack again that day, dispelled any disappointment.

Mike and Willy had been suffering from midge bites most of the weekend. Thankfully they always declined my body's invitation to lunch. Even in the bothy Mike was suffering and pulling them off one by one while saying, "Look, mate, I'm a vegetarian, don't eat me."

I mentioned earlier about bothies not having a loo. This isn't strictly true as each bothy does come fully equipped with its own latrine: a spade. I was hoping to hang on until civilisation but on waking the following morning I knew nature was in no mood for any further delay. I pulled on some clothes and picked up the spade and headed for some nearby trees. This is where I learnt one of the hottest tips for bothy life: DO NOT, I REPEAT DO NOT UNDER ANY CIRCUMSTANCES DIG IN SOFT GROUND. The reason being if it is soft ground somebody else has been there before you. Hire a pneumatic drill take a pickaxe but whatever you do not dig is soft ground. This experience put me off and I was left to carry my thirty pound sack along with the problem back to civilisation. Civilisation was a grubby pub loo but it was heaven.

The other thing bothies contain is *The Bothy Book* – a visitor's book where people can write in their thoughts, comments and funny stories. In the one in Sourlies somebody had written 'English Bastards Out'. I mentioned it to Willy, always game to talk humorously about the Scottish/English issue, and we recalled the first day I arrived in Scotland to work on the Strathclyde Police Command and Control Project was the day of the England versus West Germany semi-final of the 1990 World Cup. I made it back to the hotel on time and watched it on the TV in my room. For me it was heart breaking to see England go out on penalties, and the look on Gary Lineker's face when he was unable to console Gazza's tears has always stuck in my mind.

On getting to work the next day, I was describing my disappointment to Willy when he burst out laughing. "You expect us to have sympathy for England getting knocked out?"

Fortunately *The Bothy Book* at A'Chuil was much nicer with no nationalistic comments. Though a limerick caught my eye:

Said Queen Isabella of Spain
I like it now and again
But let me explain
By now and again
I mean now and again and again

81

Mike, Willy and I parted company at Spean Bridge. We knew it'd been a good one and were all sorry the trip was over. Seeing Willy again after three years was really good and the introduction to bothy life was a good experience and to become useful in my approach to other Munros.

After saying goodbye I intended to go off and find a place to camp for the night. I tried a couple of places I thought might be quiet and where I'd go undisturbed. Unfortunately each place had human beings in close vicinity and I began to doubt the idea. I have a general mistrust of people and I know I'd lay awake worrying if I thought my tent was visible to others. After giving up on the idea I thought I'd go for the opposite and find myself a hotel with ensuite. I soon spotted a sign for a hotel with vacancies at a price that suited. I went into the deserted, spacious, reception hall and rang the bell for attention. A neat lady appeared who on casting an eye over my unshaven, grubby, having slept rough for two days, appearance informed me they were full. I just about stopped myself from saying, "Would you like me to take your vacancy sign down on the way out?"

To be fair I probably smelt a bit too.

I drove on to Newtonmore and found a good looking hotel called the Balavil Sports Hotel – what a splendid name I thought but decided against enquiring about the type of sports that leant it the name as I was sure they'd be disagreeable. The hotel proprietor was obviously going through a rough trading patch as I was immediately made to feel very welcome. After a shower a shave and a fresh set of clothes I felt, and looked, human again.

On this trip I tried out a new device to aid nasal breathing. I got the idea from watching Formula 1 motor racing where the drivers had all taken to wearing these strips of plaster across the bridges of their nose. The idea being the gentle pressure opens the airways. However, the little strips of plaster did have a side effect –

when I removed them I had an interesting sun tan!

Over to the A9

In all I spent four nights staying in Newtonmore but, needing to rest, I bagged just three Munros. On September the 11th I took in Meall Chuaich which I started at 10:30 from a lay-by on the A9. It took three hours to reach the cloudy top and, with the Munros in this area being unappealing rounded humps, I understood why they aren't viewed as classic walks.

I added to the tedium of the day by failing to take enough food with me. By the time I started to descend the hunger pangs were jabbing at my stomach and, with no food waiting for me in the car, I felt thoroughly miserable.

Slumped in the driver's seat I decided to forego the ritual of making a few brief diary notes and instead got set to drive back to Newtonmore for food. With my foot on the clutch pedal, my stomach rattling with hunger and my trembling hand about to turn the ignition key I suddenly recalled Mike was eating a tube of Pringles during our drive up from England. I felt under the seat and located the tube amongst the debris of sandwich wrappers and drinks bottles. I felt a ridiculous level of joy as I found the tube still contained a full three inches of pure Pringles. As I made some notes of the day's walk I threw them down my throat. Thank you, Mike, you were my hero at that moment.

On the following day, Thursday the 12th, I bagged Carn na Caim and A' Bhuidheanach Bheag, starting from another lay-by on the A9. Again these were fairly tedious Munros, unlike the peaks around Sourlies I'd just been treated to. It took two and a half hours to reach the first Munro then a two-hour jaunt across barren ground to A' Bhuidheanach Bheag (longer than I thought it'd take) followed by a tedious two hours back to the car.

I also found the hotel tedious and alternated my time between the TV in my bedroom, walks down the main street in Newtonmore and looking forward to the evening bar meal.

A coach load of middle-aged and retired people stayed at the same time as me who, by chance, also came from Wiltshire. I idly listened to them exchanging stories – they were either all recently retired or in the last few years of their jobs. They spent much time describing their work, mainly blue collar and I felt they were all looking for something missing in their lives. I caught a few of the men making longing glances at retreating waitresses. On the final morning I was late down to breakfast and ate my food as the last of the coach party got set to leave the hotel for good. The waitresses were clearing the tables when one of the old guys came back in and dropped a tip in a metal dish set aside for such a purpose. The waitresses didn't hear, he picked the coins up again and dropped them from a greater height.

This time one of the waitresses looked up.

"Thanks then, we're off," he said.

"Right you are," she replied and got back to her work.

I felt sad for them. Life had come to this.

After this there were no more new Munros for the year. On Friday September the 14th my friend Kate Taylor arrived at Glen Nevis Youth Hostel. On the Saturday we did Ben Nevis, a repeat Munro for me and a hard slog to the summit amongst the crowds of people who do this mountain. It was cloudy at the top and I was disappointed Kate failed to get a view as she'd travelled to Scotland especially to do it. Just for fun I got my GPS out to see how accurate it could be with the grid reference and the height of the peak. Immediately another walker said, "Your mobile phone won't work up here mate," and nodded at me sagely while reflecting on his superior intelligence.

On the Sunday we got a train round to Loch Ossian Youth Hostel with the view of doing Stob Coire Easain and Stob a'Choire Mheadhoin the following day. Loch Ossian is a very remote hostel, only reachable on foot from a railway station and definitely no vehicular access. It is a beautiful setting with the rustic hostel next to the water and the hills surrounding it like a group of familiar friends who can just sit silently in each other's company. Unfortunately I woke up with a sore throat and the Munros had to be left for another day. Instead we hiked back to Spean Bridge.

After the walk, Kate and I stopped for a few nights in the accommodation block in Fort Augustus Abbey. Here one of those things in life happened which can only be described as uncanny. Kate's aunt and uncle were by pure coincidence in the next room to us, it was a good job we weren't having an affair!

So after a wind down from Munro bagging, I drove home on September the 19th for a flight out to Portugal with my friend, Nick Green, to watch the Portuguese Grand prix. We were hoping to witness Damon Hill winning the Formula 1 World Championship but alas he could only manage second place in this race and didn't secure the championship until the next, and final, race of the season.

Munro Count: 65

1997

Preparation

I knew in my heart of hearts that to achieve my aim of doing the Munros would require more time and dedication than I'd previously put in. At the start of the year my tally stood at sixty-five out of the 277. On the face of it this may sound a reasonable achievement but it'd taken eight seasons. At the current rate I'd complete these confounded mountains in another quarter of a century – my late fifties. With the risk of a middle-aged ailment, or my asthma, curtailing my ambition I needed to get cracking.

For the previous two years I'd been working as a freelancer for a company called Dopra, developing a 999 call-taking system for Hampshire Fire and Rescue service. I was getting a lot out of the project and enjoying the thrill of developing a computer system to deploy fire engines onto the streets as a direct result of an operator taking a 999 call. Like all *good* computer projects it was running late and I kept agreeing to extend my contract each time the project over ran. During the winter it became clear the customer would accept the project in late April, tying in with the start of the summer walking season. I therefore planned to head for Scotland in early May for at least ten weeks. It was also ten years since I'd graduated, and therefore ten years of working in an office – definitely time for a break and a chance to extend the last seven years of snatched time doing the Munros into something more fitting of an expedition.

Arrangements were a bit hectic. The first thing I decided to do was to get fit. Therefore I visited the gym regularly and on some weekends put about four hours in. I also took my mountain bike for a few spins around Savernake Forest, sometimes staying out so late I was zipping between the trees in the dusk.

I also decided to try and get some movement into the joint between my big toe and my right foot. In 1987 I'd injured it badly playing football (or to be precise, I injured it by playing football badly), it'd mended itself but weakened the muscles around the joint and down the instep. Gisella suggested massage, which I did on a daily basis with various oils she bought me from Boots. It did the trick as far as getting movement into the joint but the muscles still felt weak.

The next thing was to make sure my finances were in order for such a long trip. I needed to get all foreseeable hurdles out of the way which meant I had to come clean with my accountant and tell him what I was up to. I was expecting some talking to about how this trip would affect my income. But nothing of the sorts, he was enthusiastic and on meeting pumped my hand firmly and wished me luck.

To add to the complications Gisella and I'd decided to sell our house and had accepted an offer some weeks before my departure date. After four and a half years of DIY we'd had enough and decided to sell what we considered 'The House of Hammer Horror'. The purchasers asked if we could hold off completion until July. This was excellent, a house move any earlier would have cut short my trip. Things were falling into place.

The next task was to take a good look at my kit and decide if I needed any more goodies from the sweet shop that masquerades as an outdoor enthusiasts centre. So it was off to the Cotswold Camping shop near Cirencester I went with credit card in hand to extend my collection of kit. I was aware my mother and Gisella had concerns for my safety. Therefore I decided to buy an emergency transmitter beacon. These are devices normally attached to yachts, which during a disaster the crew can activate. Once activated the device broadcasts an emergency signal on the 121.5 MHz frequency that can be picked up by aircraft and specialised satellites. Anybody who remembers Tony Bullimore's rescue way off the coast of Australia will know what a lifesaver one of these devices was for him.

I asked at the counter for one.

"What do you want it for?" replied the assistant.

This wrong footed me for a second. I've bought many things in my life and never been asked why.

"For walking," I said. "In Scotland," I added trying to justify myself.

"They are really only for yachts," replied the assistant sternly, "walkers should rely on the mountain rescue services."

"I know," I said, "but I walk alone and go out in the wilds of Scotland." I thought what else can I say? I know, "I only intend to use it if my life is in danger, I'm not intending to use it if I am simply lost."

The assistant relaxed and said he was happy to sell me one. Apparently there have been instances of walkers using them when simply lost, annoying the RAF who have gone as far as scrambling Nimrods when one goes off. So I took possession of a brightly coloured handheld Jotron TRON 1E MKII device for a cost of about £140. Secretly it wasn't just my mum's and girlfriend's voices which drove me to buy this thing, my own fears of breaking a leg high up in the mountains also played a hand.

Earlier in the year I'd watched one of the Wilderness Walks television programmes with Cameron McNeish and the Olympic gold medallist Chris Brasher. In the programme they praised trekking poles. These are telescopic ski-like poles you carry in each hand and use to take the weight off your knees. I decided to invest in a pair so what with the transmitter, a new stove, a pair of light weight boots and various other sundries I departed from the

Cotswold Camping shop heavier in the carrier bag department but lighter in the wallet.

When I first started walking I always looked at the cheapest equipment and worked up. Time has brought an increase in experience and salary to the point I now always look at the most expensive kit and work down. Many times I have been in the mountains wet, cold and miserable wishing I'd spent an extra £50 on a jacket.

I also invested in a new camera and doubled the value of my car by buying a CD player for it. It sounds a bit extravagant but I knew I'd be spending a lot of time in my car and could do with some music of my own choice.

I was uncertain how long I'd spend in Scotland or how many Munros I'd achieve. However, I set myself the following targets for my total Munro tally:

70	because this would be quarter of the Munros done.
77	because there would be 200 to go.
88	because this would be greater than my previous total in a year.
93	because this was a third of the way.
100	because it is a nice round figure.
109	because this was greater than twice my previous total in a year.
125	because in 1992 I made this part of a five-year-plan.
127	because there would be 150 to go.
130	because this would be twice my current total of sixty-five.
139	because this would be half way.

Privately I wanted to break the 100 mark and exceeding 125 would be a bonus. Of course this all appears very sad and makes me sound like the Munro equivalent of a train spotter. This is totally untrue because I don't wear a blue Pac-a-mac and I never take a thermos up the mountains.

As a final boost to my forthcoming trip The National Asthma Campaign featured a small piece about my Munro-bagging exploits in their quarterly magazine. This was as part of a larger article discussing the sporting exploits of asthmatics.

The First One of the Trip

I set off for Scotland on Saturday May the 3rd, two days after Tony Blair's landslide election victory. I decided to spend the first night in Glasgow and trail around a few of my old haunts. Needing somewhere to park my car, I booked a hotel slightly out of town.

I arrived in the late afternoon and after a rest I decided to take a walk around the city. I started by walking towards the Central Hotel, where I used to stay. Now the Central Hotel is right on the Central Railway Station, which has its seedy sides. I took a few wrong turns and found myself in a drab and seedy area, a few streets away from where I knew I wanted to be. Ahead of me a lady crossed the road and approached me. Perhaps she needs to know the time I thought, or perhaps she's lost too.

"You looking for business, love?"

Ah, I see. I had naively strayed into the red light district. I hastily fumbled out a no and thanked her for asking. I took a few paces then, with typical male curiosity, looked back. She was nowhere to be seen. I am not very streetwise.

On May the 4th I set off from Glasgow to bag Ben Challum. It was raining and I opted to follow a track above a deep gully with the raging Allt Gleann a'Chlachain stream in its base. I soon realised I'd made a bit of a mistake because I needed to be the other side of the gully so I cut down to the stream. This was my second mistake because in the base of a gully your field of view is restricted to a few metres around you. I knew I needed to branch to the north-east but deciding at which point to take the plunge was difficult. The map showed many tributary streams but, given the OS may have done their aerial survey when some of these were dry, I couldn't rely on counting these off as a reliable method of navigation.

I switched on my GPS and found the batteries were flat – I'd forgotten to check them, but at least I carried spares. However, my heart sank when I found the old ones were stuck firm in the torpedo tube battery cases. So now it was down to my navigational skills. I decided to cross the stream at the next convenient point – this didn't come for quite a while and then only in the form of a derelict bridge. The iron girders were narrow, too narrow to walk across. Many of the wooden slats were missing or rotten. This is where the trekking poles took on an extra dimension. While crossing the bridge I was able to test each plank by striking it with a trekking pole before risking the weight of my foot. Many were unusable so I spent a while picking my way across with the stream in fast flow below. I was impressed with the poles, they helped me across this bridge and had proved very useful on the uphill and downhill sections of the walk so far. They had also given me something to do with my hands – often when walking I don't know where to put my hands.

The escapade with the bridge reminded me of a story Willy Newlands told me. A year or so ago he'd been out walking, with a friend, in the winter and it had become extremely cold. They were heading for a bothy and making steady progress before nightfall. As they were without a tent reaching the bothy was absolutely essential – spending a night out would have spelt death from hypothermia.

According to their map the bothy was the other side of a

river but there was a bridge marked. On reaching the bridge their hearts sank as they discovered all of its wooden structure had been swept away and all that remained were two six inch wide iron girders which were too far apart to straddle. This meant they had to cross tight rope style. Unlike a tight rope they weren't hundreds of feet above the ground, but their danger was in some ways more sinister. The river was flowing fast and had risen to within a few inches of the remains of the bridge. I know what Willy meant by 'flowing fast' – raging torrent. They managed to make it across but the phrase Catch-22 stayed with them for a long time. It was either death by hypothermia or risk the girders and try and avoid death by drowning.

Now back to the Ben Challum story. Having crossed the 'bridge' I headed north-east on a compass bearing. This was the hard slog bit – most Munros have a section where you encounter exceedingly steep slopes for about one to two hours. As per usual my age old question of, 'Why do I do this?' came to mind.

It was misty and raining so I took bearings off a succession of distant objects which I walked between. The lower slopes of Ben Challum were quite generous because there were many boulders to take a bearing on and walk to. Finally selecting one I put my head down and marched forth. On one occasion I glanced up and was certain the boulder I was heading to had moved. Indeed it had, it was a sheep.

I reached the summit at around 15:00 and, as there was no view, I turned straight around for the three-hour tromp back to the car. Sitting in the driver's seat with my feet swung out onto the ground I took my boots off and a cloud of steam rose from each.

I was satisfied with my first day's walk. On a couple of occasions it looked as if I'd have to abandon, but it all turned out okay. My troublesome knees gave a couple of twangs but I pacified them with Deep Heat. It was also the first time I'd carried the emergency transmitter. Paranoia caused me to check it regularly to ensure the pin, which you pull out to activate it, was still in place. I could imagine strolling along and thinking to myself 'There's a lot of helicopters about today.'

Killin

I arrived at Killin Youth Hostel where I planned to base myself until I finished the Munros in the area, to find it amidst renovation work. It was good to see the Scottish Youth Hostel Association is putting money into this non-mainstream hostel. Over the last few years quite a number of hostels have been forced to close because of lack of funds. After showering and eating I spent a frustrating evening trying to extract the stuck batteries from my GPS. I failed.

Another debate I had with myself during the close season was how many consecutive days walking I should chance on my poor knees. As I'd bought the most expensive knee supports I could find, in the hope this would alleviate the problem, I decided to do a second day's walking and then take the following day off. Therefore on Monday May the 5th I set out from the hostel to do Meall Glas and Sgiath Chuil. These two Munros live at the end of Glen Lochay, north-west of Killin. The first thing I found was the recommended parking place in the guidebook was no longer accessible, the popularity of the sport is clearly causing land owners to gate their private roads.

I started walking at 10:00 in poor visibility, the mist cleared from time to time revealing two peaks. I was confused which peak was Sgiath Chuil and took a gamble, which fortunately paid off. After a hard slog I reached the summit at 14:00, quite late in the day for then striking out to Meall Glas. The weather was poor with my face being viciously sandblasted by hail and snow. It was also really cold and I only just managed to get comfortable by wearing a

93

T-shirt, a normal shirt, a thick jumper, a thermal fleece and my Gore-Tex jacket.

At one stage the wind whipped my map and compass, which were held by cord around my neck, into the air. I managed to catch the map case but then was in a panic as my compass was nowhere to be seen. It is always a debate whether it is worse to lose your map or your compass – I think I'd keep the compass as you can just head in one direction until you find something familiar. As the visibility was so poor I really needed to find it. After a few more anxious minutes of panic I discovered it'd blown, out of sight, around the back of my neck.

About ten minutes after this incident the map case decided to change personality and become a kite, using my neck as an anchor. The scene must have been comical as I was desperately trying to catch it while its cord twirled around my neck slowly garrotting me. However, I was playing to an empty stage as, like yesterday, I had the hills to myself.

A bit further on, the map case was again wrenched out of my grasp, this time the cord holding it around my neck ended up in my mouth cutting the join between my upper and lower lips. Things were against me and I seriously considered pulling out of doing Meall Glas. I pressed on and promised myself to review the situation at 16:00. When 16:00 came I felt I'd made sufficient progress so continued and reached my sixty-eighth Munro at 17:20.

The walk back was tiresome as I misjudged a suitable crossing point over the river in the floor of Glen Lochay. I must have walked up and down for twenty minutes or so looking for a suitable place to cross. In the event the one I plumped for made my feet much wetter than they already were. I got back to the car at 20:00, damp and bedraggled but elated in having achieved the two Munros despite the conditions. I decided the trekking poles were excellent and had vastly assisted my ascent and descent.

Arriving late and soaked at a youth hostel is fairly common so I went unnoticed as I staggered through Killin's front door. On showering I discovered I'd a blood-filled blister on each of my heels. I popped them both and cleaned them up with surgical wipes and plastered them over.

Killin is a very friendly hostel and the new wardens made me feel very welcome. It was also a pleasure to encounter John Ward again. He was a chap I'd previously met twice in the hills above Loch Mullardoch. Seeing a familiar face in unfamiliar surroundings always takes one a few seconds to place.

"You're a retired school teacher," I said.

"And you're the man who hired a boat and took it to the bottom of Loch Mullardoch," he replied.

I didn't dwell too long on the double meaning behind 'the bottom of Loch Mullardoch'.

The One That Got Away

I took the following day off and visited the Teddy Bear museum in Calendar and the Motor museum at Doune. At both places I was welcomed and forcibly given a discount at the motor museum because they had the doors open and it was a bit cold! I also phoned Cotswold Camping, near Cirencester, to ask about the stuck batteries in my GPS. They straightaway knew the problem so I arranged to post it back.

One thing which occurred to me on my day off is I am bad at enjoying the moment. Whenever I get to a place I immediately look for the next thing to do and forget to take pleasure from the present. Therefore I am always hoping the future will supply the pleasure I wish for. Ultimately it means I rarely truly enjoy myself.

This perhaps is why I enjoy Munro bagging because I am doing something for most of the day and therefore there is no opportunity to think 'now what shall I do next'?

It was on May the 7th I got back to the hills, taking in Beinn Heasgarnich and Creag Mhor. This is one of the frustrating groups of hills where they are close enough to do in a day but are on different maps. Being now more relaxed about my possessions I cut the relevant part out of one map and stuck it to the other with sticky plasters.

After my experiences of Sgiath Chuil and Meall Glas I decided on an earlier start. Striking out at 08:20 I reached the intricate summit of Beinn Heasgarnich at around midday, or so I thought. I was following two other guys up in the mist by tracking their footprints in the snow. Suddenly the footprints disappeared without trace. I could only assume an alien abduction had taken place. I was a bit unsure about the peak so walked parts of the ridge and finally settled on a small cairn as being the summit. The trek across to Creag Mhor was much easier save for a very steep descent off Beinn Heasgarnich. By this stage my body was loosening up a bit and I arrived at the second peak just after 15:00 and got back to the car two hours later.

On the second peak I got chatting to two guys who were doing the same walk as me but in reverse. I bumped into them back at the car where I learnt it'd taken me over four hours longer to do the same distance.

I chatted with John Ward again in the evening. He thought perhaps I'd missed the actual summit cairn on Beinn Heasgarnich and instead I'd found the cairn marking the west end of the ridge. Secretly I was thinking 'damn, he is probably right' but spent a while in denial about the possibility I'd missed this one. Deep down I knew I'd have to return to make sure.

John was very precise about his pronunciations. Being dyslexic I am useless at the Gaelic phonetics so every time I mentioned the name of a mountain John repeated it in a different way. I think pronunciations can become a figment of people's imaginations as I have copied one person's pronunciation only to then be corrected by somebody else. Perhaps you just have to sound convincing.

Personally I think all the mountain names were made up on the spot when the nineteenth century OS surveyors asked the locals. I am convinced some of the mountain names translate to such things as, 'Go away you silly little bald man with a theodolite'.

I further chatted with John and mentioned somebody had screamed in our dorm during the night. He said it was because he'd clouted a snorer – once a school teacher always a school teacher I suppose. Actually I'm convinced the snorers are in the employ of the local B&B's to force the innocent hostel guests to take refuge in their establishments. Of course I jest but there is a classic type of hosteller who bores you to sleep all evening with tales of hostelling in the old days then keeps you awake all night by snoring and farting.

My First Walk on The Ben Lawers Ridge

The following day I decided to do Schiehallion but was thwarted by my trusty Toyota finally breaking down on me after 153,800 miles. I could have no complaints but by the time the 'very nice man' from the AA got me going again, and I'd arranged for the necessary parts to be sent up, it was too late to try for the mountain. This was the second time Schiehallion had eluded me as I was due to do it with Willy Newlands back in 1991 but, for a reason that now escapes me, we failed to start it.

Therefore my next adventure into the hills was on May the

9th with an ambitious plan of doing four of the six Munros on the Ben Lawers ridge.

It was a clear day and I set off at 08:15 from the National Trust visitors' centre and followed the well-marked paths up onto the ridge. After about half an hour of walking I felt I was missing something. I then realised I'd set off without my trekking poles – it was too late to return for them.

I reached the summit of Beinn Ghlas at 10:25 and Ben Lawers at 11:30. At this point I'd the choice of going on and completing the east side of the ridge or to double back and do the two Munros to the west of the visitors' centre. I opted for doubling back so took in Meall Corranaich and Meall a Choire Leith. In the final descent I got bogged down in an intricate area and ended up in a hollow, feeling a sense of panic when I was unable to focus on any point to head towards. I calmed myself and logic told me just to use my compass to rise up out of the hollow and find the final stretch of the walk, which took me along the minor road back to the visitors' centre.

I tried to hitch a couple of times but with no luck. I looked a bit bedraggled and any tourist driving past in their brand new Rover 620 with optional leather interior with walnut dash was sure to give me a miss.

My Second Walk on The Ben Lawers Ridge

Today I decided to complete the Ben Lawers ridge by bagging its two most easterly Munros: Meall Greigh and Meall Garbh.

The best place to start these is from the village of Lawers on the road between Killin and Kenmore. However, the local inhabitants do not favour their community being regarded as a public car park for hill walkers. Therefore the signs vary from 'No

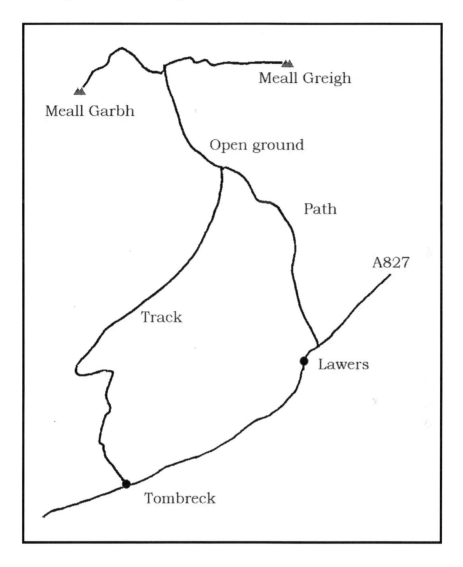

The problems of finding parking at Lawers are legendary. One chap, staying at the youth hostel, told me how he'd once parked outside a farm at Lawers and on setting off discovered the owners of the farm had a well-rehearsed plan to corner any fiendish illegal parker. This involved employing two people and an easily bribed Alsatian dog. The victim would be allowed to park his or her car and ready themselves for the hills while the farm owners prepared the ambush at a barn which the walker had to pass. It was here any feelings of 'parked car smugness' were curtailed. On some form of cue the two people would run in opposite directions around the building while the third conspirator, the Alsatian dog, was set loose for the kill, preventing any break for the hills.

I could find nowhere to park so headed back in the direction of Killin and parked near the small hamlet of Tombreck. This substantially increased the length of my walk as I now had to spend the first few hours walking up a Land Rover track to the shielings near some hydroelectric works.

A mile or so up the track a Land Rover was parked. I am always cautious and was worried about getting ticked off for cheating on the £5 parking charges at Lawers. As I got within 100 metres he started the engine. Here we go I thought and tensed myself for an encounter. Instead he looked straight through me and headed down the track.

In the area in which he'd been parked were a few animal pens. Curiosity got the better of me and I looked through the meshing of one of them to see the skin from the torso of a lamb. I reeled back in horror as I saw the rest of it, it had been delimbed and decapitated with its legs and head placed around the skinned torso in line with their original positions. Oh my god I thought, I've just encountered some inbred nutter doing tricky black magic with the livestock – the kind of bloke who reckons *The Wicker Man* is merely a documentary.

I looked back down the track and the Land Rover had parked near the bottom, near to my car. Had he seen me look into the pen? What to do I thought, press on or go back? I decided to take the chance there was some legitimate animal husbandry reason for performing this act on a lamb and decided to carry on. I kept the Land Rover and my car in view for a long time until the gathering mist gave me some confidence my Munro tally wouldn't be halted at seventy-four with my delimbed and decapitated body found a few days' later with my Gore-Tex jacket tossed to one side.

As I gathered height the wind reciprocated with ferocity. It became some of the worst conditions I'd ever encountered with the wind literally thumping the breath out of me and the snow and ice being whipped up into my face.

I had to climb up a deep gorge of a streambed then negotiate a tall deer fence. Although I didn't recall seeing any tall deer! Once on open ground I made for the line of an estate boundary fence. It was a fairly new construction but already was showing signs of the ravages of nature. I never understand why estates bother with fencing near the top of mountains. There are the remains of so many around I'd have thought by now the land owners would have got the hint Mother Nature views them with nothing but utter contempt. However, they make useful navigation routes in poor weather so I shall say no more.

When I reached the fence I piled a few small rocks near one of the posts as a reference point for my descent and then struck out east for Meall Greigh, Meall Garbh being to the west. It was very difficult to find the summit as there were a few false tops on route and visibility was appalling. I was able to follow my fence for about an hour, only dispensing with its services to search for the summit. The search took a while and I was glad when my wanderings, in the mist, bore fruit in the shape of the top. Just an isolated point in space whereas the previous day, in the clear sunlight, it was part of a grand ridge.

Once I'd taken the obligatory photograph I set straight off again – with the conditions so poor, resting meant I'd get very cold. I made some mistake on the way back to the fence and found myself in deep mist with nothing to take a reference from. In these situations it is always best to take a compass bearing and head for it, so I did this looking for my fence again. Still it proved evasive and I started to have constant hallucinations I could see it about ten metres in the distance but on getting there, each time, it'd gone. This frustratingly continued until I realised my eyelashes were icing up and every time I blinked it looked like a line of distant posts.

After some further searching, both of the terrain and my soul, I found a fence, but not the intended one. Instead I stumbled across the tall deer fence I'd had to cross on my original ascent. Nonetheless it was a welcome sight – I'd started to become concerned I was well and truly lost. I followed it around until I recognised my original crossing point.

I struck north again and found the estate boundary fence with my pile of rocks still on century duty. Now I could follow it to the west with the confidence it goes so close to the summit of Meall Garbh I never had to leave its friendly confines. I plodded on against the howling wind. Ice spikes, up to eighteen inches long, had formed on the sheltered sides of each fencepost. Footprints in the snow indicated humanity had been this way with only the fourth dimension, time, robbing me of a companion. I pulled the hood of my jacket as tight as I could to protect my face and eyes from the lashings of piercing ice being thrown at it.

> The weather is lovely
> The weather is fine
> Apart from this *blizzard*
> It's simply divine

I kept plodding, it was a trudge and my morale was low. Then all of a sudden a voice from behind said, "Hello."

I jumped out of my skin (which would have probably

thrilled the chap in the Land Rover) and turned – there was a young lady with a broad smile. A lovely Irish voice followed it up with, "I did not know how to attract your attention without making you jump. I saw you a way back and could not believe there would be another soul out in these conditions."

"That's okay," I replied as a wave of pleasure went through my body relishing the thought of a companion to share these atrocious conditions with. I privately hoped she'd be able to accompany me for the rest of the walk, not just because she was a beautiful young woman but because my need for company had suddenly become quite desperate.

"Heading for Meall Garbh?" I asked.

"Yes, then heading back to my car. I just managed to get parked at Lawers."

"Oh I'd trouble parking there and ended up at Tombreck."

"If we stick together then I'll give you a lift from Lawers to Tombreck."

This was just brilliant, company and a lift.

After finding the summit of Meall Garbh we managed to continue shouting out a conversation until we got back below the deer fence and to the relative calm of being able to speak without yelling at each other. I lapped up the company. Her name was Michelle she lived in Edinburgh and she'd just done her seventy-fourth Munro, my seventy-sixth. She started her Munro-bagging career in 1994. It transformed the day as she was an excellent companion having done a degree in philosophy, a subject that intrigues me a great deal. The lift from Lawers saved me about two hours walking and perhaps a fate similar to that which befell the poor lamb. Also she saved me an extra hour by being so quick I was virtually jogging to keep up with her.

I took a rest day on May the 11th and found a road unmarked on my road atlas. It is a private hydroelectric road, stretching from Glen Lochay to Glen Lyon, which appears to be open to the public by the good will of the owners.

I drove to the summit to get good enough reception to listen to the Monaco Grand Prix. While sitting in my car a hairy motor biker pulled up and spoke with me. He had a wonderfully soft Scottish accent. We spoke for a while and on hearing I was from the South of England and trying to get up to do the Munros whenever I could, told me of a book he was reading called *Burn on the Hill*. It is about a man called Ronnie Burn, from the South of England, who during the earlier part of the twentieth century did all the Munros by getting up to Scotland during his holidays. I resolved to locate a copy.

It was May the 12th when I set off to try and bag Schiehallion. Schiehallion is a famous mountain because in 1774 the Astronomer Royal, the Rev. Nevil Maskelyne FRS, used the gravitational pull of the mountain to try and estimate the mass of the world. Schiehallion is also famous for its pointy shape and its distinct features make it readily identifiable from many miles away.

The day was fairly uneventful with mixed weather and a long tedious pull, on slippery rocks, up. I re-christened it Ben Plod. It was a significant point as it was my seventy-seventh Munro with 200 to go. In all it took me five and a half hours. Back at the youth hostel, a chap told me he'd done it in three and a half.

One sad thing about Schiehallion is it is becoming badly eroded. The path is now so wide it could be better termed a motorway than a footpath. Being a walker myself, therefore part of the problem, I cannot grumble.

Schiehallion

The following day was another epic with four Munros planned. I always study the guidebooks carefully where routes taking in greater than two Munros are described. There is always the chance the route was done by some incredibly fit person and a mere mortal such as myself would struggle to do half the distance in the suggested time.

The group of four was the Carn Gorm group to the north of Killin. I took my recently discovered hydroelectric road to reach Glen Lyon and parked at Invervar where the local authorities had generously provided a nice little car park.

I traversed the horseshoe in a clockwise direction starting with Carn Gorm followed by Meall Garbh, Carn Mairg and Creag Mhor (Meall na Aighean). The pull up to the first Munro was laborious and meant I had to walk into the mist line.

Between Meall Garbh and Carn Mairg I followed the remains of an ancient fence across a few false summits. So indeterminate were the surroundings I began to question whether I'd inadvertently bagged it and missed the occasion.

On one pause, to check the map, a chap called Hugh caught up with me. He thought we still had a while to go which proved to be correct. In time honoured tradition he'd set out two and a half hours after me and caught up with me within an hour and a half. This is where I get frustrated because people look at me as a tall slim male and cannot comprehend how I take so long over doing the mountains. Perhaps if I'd only one leg I'd get away with it.

We parted company at the top of Carn Mairg as Hugh wanted to go on and do the Meall Liath, which is only classified as a top. I made a tough descent through a slippery boulder slope. I met up with Hugh again at the top of the final Munro, Creag Mhor. We walked back together to our cars, which were parked side by side. The company was good and as the weather cleared for the final Munro the day was finished off on a cheery note.

On the next day, my last at Killin Youth Hostel, I tackled Meall Buidhe and Stuchd an Lochain. These are unique pair of Munros because you return past your car, in Glen Lyon, half way through the trip.

I tackled Meall Buidhe first, enjoying good views from the summit. On the descent I met a couple of chaps with a dog. Dogs repeatedly run ahead and back again so I am convinced all dogs do a Munro at least twice in any single ascent.

Back in the floor of Glen Lyon I then had the strange experience of eating lunch in my car – normally lunch is grabbed on some windswept summit huddled below a pile of boulders.

After a twenty-five minute break I set off for Stuchd an Lochain, reaching it some two and a half hours later. Again I enjoyed good views from the summit.

I was tinged with sadness on my eleventh and last night at Killin Youth Hostel. The wardens joked I'd become their 'permanent resident' which, I hoped, wasn't a reference to the permanent residents in *Fawlty Towers.*

On this final night a group of us got chatting in the kitchen.

106

One was a chap who'd gone out to Australia in 1969 on a £10 passage and was now taking a holiday back in Britain at the age of sixty-two. He was a keen cyclist and had been involved in an appalling accident a few years back in which he'd lost an eye and damaged many of his joints. Nonetheless this plucky chap still rode a bike and was doing a UK tour.

He told us he'd an eighty-three-year-old sister who'd emigrated to Canada in the 1930s. He had met her only once but they still keep in touch. Also in the kitchen was a Canadian lady by the name of Barbara who joined in a general conversation about mountaineers and enjoyed my analogy doing such mountains as K2 was like crossing the M1 on foot while drunk. Later I got chatting to Barbara outside and we went for a few drinks together.

A week or so later Gisella was reading out my post to me over the phone when she said, "Bank statement – you're in credit, junk mail, junk mail, letter from such and such oh and the love letter."

"What?" I replied cautiously.

"I'll read it to you."

With that she put on a deep seductive Canadian accent. Apparently after I left Barbara had got my address from the warden and sent me a letter saying if I ever I was to find myself on the 'other side of the pond' I'd be welcome to stay.

Oban

I spent May the 15th getting my car fixed and enjoying a drive over to Oban. Oban is a beautiful place and is very accessible by road and rail. It is also a gateway to many of the islands as the Caledonian MacBrayne Ferry Company operate from there. This makes it quite a busy place with grand hotels lining the harbour walls. In turn the youth hostel is very impersonal which meant I slipped back into my default state of being very shy and skulking around.

The following day I tackled Stob Daimh and Ben Cruachan. These are unusual Munros because you have to start them from sea level: most Munros are inland where you get a couple of hundred feet starting advantage.

I was very weary climbing up Stob Daimh but I picked up speed on the ridge between the two Munros. In places it was a bit narrow which I found a bit scary. As a reward for my perseverance the weather was excellent so I was able to spend over an hour on the top of Ben Cruachan enjoying the views. Here I met a pair of middle-aged retired couples. One couple had, thirty years ago, named their house Cruachan and therefore resolved to one day climb it. I suggested they should have called it 'Lay-by on the A82' and saved themselves the trouble.

The chap also said he'd always resolved that when he got his wife to the top of Ben Cruachan he'd take her round the back of a large rock and make mad passionate love to her. He followed that up by saying, "So if you will excuse us for ten minutes."

His wife glanced at him.

"Okay then, ten seconds," he conceded.

I kept away from the hostel for as long as possible. The previous night some old guy used the sink in the room as a urinal, leaving me feeling repulsed by the thought of returning. However, it improved a bit this night but some people set their alarm clocks then made no attempt to get up. This is the selfish side of hostelling where people cannot comprehend setting an alarm clock, then not getting up may just be a tad anti-social.

The next day I targeted Beinn Eunaich and Beinn a'Chochuill. However, I nearly abandoned them the moment I got out my car – the wind was so strong I had to wrestle with my coat, managing to get one arm in its sleeve only to find the other one yards above my head flapping like a wind sock. I reeled it in, as a fisherman would a reluctant fish, before managing to slide my other arm in and bridle its anger.

I was very slow climbing Beinn Eunaich, it took me four hours in cloud and mist in complete contrast to the previous day. I think the contrast in the days contributed to my sluggish pace. After the first Munro I got a second wind and I managed to hurry across to the next Munro and took a direct line off it back to the return path. This made the descent very steep but I decided I wanted to get back to my car to hear the second half of Chelsea versus Middlesbrough in the FA cup final.

When I climb the mountains I spend nearly all of my time thinking about life, the universe and everything. Today I began to think again about why I actually do this sport. A reason came to mind, just a possibility, in that it is a sport I have found for myself. None of my family and friends are into Munro bagging so when I say I've done such and such a mountain I am spared the story of when they did it and how long it took them. Therefore there is no competition. On a similar line of thinking when I was at school I was either poor or average at most sports. At the time I got sucked in to thinking I was no good at sport at all. Although I had quick reflexes, good for in goal or playing badminton, I allowed the jeers of other pupils to get me down. Here in my adult life is a sport I can do at my own pace with my assets of stamina and tenacity seeing me through. There are no childhood echoes with this sport, it is all fresh and new and just for me.

Glen Coe

I took a rest day on May the 18th in preparation for an onslaught on the Glen Coe mountains. Glen Coe is one of Scotland's most beautiful glens and if you factor in accessibility, it has to be one of the best loved. Sadly for the Glen it is steeped in dark history. The Highland clans, who used to populate this area in their carefree and lawless way, had always been at odds with the ruthless central government. In August 1691 King William III, in London, offered a pardon to all the Highland clans provided they took an oath of allegiance before a magistrate by January 1st 1692. In the fair minded spirit of the offer King William gave them the option of the oath or death. The MacDonald's clan chief reluctantly agreed to take the oath but didn't present himself until January 6th. MacDonald thought because the oath had been taken this was acceptable, the King felt differently and unbeknown to the MacDonald's a force of Campbell's (loyal to the King) were formed at Inveraray to kill the MacDonalds. Marching north the Campbells, led by Captain Robert Campbell, reached Glen Coe and asked the MacDonalds for quarters. They were duly given hospitality for ten days until on the night of February 12th Campbell received orders to proceed to kill all of the MacDonalds under the age of seventy. The following morning the Campbells rose early and murdered forty MacDonalds, many more fled to the hills where they perished from the cold. It has always been regarded as a heinous crime as it was an act of betrayal of their hosts.

My visit to Glen Coe involved a shift in youth hostel to the less impersonal one in Glen Coe, apart from the warden who wore a permanent scowl on his face.

I'd always put off doing mountains in this area – there are so many doing the odd one or two wouldn't feel like an achievement. However, as this was to be a long Munro-bagging trip I decided to break it up and make two trips to the area. My first walk was a group of three Munros: Ben Starav, Beinn nan Aighenan and Glas Bheinn Mhor. These are way down Glen Etive, which is a glen running to the south of Glen Coe. The terrain is different to the Killin district where parallel glens have connecting roads; in this area the mountain ranges are more spectacular with no let-up for adjoining roads. Therefore although the mountains were close to the hostel as the crow flies, or should I say the ptarmigan, it was a long drive round.

I made my first mistake of the day by leaving a route card at the hostel. The idea of a route card is if you're overdue they know where to come looking for you. The disadvantage of them is it puts you against the clock and therefore encourages you to take risks if you're running late. My second mistake of the day was to cut steeply up the hillside. After a while I looked to my left and realised I was at a very steep angle and one slip would have led to a very long tumble, probably for about 1000ft. I experienced the classic borderline feelings of fear, panic and exhilaration. I had no choice but to stick with the situation of my own making and coax myself towards the ridge. This took quite some time and my nerves were fully tested.

Once on the ridge I was greeted by a black Labrador and soon joined by three other dogs. Their owner then appeared: a fair-haired bearded vision of a man. Where I wore a Gore-Tex jacket, he wore an old tweed jacket with an abundance of holes in the arms and main body. Where I wore tracksuit trousers, he wore khaki army ones. Where I wore heavy duty four season walking boots with Gore-Tex gaiters, he wore a pair of ancient army boots, scuffed and with many holes and patches. Where I wore a rucksack, he wore a 0.22 calibre high-velocity rifle. He was a stalker.

He was good company as we made our way to the top. It was interesting to chat to a 'real' Scot as usually most Scottish people you get to speak with are influenced by the tourist industry.

He had a mellow country accent and was taking a keen

111

interest in all about him. He was after foxes that prey on lambs, I also think he was simply out for a good walk. He said he loved South West England and had just been on holiday there.

Occasionally he peered into the glen below.

"Looking for foxes?" I asked.

In a dry tone he replied, "No, just looking for easy ways to bring twenty stone city types up when the shooting season starts."

He told me some of the estate's shooting customers are so fat and unfit by the time they have got them to the shooting site the deer have long since got wind of the danger and legged it.

We talked about modern day problems and despite our vastly different backgrounds we found a lot of common ground. At one stage he said, "Do you see that house in the Glen there? It is owned by a fine woman. She's got five sons and they are all afflicted with the drink bar one."

I loved the phrase 'they are all afflicted with the drinks' – such a Scottish way of putting it. When we reached the top we ate our food and passed the time. When it was time to go our separate ways he thanked me for my company – I liked that because it made me feel welcome in the hills in which he earns his living.

The second Munro, Beinn nan Aighenan, was on a different ridge to the first, Ben Starav and Glas Bheinn Mhor. Half way between I needed to head south and drop onto another ridge and climb up Beinn nan Aighenan. It was very misty and I got confused at which point on the ridge I needed to break off. Luckily two other walkers appeared and after a confer I managed to find the correct route.

With blood thumping inside my skull, the pull up the final two Munros was, due to the route card I'd completed, against the clock. I am always frightened of getting myself involved in a rescue operation because details of all rescues are published and they always find some bit of kit you were missing. Most rescue accounts

112

conclude, in a ticking off tone, with 'and the walker didn't have such and such'. Having read many rescue accounts I am now of the conclusion if you had every single piece of equipment all the other rescue stories damned people for not having, your own story would conclude with 'and the walker fell to his death under the sheer weight of having all the correct equipment'.

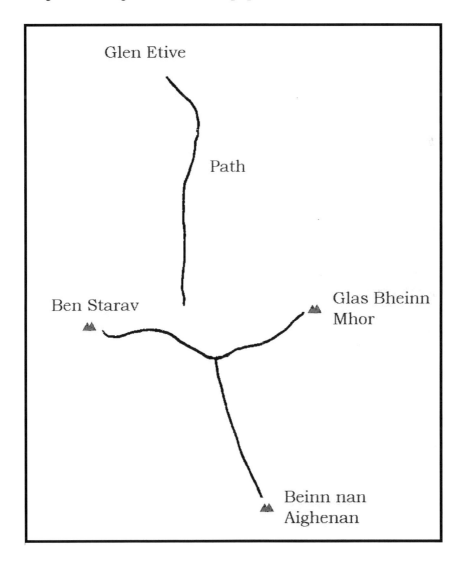

Taking in Beinn nan Aighenan made it a very long day, eleven hours in all. I could have made the day much shorter by missing this second Munro but, being one of the more remote mountains, it'd have meant another long day to reach it.

When I got back to the car it was quite sunny and I drove back along Glen Etive to the genial rasping tones of Louis Armstrong singing 'Wonderful World'. I had to pull up to allow a herd of deer to cross the road. Scotland is a difficult place to beat.

That evening, while walking to the Clachaig Inn for my evening meal, I felt pain in my knees and strains in both my ankle tendons. I carried this into the following day, May the 20th, making a tough day of tackling a singleton by the name of Beinn Sgulaird. I decided to wear my new boots in the mistaken belief the pain from the pinching would mask the pain from my knees. In contrast the weather was rain free with a combination of mist and clear views.

Whisky Galore

May the 21st brought a rest day for my knees and myself. I was wondering how to fill the day when I remembered while in Oban I'd seen a cinema advert for Whisky Galore. Therefore I took a trip down there to see this classic Ealing Comedy set on one of Scotland's beautiful islands.

One of my pastimes in hostels is to read and for the rest of the day I continued to plough my way through the *Colditz Story* with frequent pauses to shroud the volume from the vast number of Germans in the hostel. From reading the book I now realise my true vocation would have been goon-baiting in a Second World War POW camp. This is because I always like to have a go at authority when I know I am in the right and have the backing of others. Having the time to think on a long trip gives my self-awareness the chance to grow.

The Clachaig Inn is a pub geared up for walkers and climbers and many a good night is had there after a day in the mountains. So in the evening I paid another visit for my supper and a few beers with two Dutch guys. Both worked in computing and to make the world an even smaller place they worked on a seldom heard of product my friend, Graham Disselduff, was using – unbeknown to me this was to be my next contract in the computer industry. We then agreed to stop talking about computers, then proceeded to spend the next hour doing the very same.

The walk back from the pub was magnificent as the sky was cloudless and the moon was just to one side of a pair of adjacent mountains, it was simply beautiful.

Along with the Dutch guys also in my dormitory that night, was a group of cyclists from Birmingham who'd never been taught to be quiet. Their idea of a whispered conversation was to turn the volume knob back a couple of clicks on the megaphone. I was trying to get to sleep when one of them started snoring so loudly I couldn't drop off despite wearing earplugs. At about 01:00 in exasperation I yelled, "Shut up!" The entire dorm fell about laughing, clearly everybody was being kept awake by this chap so we collectively woke him up to stop him. However, he was like an alarm clock on snooze, you'd shut him up then about five minutes later he'd start off again.

To add to my sleepless night, the Birmingham cyclists woke at 06:00 and started to talk loudly. It is really annoying because although I accept you will get disturbed there is no need to talk loudly during sleep hours. One of my problems is I am a light sleeper unless I really need to be awake. For example, I slept through the 1987 hurricane that hit the South of England despite the roof of our garage collapsing. I also slept through a fire in the Central Hotel in Glasgow raging in a lift shaft just along from my room. But if a mouse breaks wind in the back garden I'm wide awake.

On May the 22nd I did Bidean nam Bian. The weather was so beautiful, hot and clear I spent over an hour on the top taking in the view and watching the traffic on the floor of Glen Coe some 3000ft below. On the way up I met a lady who was on her 260th Munro, she did her first in 1956. At the top I got chatting to two retired people still able to enjoy their hill walking despite their ageing limbs.

Again the company in the hostel was good. It was great to spend another evening in the Clachaig Inn with Kenny, a Scot, Julian a bearded violinist from Cumbria and an Aussie by the name of Mike.

On leaving the pub, at 23:00, it was still light. It took me ages to figure out the extra hour or so of daylight, which a Scottish summer evening gives over the South of England, means it is dark down south while still light in Scotland. This, of course, is perfectly obvious but it took the release of John McCarthy to make me realise this. I was working in Glasgow at the time and was sitting in the canteen when somebody walked by with a local newspaper. On the front cover there were just two words – 'McCarthy Free'. It took me a couple of seconds to realise the impact – John McCarthy was free. I left work bang on time and headed for my hotel room so I could watch the events of the day unfold on Sky News. Sprawled out on my bed, with sunlight still pouring in through the window, the news switched over to RAF Lyneham, in Wiltshire, to await the arrival of the plane carrying him home. I was surprised to see the reporter standing against the black night sky while I was still being bathed in sunlight through the hotel window.

I was amazed by John McCarthy's composure. After five and a half years, chained to walls in various 'dungeons' not knowing from one day to next if he was going to be freed or murdered, he met the press in Damascus and, with a twinkle in his eye, said 'Well Hello' as if he'd some explaining to do.

Things like that put other things into perspective. Occasionally when I reach the summit of a mountain I really appreciate the freedom of being able to do this and sometimes the thought of John McCarthy, at a similar age to myself, chained up in a cell passes through my mind.

Skinny Dipping

The following day, May the 23rd, I parked at the ski centre at the east end of Glen Coe to climb Meall a'Bhuiridh and Creise. Before setting off I had a chat with a man packing a paraglider into a rucksack. It was another beautiful sunny day and he said the conditions were ideal. I made a note to look out for him later in the day.

The great thing about totally clear days is you can see exactly where you're intending to go so there is no need to meticulously follow the route with a map and compass. Once I'd hauled myself onto the top of Meall a'Bhuiridh I could see the job in hand to get over to Creise. Once on top of Creise the views were outstanding, mountains everywhere with Schiehallion and Ben Nevis the most distinct peaks about. Snow still picked out the sheltered regions, as an artist uses shading to give perspective. I enjoyed the view so much I took photographs to make a 360 degree panorama.

During my descent I found some beautiful rock pools and went for a quick swim. Quick because only an optimist would describe them as refreshing, to everybody else they are painfully freezing. The chances of being caught going for a quick skinny dip are slim. However, on this occasion I think the men in the paragliders observed me. After drying off in the sun I became aware of the narrowing proximity of these flying machines. I got dressed before any gender identification could take place leaving the men in their paragliders to cling to the hope I was a page three girl out for a stroll basking by a rock pool.

Another visit to the pub was in order in the evening with Mike, the Aussie, and a stocky German chap called Peter. Peter was a gentle giant with an amusing accent and mannerisms. Unfortunately he was a bit naive and Mike and I struck a chord with some gentle, yet undetected, leg pulling.

At one stage Peter said, "I met this chap in Ireland who was in the army."

"The IRA?" asked Mike.

"Yah I think so," replied Peter, misunderstanding where Mike was going with this.

"Did he give you any leaflets?" I asked.

"Nooh," replied Peter.

"A package perhaps?" asked Mike.

"Nooh," replied Peter still oblivious.

Here and There

The following day was a mixed bag of driving to Fort William, stocking up on food then driving to collect my friend, Ady Glover from Inverness railway station. Shopping in Fort William is now easier than in the days of the holiday cottages. In the late 80s and early 90s the trip from the south was always pressured with having to make Tesco before 17:00.

As Ady walked down the platform, at Inverness, I could see he was holding my GPS. The shop failed to get the batteries out so they sent a new one and Ady brought it up for me. A note with the

GPS said they'd used 'extreme prejudice' to extract the batteries but failure meant they supplied me with a new unit instead. Also a letter from Gisella came courtesy of the Ady delivery service.

Ady had come up on the sleeper for the weekend and, as he is much stronger and fitter than me, I was praying he'd had a bad night's sleep on the train to compensate for my lesser strength. Unfortunately he'd slept like a log.

We drove to Inverlael then walked through the forest and set up camp in readiness to tackle four Munros the next day. Now I say four but there was actually a fifth but it'd make the day very long, so when I was showing Ady the map I carefully folded it so this fifth, very remote, Munro was out of sight. Ady immediately wanted the map spread out and noticed this fifth one.

"Steve, mate, can't we take this one in too?"

"It's a bit far," I said.

"Yeah you're right," he replied.

I was surprised Ady was so ready to accept this and started to look at the map in a bit more detail. "Well, I suppose we could take it in," I said.

Why was I doing this? I knew in my heart of hearts it was too far but I also was starting to realise this was a golden opportunity to get it bagged. We agreed if we finished the fourth by 14:00 we'd go for it.

We woke at 04:20 but I failed to get Ady to shift for a further two hours. He said he wanted to lie in until about 09:30 so I guess a departure time of 07:40 was a fair compromise. Ady wanted a coffee before we left, I didn't want to delay our start any further and tried to talk him out of it. He gave me a choice of a coffee now or to carry the stove up the mountains. I opted for the coffee now, boiled some water, promptly kicked it over, started to boil some more, ran out of gas. With the day ending up being of epic proportions I was glad to find out we'd run out of gas early on – the thought of a hot meal, at the end of the day, only to then be thwarted would have been a cruel blow.

The weather the previous evening had been high cloud with all the peaks exposed. In the morning they were all well and truly covered. By this time I had it in my head I wanted to do the fifth Munro, Seana Bhraigh, and was itching to get cracking. We followed the good path up onto the plateau that sits below the first three Munros. From there, in heavy mist, we climbed Beinn Dearg, Cona' Mheall and Meall nan Ceapraichean. We found navigation very slow and had to rely on the GPS a couple of times to confirm our position. One trick I have learnt about navigating in the mist is the wind always picks up near a ridge or a summit – we used this 'tip' on a couple of occasions today.

The climb down from Meall nan Ceapraichean was a bit hazardous as there were ledges to lower oneself down and a large rock pavement to negotiate with deep cracks to avoid. I imagined falling into one of these cracks, the chances of extracting myself unaided would be very slim.

When we got to the fourth Munro of the day, Eididh nan Clach Geala it was about 16:00. This overshot our deadline for attempting the fifth Munro by two hours. We should have stuck with our original plan as the weather was getting windy and there was no let-up in the cloud cover. If I'd been alone I wouldn't have tried for it. However, the company gave me a false confidence.

On route the wind picked up and the terrain became more barren. A couple of times we came up against dead ends with the ground dropping away to such an extent we had to backtrack to find a way through. When Seana Bhraigh came in to sight it looked very menacing – an 800ft horseshoe shaped cliff face guarded its approach.

As we staggered around the edge, to line up a 'home run' for the summit, the wind gathered pace. I had to cling on to my map case in one hand and my hood with the other. A lesser summit had to be negotiated first and after it we took a rest. The wind was howling so much I could barely open my rucksack to get at some desperately needed food. With the rain now lashing into us I felt very irritable, often a sign when approaching exhaustion. Ady opened his sandwich box and made no attempt to prevent his spent chocolate bar wrappers becoming fugitives to the wind. I gritted my teeth.

After a few minutes we pressed on into the wind and rain. We could barely stand and on one occasion I was physically blown over. I am only twelve stone in weight, but 6'1" in height so it gave the forces of nature an easy target. On other occasions I had to stand with my back into the wind and just brace myself until the wind relented enough to press on. This was wild remote country.

We struggled on with the peak in sight. From way back, the route up looked very narrow, when we got there narrow wasn't the word. It was a knife-edge with 800ft drops either side. Mist wisped over the exposed ridge beckoning us like a mysterious woman into her lair. You know it spells disaster but nonetheless you're still attracted. We could barely stand and conversation could only be had by taking it in turns to put mouth to ear, and then only by shouting.

With the wind smashing into us I just managed to hear Ady say, "We can't get over that."

I crept forward on all fours, to reduce the risk of being blown off, and made doubly sure we weren't missing an easier route. There wasn't one. I took a while to concede there was no hope of getting to the summit, literally only a few metres away, and agreed to turn back. We were at the furthest point of the entire day from the tent when we made this decision and it was 19:20 hours.

The journey back to the tent was awful. During the initial descent I was starting to suffer from exhaustion. I could feel myself starting to slip, stumble and mentally slide. Ady went ahead most of the time and, as the distance between us ever increased, I felt very angry with him for 'leaving me'.

I felt very alone, heightened by his figure disappearing into the wilds before me. I summoned my strength and caught him up by reeling him in bit by bit. I was then none too pleasant company. Friction grew further when I discovered the emergency equipment he carried consisted of a pair of shorts and sunglasses whereas mine contained bivi bags, whistle, spare food, GPS system, hypothermia blanket and emergency transmitter.

I was desperate with exhaustion and longed to be at home. I wanted out, out of hillwalking, out of this pursuit, out of the dream of being a Munroist. At this point it held nothing for me but misery. I was in a state as I realised I'd long exhausted my energy reserves and my mind was starting to break loose from reality and bring on feelings of panic about the predicament.

After losing height there was further high ground to ascend to get ourselves out of the plateau that leads to Seana Bhraigh. This was tough and it took us ages to pick up the path marked on the maps. After we lost some height the rest of the trek was a route march in constant wind and rain but manageable. As the light faded I realised I'd done Ady a disservice, he'd remembered to pack a torch. I had not.

It took us a further four hours to get back to the tent and the thing that kept me going was the thought of my dinner – a cold can of baked beans with vegetarian sausages. As ever with life the dream was better than the reality.

Fortunately the tent was still standing and we piled in and got our wet things off and had food. Later we reflected we'd have had more chance: if we weren't so exhausted when we got near the summit, if the weather wasn't so atrocious, if we could see, if we could hold the map to read it and if we'd been on the right bloody mountain! A navigational error had meant we missed Seana Bhraigh and instead attempted its hazardous easterly neighbour, Creag an Duine which isn't a Munro. Looking at the map, the approach features to the two are very similar, both having cliffs to negotiate on route. Getting the wrong peak also added about an extra three miles to the walk.

As a footnote to this story I later read Ranulph Fiennes book *Mind Over Matter* describing his epic crossing of the Antarctic continent. In this work he points out at some stages an expedition is depending on luck rather than skill or experience. At this point the party should turn back. I think Ady and myself had got ourselves into this position.

Billy MacRae

When we woke neither of us was in the mood to get out of our sleeping bags and submit ourselves to the chill air. Instead a slug, making its way across the outside of the inner tent lining, supplied the entertainment. Its sticky trail marked its wake as it made its pointless climb up and over the top. Only when it got near to the grass, just as good it'd left some hour beforehand, did we feel it was time to start making a move.

It was painful leaving the damp, yet warm, confines of my sleeping bag and, to make matters worse, I'd no spare clothes so I had to dress in my sodden garments.

We headed for the beauty of Ullapool – a natural harbour surrounded by wonderful scenery and on a calm clear day it takes on a magic all of its own. An afternoon stroll drifted into a search for food interspersed by a visit to a local bar where we were waylaid by a local character by the name of Billy MacRae. He was a fisherman, in his mid-sixties, who insisted on buying us shorts and was offended when we tried to retaliate and buy him a drink.

I get a sense of insecurity when somebody is trying to buy all the drinks as I feel morally obliged to owe something back – such as my company for the entire evening.

On each new short we had to stand as he said, "Be upstanding at all times."

He kept bursting into song which caused the barman to speak firmly to him, "Billy we no have a licence for the singing."

Billy would then go silent for a while until, like a child, he calculated enough time had passed to be able to risk a few further verses.

His accent was very difficult for me to follow and I found myself nodding a great deal only to be caught out when it was clear he was waiting for an answer to a question I'd missed. I concluded he must come out with the same stories every evening because many of the locals reacted to his stories with a resigned, "Aye Billy, Aye."

Nonetheless his tales were interesting to the virgin ear. He had worked on the dams for the hydroelectric during the 1940s and 50s and was determined to work, despite being an asthmatic, until the day he died as he thought retirement was for fools. He was proud his dog was called 'Askhim' for the very simple reason when people enquired of his dog's name he could say, "Askhim."

Ady asked him, "Are the Spanish fishermen a bunch of sods?"

Billy said no and added they are just trying to make a living like the rest. Some other fishermen in the bar rolled their eyes. Billy said the comradeship amongst the fishermen is high and you'd always go to the rescue of a fellow man whatever his nationality. The other fishermen in the bar rolled their eyes. On more than one occasion Billy came out with a rhyme that went something like:

124

Take yourself a good wife
And give her no tears
Be good to your wife
And she'll last you for years

Each time he said this he winked at me metaphorically repeating
the entire rhyme with a wistful, "Aye, aye." The other fishermen in
the bar rolled their eyes.

A Walk Without A Munro

The following day I dropped Ady at Inverness railway station and
met up with another friend, an ex-work colleague, Steve Hampton.
Steve had just separated from his wife and had also badly sprained
his ankle. Therefore we had lots of time to talk and spent a few
days together touring my old favourites of Loch Mullardoch and
Glen Cannich followed by a trip over to Skye.

While on Skye Steve bought a book of walks and we
attempted a modest coastal one. After about an hour it became
clear I was struggling. If I am off to tackle a Munro then my body
gears up for a day's hard slog whereas for a gentle coastal walk my
body thinks 'no trouble' and after only a short distance says 'okay
you can feel tired now'.

Unfortunately I think I did Steve a disservice because my
enthusiasm for the Munros caused him to say, "I can see this is the
sort of thing I could get into as I like ticking things off."

Whoops, possibly I've landed somebody else with the same
bug.

After a three day break I returned to the hills on May the
29th to tackle Beinn Sgritheall. This entailed first negotiating the
road from Shiel Bridge round to Arnisdale. This is a most beautiful
drive with great views of the sea, islands and mountains. It was a

hot day and I forgot my trekking poles so found it tough going. At one stage in the ascent there was a large boulder come scree slope to negotiate. I found this very difficult, as it was quite hard on my knees. Once the scree was safely negotiated there was a minor top to cover before a superb ridge walk, with one nerve testing exposed section, out to the true summit.

On the route back I dislodged a football-sized boulder which took off and bounced, with ever increasing vigour, on the slopes beneath me. This cannon ball of nature narrowly missed a fellow walker a few hundred metres below me – even on the calmest of days there is danger in the mountains.

Following this I drove for three hours in the evening sun to Glen Etive, stopping on route a few times to just take in the views. Glen Etive is a classic place for rough camping as it has good ground for pitching and there is plenty of water around. I followed the classic camper's sequence of events which are to:

- Find a suitable pitch
- Put bottles of beer in stream to cool down
- Erect tent
- Drink beer
- Trip over guide ropes

Unfortunately I had a lousy night's sleep. After finally dropping off I woke to find my back welded to the ground, each way I moved I couldn't raise myself. Fortunately the tent was on a slight slope so after some forty-five minutes of testing the water I was able to roll over on to my stomach.

The reason for camping was to try and get my tent dried out from the soaking it got a few days previously. Unfortunately the outer of the tent had got wet in the night so I had to wait until the sun rose above the mountains to dry it off before I could set off for my day's climb and my 100th Munro.

Century Reached

This was a glorious day to attempt my 100th Munro on. I chose Buachaille Etive Mor as it is a classic Munro proudly sitting on the left of the road as you sweep into Glen Coe from the south. The pull up to the higher ground was via a steep, scree-filled corridor. In wintertime this area is prone to avalanche and has claimed many lives. One entire family was lost in this region after just a low level stroll ended in tragedy as they were engulfed by snow and their bodies lay undiscovered until the thaw began, some months later.

Once through the scree it was a gem of a straightforward sunny ridge walk to the summit. I spent about an hour on top chatting with people and admiring the view across the famous Rannoch Moor. Sadly one person told me somebody died on the mountain a week before on an attempt to negotiate a descent of the hazardous east face.

My descent took me back via the safer scree slopes on which I invented a new sport of scree surfing. This involves standing on a slab like rock and skidding over the surface of the smaller scree below. Though I figured I'd more chance of taking off than my newly invented sport.

Buachaille Etive Mor was the start of my second visit to Glen Coe of the trip in an attempt to complete all of the Munros in the immediate vicinity. Again I stayed at Glen Coe Youth Hostel and on arrival I presented my pre-booking form for a nine night stint. The warden was quite peculiar about me staying for this length of time.

"I know your sort, if the weather turns nasty you'll want

straight out," he said.

"If the weather turns nasty this is the very place I'd want to be," I replied.

With that he begrudgingly entered my details into his ledger and said, "I can't say I can keep you in the same dorm every night, we get groups in you know. You'll have to come and check every morning to see if I want you to move."

Needless to say I never bothered checking and he never stopped scowling at me.

In the evening I revisited the Clachaig Inn, this time with a German chap called Christian. He was enjoying some time to himself having just finished a tedious stint of national service. Apparently you get drafted then sent to some camp where you either do nothing or totally mundane jobs. One of his friends had got out of it by presenting the medical board with some chest X-Rays showing a tricky illness. The X-Rays were supplied courtesy of the chap's father who was a hospital doctor.

Christian also told me the chap who'd been killed on Buachaille Etive Mor was a police officer and it'd been quite a local news story. We chatted for ages, his English was superb and he knew more about English football than I did. He also told me about a guidebook he was reading which described mountains called *Munros* and how it is a strange sport amongst certain British people to climb them all. You can go right off some people you know. I gauged how far I should let him dig himself into this hole before I confessed to being one of this strange breed.

The Aonach Eagach Ridge

May the 31st was clear and calm and very warm. Ideal conditions to take a look at the Aonach Eagach ridge. This is the most exposed mainland ridge in the country and connects the two Munros of Meall Dearg and Sgorr nam Fiannaidh. I had read the guidebooks and had been totally put off by their warnings of the danger for the novice climber. Therefore before setting out I'd decided to just climb Meall Dearg and miss the ridge and then climb Sgorr nam Fiannaidh another day from the other side. Of course this is less than efficient but I reckoned attempting the Aonach Eagach may well have meant I wouldn't have another day.

I set off from the unusual starting point of Caolasnacon, on the road to Kinlochleven, with the aim being to avoid as much of the exposed ridge as possible. Unfortunately due to a basic navigational error, I took three and a half hours to reach the summit.

On my final approach I could see the Aonach Eagach and, as I reached the summit, its full horror lay before me: a jagged ridge of knife-edged rock stretched for about a mile between me and the Munro of Sgorr nam Fiannaidh.

Any secret thoughts I still harboured of doing it were quickly expelled. As I settled down to my lunch and the prospect of a leisurely walk back to my car, a group of five chaps joined me and began to tuck into their lunch. We got chatting and they were surprised at my route up.

"I didn't fancy doing the first bit of the ridge from the Glen Coe side," I explained, "so chose this route to avoid any of the exposure." I then paused and asked, "Have you done the Aonach Eagach before?"

Four of them said, "Aye."

"How bad is it?" I enquired. Mistake, mistake, mistake.

"Aye nah as bad as it looks – yee can do it with us if you like."

"Thanks so much but me and that kind of risk don't get on so well," I said.

"You'll be all right, you can walk amongst us and we will talk you through it."

How could I refuse?

The first thing I had to do, on their advice, was tie my trekking poles to my rucksack – I'd need my hands free for what lay ahead.

The ridge is a mixture of chimneys, steep-sided faces, traverses and narrow interconnects. The memory is now a blur but I can remember having to raise and lower myself and sideways traverse over-exposed sections with 500ft drops if I were to slip. I can remember having to lower myself onto ledges with my feet out of sight desperately seeking purchase. I can remember blowing my nose a lot, something I always do when I am nervous. I can remember the scratch marks on the rock, which I assume were from winter crampons and not finger nails! I can remember sideways traversing and being talked through it as I began to panic as I looked down between my legs to see the ground very far away. I can remember being out of water and very thirsty, no stream ever graces a ridge. I can remember an alarming moment of my rucksack shifting on my back. I can remember being very scared.

Once started the point of no return soon comes and you realise just what you have let yourself in for. There were places to rest but this wasn't a good idea as the longer I rested the more time I had to dwell on what had gone and what was to come. The guys were great, they always talked me through the difficult bits and made sure I was never at the back.

However, all of their reassurance went to pot when one of them said, "This is about where the guy fell."

"What guy?" I said with alarm.

Apparently when they'd done the ridge the previous September there was a cry from the party behind them. Somebody had fallen to their death, paying nature's forfeit. I thought, 'Thanks a bunch for waiting until now to tell me'. The incident had happened late in the afternoon and the rescue services were unable to recover the body until the next day.

A section of The Aonach Eagach ridge

When completed I was a relieved man. In Muriel Gray's Munro book *The First Fifty* she describes the Aonach Eagach ridge as a 'brown underpants job'. This is an observation I can now fully understand. I couldn't have done it without the company, if I'd attempted it myself I'd have wound myself up so much I'd have either come a cropper, got cragfast or have followed Ms Gray's advice.

The views from the top of Sgorr nam Fiannaidh were tremendous, the Ballachulish Bridge which spans the mouth of Loch Leven looked a real spectacle from my 3200ft vantage point. The islands of Rum, Eigg and Skye in the distance were just outstanding against the perfect blue sea and sky. I think I was on a high!

If you're intending to do the Aonach Eagach for the first time then these are my tips:

- Do it east to west as this is supposedly safer.
- Walk with somebody who is a climber and has done it before.
- Pack away your trekking poles.
- Don't do it in icy, wet or windy conditions.
- Pack a spare pair of undies.

Brutal Sun

June the 1st was another allotted rest day. I parked in a Glen Coe lay-by and climbed about 300ft above the road. I spent hours reading and watching the holiday traffic. The weather was, again, perfect and I could virtually join in the thrill the many motor cyclists were getting from being able to cruise through some of the finest scenery Britain has to offer.

I started to reflect on my trip and tried to understand why I was enjoying it so much. Despite having such a solitary day I began to realise travel isn't just the things you see it is also the people you meet. A week's holiday doesn't give the time to wind down enough and really get into it. I reflected hillwalking gave me the time to think, to really analyse things that had happened to me and to suss things out which ordinarily you wouldn't get the space or time to do.

I got back to the hostel and found the warden had changed the key code on the main entrance door. I had to press the buzzer until he appeared. He told me the new key code and, with a dour smile, explained this was a date when the Scots stuffed the English in some long forgotten battle.

Before my evening visit to the Clachaig Inn, with Christian and two other German chaps, I took a shower. It was here I began to notice my interesting sun tan. I was tanned on my arms, save for where my watch sits, but not my T-shirt-covered torso. I was tanned on the tops and bottoms of my legs, but where my knee socks protect me during my climbs I remained pale. I was becoming quite multi-coloured. Even as I write this account, in the following November, I can still see the tide marks on my legs.

We had another good chat in the Clachaig Inn and unanimously agreed the male warden was a bit unfriendly. A few years later, while ascending Gulvain, I got chatting to a lady who knew the couple who ran the hostel. She told me the warden was a nice chap and was surprised to hear of the problems I'd had with him. I explained how he scowled at me daily and had, on more than one occasion, changed the key code to a date in which the English took a good beating from the Scots.

June the 2nd saw me tackle Stob Coir an Albannaich and Meall nan Eun. The sun was brutal especially during the first section where I climbed for over two hours on a steeper than a 1 in 2 ascent. Cameron McNeish's *Munro Almanac* guidebook states the navigation between the two summits is difficult in poor weather because of an awkward dogleg in the route. Fortunately the beautifully clear weather showed me the obvious path and the map and compass were only needed for confirmation. The map also confirmed that the guidebook incorrectly puts the grid reference of Stob Coir an Albannaich 1km to the south.

The walk took a shade over seven hours and I didn't see another soul all day. The views were tremendous and I was able to pick out many of the mountains I'd walked on previous days. It's a nice feeling to think, 'Ah I was on that peak just the other day, and that one five years ago'.

In the evening I phoned my friend Willy Newlands, an inspector with Strathclyde Police, to arrange for him to come up for a day so as we could do some walking together. On answering I said, "Hi Willy, it's Steve, how are you?"

"Not so good, Steve," replied Willy. "See one of my

sergeants was killed on Buachaille Etive Mor the other day."

So that completed the picture. I had been hearing snippets of information about the death of the police officer, now it'd come to light he was a friend of a friend. Willy sounded gutted, having been abroad on holiday he'd only just learnt the news. He had under three hours to get ready for the funeral. Despite that Willy said he'd come up for the day on Friday so we could get a Munro in together.

Another Aonach Eagach

On June the 3rd I took in Stob a'Choire Odhair and Stob Ghabhar. I started from Forest Lodge and enjoyed what was another gorgeous day. The route between the two mountains took in a short stretch of exposed ridge called Aonach Eagach. Thinking back to my experiences on the ridge of its namesake I can only imagine this is Gaelic for dangerously exposed ridge.

On the top of the second peak I got chatting to a sixteen-year-old lad who was doing a two week solo walk across the Highlands in preparation for a career in the Royal Marines. I was impressed by his pluck, I couldn't imagine myself going off alone at that age.

Fortunately my knees had finally got a routine ironed out between them. Like two people having a conversation on adjoining swings they negotiated a truce whereby only one hurts at any one point in time, allowing me the opportunity to hop when things became too much.

The trip back to the youth hostel took me past the east face of Buachaille Etive Mor, it stood proud in the sun but a shiver went through me as I thought of its recent victim.

Buachaille Etive Beag (Stob Dubh)

June the 4th took in one of the more straightforward Munros with a mere two and a half hours getting me to the summit of Buachaille Etive Beag (Stob Dubh). In glorious, sweltering, sunshine I soaked in the unbelievable views, reminding me of the attractions of this pursuit.

The End of Glen Coe

June the 5th was a rest day so it was on the June the 6th I met up with Willy to set foot in the hills once again. We met at the youth hostel at about 09:00, Willy having driven up from Glasgow in his new car, a White VW Golf GTI convertible. He got in the joke about it being a hairdresser's car before I could.

He needed the loo and had to suffer the scowling glances of the warden as he went inside the hostel to relieve himself. But Willy, having listened to my warnings, said a friendly, "Hello."

When Willy returned I said, "Do I have a problem with that guy?" I then paused. "Yes I think I do."

Willy said I should have got that recorded for a 'Video Nation' clip.

We tackled Sgor na h-Ulaidh as it was one of the few left in the Glen Coe region neither of us had climbed. The weather was more typically Scottish with rain at first, some clearance and a slight view at the top.

As ever Willy brought lots of food to share. This reminded me of the days on the Strathclyde Police Command and Control Project when he always brought enough grub for me to share when walking in the hills.

We recounted the story of when I first arrived in Scotland to work. I had got on the plane at Heathrow in the blazing heat so turned up in just a shirt with a last minute jumper stuffed in my bag. At the end of the first day Willy walked me to my hotel in the drizzling rain. Eyeing me up he said, "You no bring a coat, Steve?"

"Ah no," I replied. "It was hot in London this morning."

He laughed at my naiveté about the Scottish weather and relentlessly pulled my leg. Next day he brought me a coat to borrow for the rest of the week.

Willy chatted about his friend the police sergeant, Graham Munro. I was trying to judge what to say. I didn't want to ask questions like some tabloid reporter, whereas remaining quiet might sound like I didn't care. Sadly he'd left a wife and two children. We commented on how most accidents happen when you take your eye off the danger.

Willy mentioned how much my fitness had improved and how well I was managing the steep bits. We kept pace together even though I knew he could out walk me. I can manage walking with one other person who is faster than me because they will always slow to my pace; with two or more I soon lose them to the ground ahead.

According to Willy I was starting to use the term 'Aye' instead of 'Yes' with quite a Scottish slant on it. We had good conversation and at the end of the day we stopped for a drink in the Clachaig Inn followed by Willy doing a wheel spin out of the youth hostel car park – I put my head in my hands as the warden peered through the window.

June the 7th was my last walk in the Glen Coe area, as the bagging of Beinn Fhionnlaidh would complete all the Munros in the glen. This Munro can be tackled from more than one approach. As the weather forecast, faxed to the youth hostel from the Met Office, said there'd be morning rain in the west, I chose the easterly approach from Glen Etive.

As I ascended a hole appeared in the cloud, allowing the sunlight to pour through. The hole then swirled around with the wind, causing a patch of sunlight to pan around the hills like a searchlight.

Most of the rest of the walk was in the rain and strong wind. At one point the wind was producing eddy currents beneath my nose to such an extent I experienced the strange sensation of air being sucked out of my nose. The weather cleared at lunchtime, as per the forecast. On the way back down I looked on the skies as one would a naughty child. 'Don't you dare open up', I thought – I'd dried out and didn't want to get wet again.

That night was my last at Glen Coe Youth Hostel on this trip. An Aussie guy was in the same dorm as me and was snoring very loudly. I knew he was Aussie even before I first spoke to him because he was unshaven with blond hair and wore a brown leather cowboy hat and a brown leather jacket. With my pressing need for sleep I threw a pillow at him. He came to and looked at me.

"You were snoring," I said in explanation. At that precise

moment another person, who'd previously been quiet, let out a snore.

"Wrong target, mate," he retorted.

I finally got up, feeling very stressed, and headed down to make my breakfast. In the kitchen was a group of middle-aged people I'd encountered the previous evening. Between them they'd two N registered Citroen Xantias and a P registered large BMW which they'd used to block in around seventy-five percent of the other cars parked in the tight car park.

At one stage I'd popped up to get myself some pepper, leaving a large plate of steaming food on the table as a rather obvious placeholder. When I got back one of them had stolen my chair. I guess it was just more convenient for them than walking the five yards required to get a free chair. They then proceeded to run the hostel down. Looking at their wealth I couldn't understand why they didn't go into a hotel if the hostel bugged them so much. Hostels, as you can imagine, are run on a shoestring budget so cause for complaint about their amenities is very unfair.

After eating my breakfast I was itching to get going, not wanting a late start in the hills. While exchanging the sheet sleeping bag for my membership card one of the middle-aged party appeared. I asked, "Are you one of the Xantia, BMW party?"

"I might be," he replied with all the help of a skunk in an air freshener factory.

"I need to get my car out, can you organise some shunting?" I asked.

"We are all going this morning," he replied and walked off.

'Oh I'll hire another car then', I thought, seething. Most acts of violence in the world come as the result of feelings of disrespect. Fortunately I'm not a violent man.

The lady warden looked at me and said wryly, "Now that was helpful wasn't it."

138

The party were far from ready so I went and asked another member, who could see the sense in my suggestion, and got some shunting organised.

The lady warden gave me the thumbs up and said, "Good for you."

When outside, waiting for them to complete the movements of their cars, two of the party came up to me and started criticising the way other people had parked as the reason for why they blocked everybody else in. When I didn't respond one of them started to say, about his friend, "These BMW drivers eh?"

I could sense they knew they were in the wrong by their use of dismissive language and blaming others and trying to triangle with me to overcome their guilt. By the size of their cars they were clearly flourishing in life, something which left me feeling a double sense of injustice. I really felt they considered me an insignificant nuisance when I asked to get my car out.

That was the end of my stay in Glen Coe for the year and as you can imagine I left with some mixed feelings. Two minor things tickled me about a chap named Ian I shared a dorm with during my stay at the hostel. I didn't record the exact day on which they occurred and hence I cannot neatly fit this into the text above so will just add it here in the hope nobody spots my sudden addition of an extra story.

Ian was a very pleasant chap, a retired lecturer in his early sixties. He was up doing the Munros and when I asked him how many he'd done he said, "Two hundred and forty, but I don't know if I'll finish them."

Being able to give the exact number you have done implies counting, to count you have an aim and what else could the aim be than to complete?

Ian was very organised and during his stay a friend of his, Dougie, joined him for a few days. One morning Ian was waiting for Dougie to get ready and said to me, "Never have I met a man more prone to procrastination."

It tickled me because they were about the same age and had obviously been friends a great part of their lives but still hadn't sorted this one out. I thought of my friends Andy and Ady Glover and realised that'd be me with them in thirty years' time, still waiting for them to get ready, suffering stress while they take their own time in their own worlds.

Wanderings

I'd arranged to meet my friend Andy Baxter in the Grand Hotel Fort William on the night of June the 8th. My intention during the day was to finish off my last Munro in Glen Coe, meet him in the evening and then set off the next day and do some Munros from bothies. However, I finished my last Munro in Glen Coe a day ahead of schedule and so decided to take the extra day bagging Stob Coire Sgriodain and Chno Dearg which sit south of the A86 Spean Bridge to Kingussie road.

I started from Fersit and crossed the broad open peat land before making the ascent proper of Stob Coire Sgriodain. To my right was Loch Treig with the West Highland Railway running along its shores. At one point the loch gave a fine display of white horses while one of the most beautiful rainbows I'd ever seen arched over it.

The walk up was difficult in the strong wind and I experienced a new phenomenon relating to the wind and my nostrils. This time it was all a bit unpleasant as the wind caused mucus to be sucked out of my nose and at one stage I was trying desperately to sever a foot long piece snot waiving about my face – I was thankful this was a solo walk.

I was delighted when I got to the cairn of Stob Coire

Sgriodain after two and a half hours and found myself yelling, above the wind, "Hello Munro 110" and gave the cairn a big hug – I was thankful this was a solo walk.

The weather deteriorated on the approach to Chno Dearg, I could barely stand up in the wind and literally got blown over twice. I did take some comfort from the wind being a lot warmer than the bitterly cold blasts I'd experienced at the beginning of May.

On approaching the summit I got the sense there were two large cairns. Looking at the map was very difficult in the conditions so I pressed on with the compass bearing I'd previously taken in a more sheltered spot. The hood of my jacket was blowing at such an angle it was pulling on my right eye. After a further ten minutes of worrying about the two summit cairns I realised it was merely a phenomenon caused by distortion of my right eyeball. On closing that eye I could see I was heading to a single summit cairn which, on reaching, afforded some shelter where I enjoyed the relief of getting my head out of the firing line.

I delayed my departure until seizing joints told me the present luxury was going to be doubly paid for unless I started to make progress. As soon as I moved, the wind whacked into me with the same force as before. On the descent the rain started to lash down, I didn't bother with my over trousers as awaiting me was a hotel room in the Grand Hotel Fort William and my first hot bath in over five weeks. I also felt quite thirsty but didn't feel like wrestling with my rucksack in the howling gale to retrieve my water bottle. I pressed on and my mouth began to feel very dry but I really didn't want to take my rucksack off. In the end I hit on the idea of sucking the water from the tassel on my jacket's hood. I managed to extract just enough to wet the inside of my mouth and satisfy the immediate problems of thirst.

When I got to my room at the Grand Hotel the first thing I

141

did, like a heroin addict being drawn to a needle, was to switch on the TV. Why oh why did I need to do this? Over five weeks without missing the thing one iota and as soon as I see one on it goes. After a long soak in the bath I put on some clean clothes and, with my jeans now very baggy, realised the extent of my weight loss.

I met with Andy Baxter in the evening. I had trouble eating as I was suffering from mouth ulcers. These were probably caused by my eating too much chocolate to give me energy up the mountains.

Bothies Revisited

I'd a lazy morning on June the 9th before driving along the twisting B8004 and B8005 roads, following the shores of Loch Arkaig. A stag was paddling out in the loch, natural and peaceful with his environment.

I parked where the road ended, near Strathan. I glanced at a tin shack all locked up, remembering it from when I'd parked with Willy and Mike the previous year before my first taste of bothy life. I would have never been able to remember it without seeing it again. I later found out it was the old school house serving the once local community.

I spent quite a while getting my stuff together before the fully laden walk into A'Chuil Bothy. It took just an hour and twenty minutes but I was relieved to get the pack off of my back. I then felt an overwhelming sense of 'what have I done?' A sense of remorse hung over me. Bothies are great in a group but on your own the drab surroundings can dominate your mind. This was not helped by having had a difficult phone call with Gisella the night before. She informed me she wanted to move back to Exeter (where she studied for her degree) and I got the impression I wasn't really part of the plan. I think a prolonged period of solitude in one of these places could have you eyeing up the drop from the rafters.

A tip for bothy life is to fill up your water bottles before arrival, this is because the streams near to the bothy are reported to have a high bacteria content. I'll leave you to work out why.

I thought there'd be a good chance of getting the bothy to myself, it being a week day evening. Although the solitude was depressing I didn't fancy sharing space with strangers. During the course of the evening the numbers swelled to nine including a clan of kilted Scotsmen on a sponsored walk through the glens. These were real kilts, not your Marks and Spencer look alike types. They also boasted a full clan flag which they held proudly as they marched – if you saw them marching in the distance you'd truly believe you were looking back in time.

On unpacking their stuff they produced what could only be described as a mobile catering unit. They got a good fire going, a task I'd failed in all afternoon. The evening passed pleasurably to the haunting melodies played out on their mouth organs.

After I ate I decided I'd walk high up the stream to wash my cooking utensils. Here I was attacked by 633 airborne mosquito squadron on a mission to hound off the Sassenach spotted in the vicinity. Another animal that can spoil bothy life are mice. A tip, that can be learnt painfully, is it is essential to hang all your gear up to avoid the attention of the resident bothy mouse.

On returning the clansmen spent part of the evening discussing who of them snored the loudest so, when I woke at 04:20 I was relieved to have slept that long. I got up and had my bothy breakfast of:

- A cup of tea
- A quarter of a cake
- Digestive biscuits

My bothy evening meals consisted of a repeat breakfast plus pasta and a reconstituted meal.

I set off at 05:50 thinking I'd plenty of time, indeed I did but the walk took me out on a long ridge taking in Sgurr nan Coireachan (which is a must for any *Man from U.N.C.L.E* fan) and Sgurr Mor. These two Munros were the ones I'd have done with Mike and Willy the previous year if I hadn't been so exhausted carrying my rucksack.

Early on in the day I saw a fox, I'd never seen one before in the Highlands and soon after I came across a stag. We just stood for ages, no more than twenty feet apart, staring at each other. I started to speak to him saying I was his friend and I wasn't going to shoot him. You probably think I am nuts but the solitude of the mountains changes you. Some city types might get pleasure out of murdering a defenceless animal in cold blood. I think if they lived in the mountains they'd just realise the cull is a necessity and not something to take direct pleasure from. This area is recognised as one of Europe's last great wildernesses – I hope it stays that way and my friend, the stag, can live out his days in peace and his antlers will never adorn the walls of some city slickers house.

The ridge walk between the two Munros was great, the approach to the first Munro took in a few false summits so when the ridge finally opened out before me it was a welcome sight. From the first Munro to the second was well over three hours of ridge walk away from the bothy. Willy had warned me of this but I didn't quite appreciate it until I got to the second Munro and surveyed the journey back. The normal approach to a ridge walk is to start fairly central and traverse up to one end, walk along then cut back to the starting place. Due to the geography of the area this wasn't possible and hence the long day, totalling ten and a half hours of walking

I tried a bit of a short cut on the way back by trying to miss out a rise in the ridge by traversing around it. This was a mistake as I painted myself into a few corners and had to heavily backtrack. The return trip allowed me to discover a new use for the trekking poles, this is to steady yourself when going to the loo!

When, after another three hours, I got to the bothy there was no company and the place looked depressing again. Later a Dutch chap arrived and proudly announced he held some sort of internationally recognised record for snoring. We slept in separate rooms and I discovered he wasn't kidding for through feet thick stonewalls his pneumatic snoring could be heard.

During the evening I kept putting off going to wash my cooking utensils in the stream. When I gave in and emerged from the bothy to do this chore I thought I'd avoided the midges. However, after just a few minutes word had got about and 633 mosquito squadron had been scrambled and were on a furious attack. Obviously some regrouping had gone on since the previous evening's attack and a detachment of the squadron had been deployed to fly into my ears. The little bastards.

Mr Pean

The following morning, June the 11th, I packed up my kit and set off for Glen Pean Bothy. The walk from A'Chuil started on a good track, through trees, dwindling to a mudslide as I advanced up Glen Pean to its bothy.

All the way I struggled with the weight of my pack, often just stopping to allow my body to catch up. With a sense of relief I approached the bothy and said hello to a chap hanging out his washing. He seemed very pleasant and offered me a cup of tea which I readily accepted. I asked him where he came from and he told me he didn't belong anywhere as he'd dropped out of society in 1985 and had been on the road ever since. Most of his family had shunned him for his change in lifestyle, as it might be a bad influence on their children.

He asked me what I was doing and I told him of my ambition to do the Munros. After listening intently he said, "You're wasting your time doing that are you?"

'I'm going to have fun with this guy', I thought.

Still sipping the sweet tea he made me, with my pack dumped, unopened, in the doorway he began to tell me more. Issues from his childhood that gave genuine reason for his adopted lifestyle. One of the things that still angered him the most was his brothers always gave him their opinions but wouldn't listen to his. This was my first inclination of hypocrisy as he'd given me his opinions on my choice of doing the Munros.

He was very anti-capitalist and referred to money as a, "False economy." I could see his point, I'm not a complete capitalist convert myself. But as we talked more he told me of his travels around the world – involving flying. Just how would airlines function, or ever have existed, without money? You can imagine the cockpit PA announcement. "Hello Ladies and Gentlemen. First Officer Johnson here. We are now approaching Sydney Airport and I'd once again like to ask you to return to your seats, ensure your seat belt is fastened and your seat back upright. Also all luggage is either stowed under the seat in front of you or in the overhead lockers. By the way if you could all have your pigs and goats ready, as payment for this flight, then the cabin crew will be pleased to collect them upon landing."

I settled into the bothy and did my own thing for quite some time. Sorting kit, checking maps. I felt he was a fine balance between my wish for solitude and a wish for company. Later we began to chat again, he told me he hitchhiked about and he could sense I felt it hypocritical to accept lifts off such a capitalist item as a motorcar. He justified it by saying, "Well it is public transport isn't it? You're getting a lift off of a member of the public."

Glen Pean Bothy

I could imagine somebody picking him up in their brand new Rover 620 with optional leather interior and walnut dash then throwing him out within two miles as he slated the use of a tree to make their dashboard and a cow's rump to form the seat covers.

However, it was an experience to meet him and we sat very late into the evening talking over candlelight. He had strong beliefs in nature and said he was anti books because you could learn more from a living tree than a dead one. True but then I did notice he had a newspaper with him. He also believed the education system is a conspiracy by the money makers to control people. He thought forcing children to change classrooms after each lesson and bombarding them with the work ethic was just there so the money makers could use them in their adult life without them knowing they were being exploited. He said if he had kids he'd not teach them to read or write as this wasn't natural and more bad comes of it than good. This got me thinking perhaps more bad does come of the ability to read and write than good. You need to let your mind go right back, as not be able to read and write in today's society would be a serious disadvantage.

He said the solitude of the last twelve years had given him these views, in 1985 he was just mixed up and knew he had to get out. As I'd previously mentioned he wasn't adverse to criticise my chosen lifestyle and when I told him I worked in computers he gleefully told me he was looking forward to the possibility of meteor storm that'd wipe out the world's computers. Just how would modern airlines work without computers?

I found his selective choosing of bits of the modern world annoying. He said maths was just invented to manipulate. Now he had me going: he was trying to convince me he was right about many things but maths is my home ground. I said maths could be used to prove most things; it's just a method of understanding nature. He started to slate Einstein's theories of relativity saying it is just a manmade theory and cannot be proven.

"Imagine it was daylight," I said, "and you were sitting at that window and I was outside looking in. Now imagine I ran backwards at the speed of light and looked back at you. I'd only ever see you as you were when I left you because I am going at the same pace as the light rays."

"That is only for you I could still move around, it is all relati..."

After that he started to respect me much more and not see me as somebody to talk at. We started to talk more deeply, well into the night. He made better points such as love is to give somebody your time, not your money. We also started to talk about the ills of modern society. He felt we'd lost the community spirit and the way we led our lives out of close communities brought about many of our troubles. I basically agreed with this but added communities of the past rejected newcomers, so it wasn't all roses and mutual support. I also told him about a theory I have which is in centuries to come archaeologists will unearth neighbourhood watch signs, epitomising the woes of life in the late 20th century. Neighbourhood Watch should be implicit, not an invented concept to patch up where we have gone wrong.

During our conversations I wanted to ask him his name but I refrained as I felt he might say he didn't believe in names as they were capitalist labelling to manipulate and control people – so I privately thought of him as Mr Pean, after the glen.

The following morning I woke at 05:30 to rain drumming on the metal roof of the bothy. I half cursed myself for not having tackled the Munros when I arrived in clear weather on the previous day. I lay in my sleeping bag until 08:00 when I could stand no more of the hard floor and got up. It was only when I stuck my head out of the door I realised the weather wasn't so bad, the tin roof had amplified the noise of the rain.

I set off at 08:40, crossing the River Pean by way of some stepping-stones, into a day of almost constant drizzle.

On starting the ascent I was desperate for the loo but was aware Mr Pean was watching me from the Perspex window of the bothy. I began to feel guilty, I felt in some way he was watching my every move for some environmental slip he could gleefully correct me on later. I kept looking back and he kept looking at me. I was desperate, the ascent was churning things about. There was no cover for secluded relief.

I looked back again and he was still there – motionless. I was far from motionless and I needed seclusion and five minutes of sheer heaven very quickly. Perhaps I am travelling at the speed of light I thought, and all I am seeing is the image of him when I left and he's actually having a ball burning plastic, chopping down trees and tipping chemicals into the Pean.

I looked ahead to the ascent and the refuge of the cloud line in the distance. I pressed on trying to hold it all together. Mr Pean had told me how he hated the type of people who ventured into the hills without a plastic trowel with which to bury their faeces. He told me he always made a point of digging down to the bedrock to reduce the environmental impact of his turds, well something like that – deep anyhow.

A group of hinds (female deer) heading high up into the coires distracted me, it is about this time of year they give birth so they head for the seclusion of the high ground. It was a welcome diversion and soon after I made the cloud line. I then stumbled across some rocks which formed a natural seat for the required job, giving me seclusion and five minutes of sheer heaven.

In total it took me about three hours to get to the top of Sgurr Thuilm, the first Munro of the day, involving a last minute game of 'hunt the summit cairn in the cloud' to complete the climb.

From the top I'd great difficulty finding the ridge path that'd lead me to my second Munro of the day. Initially I headed south with the intention of then turning west to head along the ridge but I failed to find the path. I retraced my steps back to the summit cairn and this time took a bearing directly to the next peak on the ridge. I soon encountered an impassable sharp drop so turned east and still had no luck. I fumbled for ages in poor visibility and seriously began to consider I should give up when suddenly I came across an iron fence post. I then remembered reading about the remains of an ancient fence on this ridge. I was thankful to recall this snippet of information, normally things I read don't stick. Therefore I was able to follow this and count off the minor summits until three hours later I reached the trig point marking the Munro of Sgurr nan Coireachan which shares the same name as the peak I'd climbed two days previously.

The only one view I got was when I looked back along the peaks and the troughs of the ridge at clouds hanging like cotton wool blankets in the dips.

I learnt from today's experience that on misty days you should only tackle pointed singletons, not flat topped Munros or ridge walks as navigation is difficult. Despite the weather I was quite elated as this completed the fiftieth Munro of this trip after forty-one days.

When I returned to the bothy the River Pean had risen to such an extent the stepping-stones I'd used eight hours previously were now almost submerged. The rain that had hampered me on the high ground had flowed down the river and was now hampering me on the low ground.

These stones had been put down some one hundred years before when the original house, now just a ruin, was deserted due to flooding and what is now the bothy was built on the opposite banks of the river. The bothy contained some notes on the history of the place. The last family living there had seven children, three of which were sons and were all lost in the First World War. This apparently broke the heart of their shepherd father, Ewen Campbell, and they left in the 1920s. The last family member, and the last to be born in the glen, died in 1986. Gone forever a way of life that had survived for century upon century.

In the evening, and the following morning, I continued my chat with Mr Pean. He told me he didn't believe people should be able to live in the city for fifty-one weeks a year then come to the country for a week because the city is made of stolen nature. I could see his point but I still fantasised about him being held hostage for five years with Margaret Thatcher in a Beirut dungeon.

He also returned to his favourite topic of how the state educates children and, in his considered view, last year Thomas Hamilton had, "Done those kids in Dunblane a favour."

Yeah right. Somehow I doubt the parents quite see it that way.

It was Friday the 13th I returned to civilisation. When I say civilisation I really mean one and a half hours of contemplation sat in my car, still parked miles up a minor road built to every contour of the terrain. Minor roads leading to hydroelectric dams have been smoothed out but the others retain their original construction technique of laying the tarmac wherever the land was.

I looked in my rear view mirror and took stock of five days of facial hair growth and the effects of too much chocolate.

Given the superstitions of the day I decided a Munro wasn't in order and instead a tearoom might be more civilised. I decided to go in search of some lunch and came across a roadside tearoom come restaurant popular with coach parties. All the staff were stressed and the current coach party, mainly retired people spending their grey pound, were wolfing down their food to try and be ready for the off. The off probably being a visit to another tearoom with some arrangement with the coach company. Nobody was smiling, the staff were probably all on a minimum wage level. I realised what Mr Pean meant which is the education system encourages people to work so hard they are bombarded and cannot see the wood for the trees. Therefore the bosses do the same to the work force and nobody can see it. He called it a conspiracy. I think it is just a sad indictment on modern day living.

After my lunch and some killing of time I drove to Loch Lochy Youth Hostel.

Loch Lochy Youth Hostel was very pleasant with friendly staff and lots of homely touches about the place. I got chatting to a chap in my dormitory who'd 'retired' about ten years previously when in his late thirties. He figured his investments brought in about £100 a week which was enough to survive on. He looked so relaxed I could only admire his pluck for saying no to the modern world and doing it his way.

Still his life can't be as complete as he'd like because he was on a singles club trip up from Glasgow. Some of the party were booked in to the hostel (not very optimistic in my opinion) others were in tents (kind of optimistic but could take a bit of persuasion) others had played the full optimist card and checked in to a hotel.

After my day of rest June the 14th took in Gleouraich and Spidean Mialach. Good views were had of the Glen Shiel ridge, which I climbed back in 1992. This is where I took in seven Munros in a day and started my knee troubles in the process.

Today the cloud was high therefore I could also see across to Sgurr na Ciche which was very pleasant to see from an alternate angle. It was a great ridge walk between the two and it was a delight to meet two chaps by the names of Geoffrey and James. They were frightfully nice and definitely public school. I guess they were in their forties or fifties. Geoffrey was an accountant and James a barrister. They took a real interest in my walking and were very kind to me giving me a cup of tea and food when they brewed up.

On the ridge between the two Munros, James looked back towards the first Munro and said, "Looks like a big party up there."

"That's a singles club up from Glasgow," I replied.

With that James came out with the following line – try and say it aloud with your best Terry-Thomas public school accent – "You're kidding. Geoffrey, Geoffrey did you hear what Steve just said there? That group of people up there on that peak, singles club up from Glasgow – what a hoot."

They were great guys and definitely some of the kindest people I met while out walking.

Me and Geoffrey

June the 15th took in Gairich which was a bit of a haul. I felt weary and, with the initial leg crossing boggy ground, I didn't feel I was making very good progress. However, the weather was good and with the cloud staying high I got some views.

June the 16th took in Sgurr a'Mhaoraich. As the weather was so good I took less kit and wore my lighter boots, giving me a real spurt in the early part of the walk. Boulders the size of houses had fallen on the ridge around to the summit. I hoped no more would choose to fall as I walked briskly by.

I spent over an hour on the top taking in the superb views. Having time on my side meant I could relax and enjoy sitting at the top – it's all too easy to get to the top and set straight off again. I met two chaps at the top who both work for Strathclyde Police. One of them, Ian Maitland, knew Willy and was also a friend of Graham Munro who was killed on Buachaille Etive Mor.

June the 17th was a rest day. I gave an Aussie girl a ride from Loch Lochy Youth Hostel to Spean Bridge. She had been travelling for two years and had just decided to return to see her parents in the Snowy Mountains in Australia. After that I drove over to Kingussie for a much needed haircut and then on to the independent hostel in Newtonmore.

Newtonmore

June the 18th saw me back in the mountains for the four in a day trip of Geal-Charn, A' Mharconaich, Beinn Udlamain and Sgairneach Mhor.

I started at 07:25 in the wet and mist, neither of which abated for the entire day. This made the going a bit miserable but the big advantage of this group of Munros is you start so high up the Dalwhinnie pass there isn't so much climbing to be done.

My main source of entertainment on the way up was the large number of grouse I disturbed. The first summit was difficult to find because as I neared the peak, I started to look at the wrong part of my map and was therefore confused until I realised my mistake. I made rare use of my GPS to confirm my position. It told me where I was – on top of the Munro. I carried on for ten metres and found the cairn.

By pure luck I hit the second Munro on a compass bearing I'd taken. A good old fence between the second and third peaks made navigation easier. The fourth I found with relative ease so I was satisfied with my exploits in the mist.

The mountains in this area are really grassy slopes with few rocky bits, making them some of the easier Munros. I needed to use the compass a lot but the windy conditions, combined with the walking poles, made its use difficult due to the lack of hands. I dreamt of building a compass into the top of one of the walking poles. In the other I fantasised building in a microphone and being able to say, "Ah, Miss Money Penny."

The end of the walk involved a lengthy stretch along the A9. This is a very busy trunk road and I couldn't help but notice the vast quantities of rubbish. Cans, crisp packets, debris from car accidents and evidence associated with just about every conceivable bodily function apart from conception. I guess even the Japanese haven't thought of a gadget to allow that to happen while travelling up the A9. The cars and lorries were throwing up masses of spray so it was a miserable return to my car at 15:50 where I then became part of the A9 procession I had just been slating.

The private hostel in Newtonmore provided excellent facilities. I had the entire place to myself so enjoyed the quiet luxury. In the hostel was a Scottish Mountaineering Club (SMC) Journal for 1991. On page 702, under the list of accidents for 1990, it said:

May 7th – wearing Doc Marten boots and glissading from the Carn Mor Dearg Arete, Adrian Glover (23) lost control and cut his scalp on a rock. Lochaber MRT & RAF Wessex. 12 [man hours].

So my first Munro actually has a record against it in the SMC journal. Subsequently I wrote to the SMC and got a copy, sending it to Ady for Christmas. The SMC were generous in their interpretation of Ady's accident, a more appropriate description would have been:

May 7th – Proudly wearing Doc Marten boots and bum sliding from Carn Mor Dearg (which he impressively, yet mistakenly, described as the Arete), Adrian Glover (23) while completely out of control cut his scalp on a rock rather predictably at the end of the snow field he was bum sliding through. Lochaber MRT & RAF Wessex. 12 [man hours].

June the 19th saw me take in Geal Charn. It rained at first then cleared on top where a massive cairn marked the summit. I saw a tiny lizard on the way up, I'd never seen one in the wild before so it was great to see the little chap (or chapess) looking up at me.

June the 20th was a classic walk as it took in some inland cliffs. I started in the mist and reached Carn Liath, bringing my Munro tally to 125, one of my biggest aims of this trip. Then on to Stob Poite Coire Ardair and then to Creag Meagaidh via Mad Megs Cairn, a huge moss-covered structure, which in poor weather could easily be mistaken for the summit. I saw a grouse on the way up and as ever it tried to lead me away from its young.

At the summit I met a chap with a lady acting as his paid guide. I had never come across this before in the mountains. They told me the window between the second and third peaks was navigable so I descended to it and then cut down the boulder slopes towards some spectacular inland cliffs. I had to pick my way carefully as one slip on the boulders would have meant I'd have been a welcome victim to gravity. The cliffs over shadow Lochan a'Choire which has a breed of arctic fish still surviving from the ice age.

Back at the car I chatted to a guy who I'd spoken with at the start of the day. Then he had said he'd slow me down if we walked together but, as is normal with my pace, he, having done the same walk as me, got back one and a half hours earlier.

He was ridiculing my speed, but I managed to shut him up by revealing I'd asthma. Well that is until he started to tell me his life story. His yellow Bedford Rascal van, which he travels around in and sleeps in, was bought eleven years ago with the money he got after he divorced his wife.

He further told me he was Scots in origin but had spent the last thirty years living in North Wales. His accent was very interesting and at one stage he came out with, "Aye, Aye, yes indeed."

This was my last night in the Newtonmore Private Hostel and this time I wasn't alone as a really nice group of people were up from the YMCA in Edinburgh. We went out to a local pub and they wouldn't let me buy a drink.

The End of 1997 Munroing

On the Saturday morning I wandered into a hotel and booked three nights, starting from the Sunday evening. I then left Newtonmore and drove down to Dunoon to see my friend, Graham Disselduff, who was up staying with his mother.

We had a good time and I was interested to see Dunoon as my gramp, a submarine ASDEC and wireless operator, was stationed there, and in other Scottish bases, during the Second World War. My gran tells of a story where one submarine was feared lost, it'd been out on patrol and they'd lost all contact with it and after a few days the base had resigned themselves to all hands having been lost. Then a friend of my gran was pushing her child in a pram out on the edge of the water and in the distance a shape came into view and slowly the realisation dawned on her it was the lost submarine, with her husband on-board. It had been badly damaged by the enemy but had enough reserves to limp its way home under its own power, but out of wireless contact. I would never wish peacetime away but there are certain wartime stories of bravery, humanity and gut determination peacetime can never surpass.

On the Sunday I travelled back to Newtonmore and arrived at the hotel and enjoyed my evening meal in the bar. I eavesdropped on a late thirties couple talking to the barman, they were holidaying in Scotland for the first time having driven up to Fort William the day before and then on to Inverness and down to Newtonmore on this day. They obviously enjoyed the scenery but I sensed they wouldn't be back, at least not for a long while. Scotland is usually cold and damp and like a grumpy old live-in relative the weather deters a visitor calling again. After two hours of driving with the wipers on intermittent the chances of getting out of your nice warm car for a stroll is about the same as a Scotsman supporting England when they play Germany. A tearoom or a trinket shop is about the limit and explains the vast number of them dotted about the Highlands. However, if you actually go walking getting wet, then drying off in the wind is just part of the experience.

    Later in the evening I phoned Gisella and immediately sensed something wasn't quite right. She tried to hide it from me, to not spoil my trip, but soon she started to cry. The day before, while out in her car, she'd had the misfortune to find herself in the path of a testosterone-filled time bomb. He had lost control of his car and veered onto her side of the road spinning her car though one hundred and eighty degrees and depositing it on the kerb. She was lucky to escape serious physical injury or even death. I headed straight back home on the Monday morning.

    So I returned to helping Gisella through a particularly

painful time, a 'mountain' of paper work, seven weeks of junk mail, wearing shoes and driving in traffic.

One morning I woke at about 03:00 needing the loo and made a slight navigational error at the foot of our bed and turned left instead of right. Gisella woke to find me desperately looking for the bedroom door on completely the wrong side of the room – 62 new Munros navigated to in all conditions, yes. Finding the loo in the night, no.

I'd lost over a stone in weight, this must be the only sport where you can eat four Mars bars a day and still lose weight. I also noticed a change in attitude towards the Munros. Previously I found admitting to doing the Munros was often a taboo subject with people climbing their soapboxes and telling you peak bagging is a lesser form of enjoying the pleasures of the mountains. It is an attitude that irritated me because what suits one person doesn't always suit another. However, during this trip it was a lot easier to be open about doing the Munros. This I found relaxing, I hate being amongst people where you cannot be yourself. Not being yourself is stressful, almost a lie you buy into and have to continue, watching out for slip-ups in your act, for what? Just to fit in with others who are being themselves – opinionated and awkward.

Perhaps being able to be more open about Munro bagging (or should that be Munro bragging?) this year was more down to me than a change in other people. Perhaps I'd felt what I was doing was less worthy than other walkers but this year confidently saying, "I am doing the Munros" halted any negative reactions. Who knows? But it did mean I enjoyed the trip all the more for it.

Munro Count: 127

1998

An Incident at Reading Station

Disaster struck at 08:00 on July the 29th 1997 on Platform 9 of Reading Railway Station. That morning Gisella had received a birthday card from her aunt and uncle in which they'd included a cutting from *The Times* for me. Between changing trains, on my daily commute from Swindon to Slough, I plonked myself down on a seat and read the article – The Scottish Mountaineering Club had promoted eight previous non-Munros to Munro status and declassified one other, thus moving the total from 277 to 284. This in itself was a minor annoyance but then the real horror struck: four of the 'new' Munros were on ridges I'd been on during the previous two months. For the sake of a few extra hours, on each walk, I could have done these four Munros but now each one will require a separate day-long expedition.

Legend has it T.E. Lawrence lost an early draft copy of *The Seven Pillars of Wisdom* at Reading station. At least he had hope of finding it. The despair, for once, even made the arrival at Slough bearable.

Life Moves On

During the winter, life changed for me. At Christmas Gisella and I decided to go our separate ways and, feeling a bit lonely, I responded to Barbara's letter – she was the Canadian lady I met at Killin Youth Hostel. She gave me her email address and, having just got online at home myself, we began corresponding – casually at first but after a while we decided perhaps a holiday together would be nice. Barbara said she could come to Scotland for three weeks in April.

We took a holiday cottage in Aberfeldy and, on April 9th, made the two-hour drive up to Glen Clova to tackle Driesh and Mayar – starting from a good height these are two relatively straightforward Munros.

Early on our navigation let us down but we found ourselves on the excellent Kilbo Path which appeared a better route than described in the guidebook. There was quite a bit of snow about on the high ground but it felt fairly safe and the sun made for a pleasant day until the cloud set in on the approach to Mayar. It then started to snow which made things a bit miserable.

At the top Barbara put a stone on the cairn and said, "Ohm Mani Padme Hum."

"What does that mean?" I asked.

"Hail to the Jewel of the Lotus."

I left it at that.

During the winter I'd purchased a new black and gold Gore-Tex jacket. I deliberately wanted something with better neck protection and something a bit brighter in case I ever needed to be rescued. However, on the descent from Mayar I couldn't get the neck done up properly and, while attempting to adjust it, I lost concentration which contributed to us wandering off course. I really needed to adjust it but as Barbara suffers from Raynaud's disease, causing her to cool down very quickly, we had to keep on the move. Therefore we weren't a brilliant combination as I needed more rests due to my asthma but realised in the very cold conditions, I couldn't do this due to the risk of Barbara cooling off.

Barbara tried to adjust the neck of my jacket for me. "Thank you it's better," I said.

However, in the strong wind it must have sounded like, "Can you make it better", because she immediately tried to adjust it again. I was too cold to repeat myself.

We then picked up a fence to get ourselves back on course.

It is interesting walking with somebody new as you pick up different techniques and ideas you wouldn't have thought of yourself. Barbara gave me some thermal gloves to go under my lined Gore-Tex ones. Not only did they give an extra layer of protection but they were also useful for routing about inside my rucksack. Thick outer gloves have to be removed when groping around for items, making your bare hands very cold. The thin inner ones are just thick enough to remove the discomfort of the cold and just thin enough to enable Mars bar shaped objects to be extracted.

Also she convinced me to buy a chest strap for my rucksack to hold the two shoulder straps together to stop them sliding on my Gore-Tex jacket – in high winds she'd noticed I'd been holding them in place. Finally I purchased a neck tube which is a tube made from thermal material to protect the neck from the cold.

On April the 11th we planned to do Glas Maol and Creag Leacach. The first thing to thwart us was Cameron McNeish's Munro Almanac guidebook which has this pair of Munros on OS Sheet 32 (which covers the Isle of Skye) whereas they're actually on Sheet 43, Braemar. The second thing to thwart us was snow. The drive up from Aberfeldy was going well until we started to climb up the A93 at which stage the snow set. At the summit of the road, the recommended starting place for these two Munros, we pulled up and surveyed the miserable scene: we didn't even get out of the car.

So our next attempt was to do A' Chailleach, Carn Sgulain and Carn Dearg on April the 13th. In the event we only managed A' Chailleach due to the conditions. The snow was thick on the ascent and I had to follow Barbara's footprints to save myself from having to cut in.

At the top we paused for just a few minutes before setting

off down a steep gully for the ascent of Carn Sgulain. The downward slope of the gully was north facing and the sun-starved narrowness made it more dangerous because of ice. Sheets of the stuff in fact, dropping into the abyss we had to cut across. We negotiated the first but when crossing the second Barbara slipped and with a cry she shot off down the slope towards the stream below. I took a moment to take in the situation then dived after her. After a few seconds I managed to catch her leg. In the event she'd managed to stop herself which is probably how I managed to catch her up, if she hadn't stopped herself then we'd probably have both slid for a few hundred feet into the freezing stream below.

Even though she said she was okay I still held on to her leg until she repeated to me she was okay. This irritated her a bit (as did many things), but I was in no mood for social pleasantries.

We decided to turn back but first waited for some people we'd seen ahead of us on our way up A' Chailleach, who had now disappeared in the gully. We had to wait a long time before they emerged at the head to start their ascent of Carn Sgulain – they looked very slow and exhausted which backed up our decision to turn back.

On the way back we had some fun jumping in the snow on the more hospitable south face of A' Chailleach. There were also some arctic hares, which were nice to see.

On the final stretch to the car Barbara went up to her waist in a bog, rounding off a partially successful day's walking. Once in the car Barbara's core body temperature began to drop, due to the Raynaud's, so I had to put the heater on full blast and as I sweltered she slowly shivered.

When encountering ice you should turn back, unless you are wearing crampons. The other useful piece of equipment is an ice axe.

April the 18th was the first trip to bag one of the newly promoted Munros, An Stuc on the Lawers ridge. We made a late start, around 14:30, from the Ben Lawers visitor centre. The route took in a repeat of Beinn Ghlas, a Munro I'd bagged last year. Repeating a Munro isn't high on my list of priorities and, given how tough I find them, I find people's passions for return visits a strange and interesting concept.

However, we were able to avoid Ben Lawers by traversing its snow-covered westerly slopes. After finding ourselves at the foot of An Stuc at just after 18:15, we turned back.

On resting on the re-traverse of the westerly slopes of Ben Lawers, Barbara got out her plastic bag of gorp (mixed raisins, nuts, chocolate, peanuts and dried apricots which, when Barbara wasn't looking, I picked out the bits of chocolate from) and tossed it on the ground. It shot off into infinity backing up our decision to turn back before too much ice formed.

We had to visit the Munro of Beinn Ghlas for a second time then, on the final descent, I enjoyed running down the snow slopes and jumping forward to be carried a few yards by the frictionless surface – it felt a bit like the dream of flying.

We got back to the car just after 20:45 (which would have been after 22:00, dark and icy if we'd done An Stuc).

Despite no new Munro to add to the tally it was a beautifully clear day, the fantastic views made up for the disappointment and we capped it all with a meal at the Ben Lawers hotel.

April the 20th saw another failed attempt at An Stuc. This time we started from the village of Lawers but instead of cutting up to the end of the ridge we decided to join it between Ben Lawers and An Stuc. After much walking we headed up a steep slope to meet a spur which we thought would take us onto the ridge proper. From here we were in complete mist and I took a bearing of 275 degrees and we set off on it up 'our spur'. After a while a path became obvious with marked cairns. It then hit me we'd inadvertently got ourselves onto one of the approaches to Ben Lawers.

"Barb," I called back, "bet you a million quid there is a trig point at the top of this path."

"Why?" she replied.

"Because we are on a path up Ben Lawers and nowhere near the ridge spur we wanted."

Barbara said fuck four times in the space of a minute, being a lady who seldom swears I could sense her disappointment.

The more obvious path and the frequency of summit cairns, put the evidence beyond circumstantial. So we agreed to turn back – the length of the walk from Ben Lawers to An Stuc would again have left us finishing in the dark.

I said I may as well just walk to the summit of Ben Lawers, so Barbara elected to stay put while I went on. After just a few minutes the path narrowed and became unnervingly icy.

Turning back I could just make out Barbara, sat below me. I called out, "What begins in B and ends in S."

A few seconds later came her reply, "Ben Lawers."

"Good answer," I said, "I actually meant bollocks but Ben Lawers it is."

April the 23rd saw our final trip into the mountains taking in Glas Maol and Creag Leacach, these being the two we didn't even attempt on April the 11th due to the snow. The day was kind to us and the twelve days since the first attempt made all the difference as there was only a bit of snow this time.

From the tops we were treated to clear views, and some mild to strong wind to contend with. The final route back to the A93 required us to ford a stream. Barbara crossed quickly, but, given it was fast flowing with meltwater, I took my time to find a place where I felt comfortable.

Me stretched out on Creag Leacach

We got back to the A93 about a half hour walk from the car. Before I could drag my heels Barbara started hitching and literally got a lift within a matter of seconds from two Australians. She picked my car up and came and collected me. All in all a much better day than our recent trips.

Between Trips

So ended our trip away together and, so I thought, my Munro bagging for 1998. Barbara asked if I'd like to go to Canada for a holiday later in the summer and I said yes. However, as I wanted to be in England for the World Cup which ran through most of June and early July, I started to look around for a short-term contract. Then Unisys, who I'd been with from July 1997 to March 1998, got in touch and said they'd like me back in July to do systems performance tuning. So that was brilliant, go back to the mountains for May and early June, watch the World Cup for the rest of June, work during July and go to Canada for August. So that's what I did and the following describes my four bonus weeks in Scotland.

East of the A9

For this trip I decided to take my mountain bike to help out with the Munros that start with a time-consuming walk along a track. I spent a couple of evenings burning the midnight oil poring over the Ordnance Survey maps of the remaining Munros and worked out forty-five that'd benefit from an approach via a mountain bike. It is amazing how some things can absorb you as at one stage I glanced up to see the time was 20:00, the next time I looked it was 02:00.

I was due to set off on May the 13th but during the night of May the 11th I was kept awake by toothache. I phoned my dentist and they got me in and found a suspected abscess. I don't know what it was suspected of but nonetheless it was hiding beneath one of my teeth. Explaining my desire to head north they patched me up with a steroid dressing, a temporary filling and a bottle of penicillin, a spare prescription and some good wishes for my trip.

Therefore I was still able to set off on May the 13th. Although I had a roof rack for my bike I did not risk it on the M5 and M6 and instead kept the bike in the car until I reached Pitlochry Youth Hostel.

May the 14th saw me back to the Munros with a drive to Old Blair near Blair Atholl, to attempt Beinn Dearg. I found a brilliant parking space and was immediately told off by a passing estate worker for using such a brilliant parking place and instead I was sent packing to the public car park some one mile back.

After assembling the bike I rode for about two and a quarter hours. I found it very hard going as, now coupled with a sore throat, the abscess and medicine were draining my energy.

I abandoned the bike where the direct track from Old Blair to Bruar Lodge crosses the Allt an t-Seapail stream and ventured across boggy ground made up of peat and small streams. I was fooled by an uncharted track, recently bulldozed out of the hill below Beinn a'Chait, until I reached the correct path that climbs Meall Dubh nan Dearcag on the way to Beinn Dearg.

I found it a real struggle and it took the best part of four hours to walk from my bike to the summit.

On the walk back I took a lot of care with the compass as I didn't have any spare energy for mistakes. In the event I managed to get back to the bike in under two hours and then converted the question if the bike was worth the trouble into an emphatic yes as I hurtled back down the track – still the dare devil from my childhood days of cycling. I hadn't realised how much uphill there was on the way in.

Apart from a quick chat with two guys at the top the only other person I met was an old chap sat by a large cairn on the side of the track. He was doing a mammoth walk across the remote highland tracks with just his pack and tent for company. He said he'd seen my bike and was tempted to take it for the ride. I had it well locked to prevent anybody from using it as an easy means of transport.

Back at the youth hostel I realised just how much I'd struggled during the day and decided to take the next day off. Also I began to think the forty-five Munros I planned to get to the foot of by mountain bike might be a bit ambitious, and perhaps instead I should consider finishing off all of the Munros to the east of the A9, including the Cairngorms. Although this plan meant fewer

Munros, and slightly less use of the mountain bike, it'd stop me having to come back to some areas, involving long drives for just the odd Munro. So with this slight change in plan I took Friday May the 15th off.

Saturday May the 16th brought another single Munro, Carn a'Chlamain which I tackled by cycling up the Glen Tilt track from Blair Atholl. I looked forward to seeing Marble Lodge which lies up this track and gets mentioned in many of the walking guidebooks. I expected to see a glorious Highland hunting lodge, unfortunately I was disappointed because Marble Lodge is a modest single-storey building but probably gets mentioned a lot due to it being one of the few buildings in the area with an easy to pronounce name.

I padlocked my bike to a telegraph pole just short of the dwellings called Clachghlas and cut up onto the path which heads west then north-east up Carn a'Chlamain. I plodded up an eyesore of a track which had been newly bulldozed out of the hill, resting often in the heat and taking in the good views.

I was satisfied with the day's effort, I still found it a bit of a struggle but nothing like the ascent of Beinn Dearg. The mountain bike was very useful both on the cycle in and the cycle out.

In the evening I phoned my friend from Glasgow, Willy Newlands, to see if he wanted to do some walking on the following day. Unfortunately his mother was sick so he couldn't make it. However, we had a good chat about things and soon got on to the subject of the forthcoming World Cup and whether the Scots will always support whatever team England was playing.

"Willy, I guess you will be supporting Tunisia when they play England in their opening game?" I asked.

"Aye, Steve, aye" he replied.

I'd a hidden scheme here as I knew Willy had been the victim of a terrorist incident in Tunisia and felt very satisfied with myself for having cornered him. "Willy," I added after a deliberate pause, "weren't you on a bus that was blown up by a terrorist bomb in Tunisia?"

I really thought I'd got him this time but seconds later I was left reeling by an all-time Willy classic. "Steve, it was just a flesh wound."

Sunday the 17th brought my last daily commute to Blair Atholl to tackle Carn Liath, Braigh Coire Chruinn-bhalgain and Carn nan Gabhar. I parked my car in fog at the end of the public road near Loch Moraig. As I lifted the bike off the roof I felt it was going to be a nice day. You start to sense the weather when you spend a lot of time outside.

I pedalled off down the track towards Shinagag but stopped after just over a mile and set off on foot for the summit of Carn Liath. I found the climbing tough but the fog started to lift to expose a glorious day.

I was soon caught up by a middle-aged woman and her two dogs. I accompanied her for about five minutes before I gave in to the inevitable and let them go on ahead. A trail of people then began to overtake me.

This walk was a classic ridge walk with ups and downs and changes of direction as the ridge plots its way between the three Munros. On the ascent of the second peak I was regularly being overtaken. Looking back I could see hordes of ant-like figures marching down the ridge I'd recently descended.

On the approach to Carn nan Gabhar there is a point at which you can drop into the glen below. Unfortunately a dog called Becky had decided some interesting mountain hare lived down there and had taken off after it. Her poor owners were standing at the top trying to spot their dog. After some further minutes one of them took the decision to descend 1000 feet to reclaim the beast.

I really struggled in the heat on the approach to the third

Munro and felt ill a couple of times. To compensate there were some beautiful views especially over to where I'd walked during the previous few days.

I spent over an hour at the final summit chatting with a chap called Jeremy who was a structural engineer working on the design of oilrigs. We descended together by going over Airgiod Bheinn and cut round Beinn Bheag and re-joined the track where I'd left my mountain bike. The summit of Carn nan Gabhar has three rises, the most north-easterly being generally recognised as the highest. As we descended a man was just settling himself down at the first summit so we had to wave him on by shouting out, "That isn't the highest point", while gesticulating off to our right.

The descent with Jeremy was nice as it was company and he set a better pace so I managed to save at least an hour on the route back. As we walked back up the track I was hoping my bike would be okay as a great number of people had passed it during the day. Jeremy told me of a case where two guys had got benighted because some estate workers had carted their mountain bikes off in a Land Rover. A stupid thing to do as it'd put their lives at risk.

Luckily my bike was okay save for a direct hit by a bird on the saddle. I pedalled back to the car park area where my car had been joined by quite a gathering of vehicles. I spied a note on my windscreen and immediately thought I was being told off for having parked illegally or something. The note simply said 'That was a long walk – hope you enjoy rest of your holiday. Munro bag lady + dogs'. This was the first person to overtake me and it was nice she'd wanted to say goodbye by leaving me this most welcome note. I initially wondered how she knew my car but then the obvious struck me – I was the only other car there when she'd parked up. The entire day took just under ten hours and, as I piled into my car, I felt very weary.

Braemar

I left Pitlochry Youth Hostel on the morning of Monday May the 18th and drove towards Braemar on the A93 and stopped just north of the Glen Shee ski area. From here I tackled Carn an Tuirc, Cairn of Claise, Tolmount and Tom Buidhe. It was another hot day with good views but this time I didn't struggle so much. It was the first time I hadn't needed the mountain bike, which may have had a bearing on things. I got good views on what really was a route march between four summits of a large raised area. I could see over to Glas Maol where Barbara and I didn't even attempt to get out of the car just the previous month. Now it was all in sun and no sign of snow let alone a blizzard!

After the walk I arrived at the delightful Braemar Youth Hostel which is an old hunting lodge. I must have been hungry because some chap commented on the amount of pasta I'd piled on the plate for my evening meal.

I had a stroll around in the later evening, passing the Mountain Rescue Centre alongside the hostel. It reminded me of a funny story about the Braemar Mountain Rescue Team. It involved an Irish climber who had gone missing on Glas Maol one spring. A rescue mission was mobilised and he was located at dawn dug into a snow hole near to the summit. While the team was warming him up with hot drinks he asked which road they could see snaking its way along the floor of the glen below. On being told it was the A93 he commented he'd been down by it the night before but had become lost. He then remembered a training course he'd been on which taught him that when lost in the mountains you should dig a snow hole in which to keep warm. But he had to climb all the way back up the mountain to find snow deep enough to dig such a snow hole. I guess the Mountain Rescue Team was mad at him at the time but can only assume over the years this has become a tale of almost folklore proportions. For myself I find his innocence rather touching.

The Botanist of Geldie Lodge

The following day I had to rest, the four Munros of the 18th having taken their toll. So Wednesday May the 20th was my next expedition into the hills. I teamed up with Tony Wood, staying in the same dormitory as me. He was excellent company, a retired schoolteacher and like me he'd brought his mountain bike up for the first time to try and pick off some of the more remote Munros.

We started from the Linn of Dee and cycled out to the ruins of Geldie Lodge, a trip of something just short of eight miles which took over an hour and a half. At one point we were treated to an eagle swooping low in front of us. I have seen many birds in the mountains and always wondered if I'd seen an eagle before. I had not, this was so obvious by its wing span. From there we took in Carn an Fhidhleir and An Sgarsoch. Carn an Fhidhleir was Munro number 142 for me, number 242 for Tony, and of course my half-way point.

It was a relatively dull day with not much of a view until we dropped down below the cloud line on the descent of the north slopes of An Sgarsoch. Tony pointed out different types of bird to me, such as dotterel (a rare Europe-Asian shore bird) and ptarmigan (an arctic grouse with a silent 'P', presumably so it isn't eaten by a predator while it is relieving itself). As botany was his great love he also pointed out various plant life.

The walking part of the day was about another nine miles on top of the ride so the bikes really helped because it'd have been a twenty-five mile walk without them, pushing it a bit for one day. We had left our bikes chained to a fence close to Geldie Lodge and, as we turned round the edge of the ruins, to reclaim them, we were

174

presented with two guys standing by a four-wheeled drive jeep type of vehicle. I sensed something was not quite right. Initially I thought perhaps they were estate workers waiting to tick us off for bringing our bikes along their track, but as we got chatting it didn't appear that way. One was middle-aged, the other younger, perhaps in his early twenties.

"Are you estate workers?" I asked.

"No, I'm just the driver here for this chap doing a vegetation study," replied the older one, scuffing the ground and looking at his feet.

This reply should have put me at ease, as there are notorious stories of hostilities between walkers and estate workers, but it didn't do much to comfort me. After a few more minutes I was relieved to see them drive off.

"Tony, that didn't sound very plausible," I said.

"No, for a vegetation survey you'd need lots of people and various bits of equipment," he replied.

We reckoned the most innocent explanation was they used the vegetation survey as an excuse to borrow a key, from the estate, to the gate at the end of the track – avoiding sixteen miles of walking. Either that or they were international drug smugglers.

On the cycle back I took a run at a stream crossing the track. It went a bit wrong and I ended up landing sideways in the water wishing I could rerun the last few seconds of my life again.

When we got back to the Linn of Dee the two 'botanists' were stuck with their jeep as the key they'd used in the morning no longer fitted the padlock. Was the estate wise or was it just a faulty lock?

Excuse Me Cameron but I Think That's a Bit Ambitious

Cameron McNeish is a Scottish Mountaineer held in esteem by

some outdoor folk. Amongst other things he is the author of *The Munro Almanac*, a handy (but not without errors) pocket-sized guidebook to the Munros.

Most of the routes he describes are split into sensible day walks. However, he describes doing the five Munros at the end of Glen Ey in one day – a twenty-six mile route with approximately 6000 feet of ascent. Just looking at the map was enough to put me off, therefore on May the 21ˢᵗ I set out with the idea of splitting it into two or perhaps three separate days.

I parked at Inverey and cycled up the track to the ruin of Altanour Lodge. In this area are the remains of a few dwellings mirroring the graves of a small community long since dead and gone.

I was procrastinating over locking up my mountain bike when Tony arrived. My aim was to do Beinn Iutharn Mhor and Carn Bhac then have a think about An Socach if time allowed. Tony was setting off to do Carn an Righ, Beinn Iutharn Mhor and Carn Bhac. Therefore we walked for a short distance together and then went our separate ways.

I took the north-east face of Beinn Iutharn Mhor which was very steep in places before it opened out into a long ridge leading to the summit. I had to battle with the wind on the final stretch. Quickly forcing my sandwiches down at the summit I backtracked to a lesser summit of the ridge and took a bearing across to Carn Bhac. The ascent of this was straightforward in comparison, followed by a drop back into Glen Ey where I started to wander towards the foot of An Socach. I soon realised it wasn't to be, my mental state wasn't up for another 1300 foot of ascent so instead returned to my bike.

When I got within sight of the ruin of Altanour Lodge, which incidentally is a haven of a place surrounded by Scots pines, I could see Tony unlocking his bike. It was quite a coincidence we both started together and finished within a few minutes of each other despite him having done three Munros and me just the two. It was good to have some company for the cycle back.

During the evening I got talking to the assistant warden, Dave Hewitt, who was a guy of about my age and similar outlook on life – we spent many a spare minute chatting about this and that. The previous night there had been a hairy climber in. When I say hairy I mean a mass of grey hair, a big bushy beard to match and middle-aged stocky frame. He was a climber of the old school, not one of these slim youngsters who skip up a rock face. He was checking in again this night after having done Glas Tulaichean and Carn an Righ. He was talking to Dave and said all day the only person he'd seen was a distant figure on Beinn Iutharn Mhor at around midday.

"That was probably me," I piped up.

We started to have a chat, he was quite a character. With an accent from the Lake District and fingers like a bunch of bananas he sat down and we chatted about our day. He had started from the Dalmunzie Hotel near the Spittal of Glenshee and everything was a bastard. The two mountains he'd done were both bastards. When he'd got back to his bastard car he went for a bastard drink in the bastard hotel. Actually I agreed with him about the hotel as they said they weren't doing food and could only sell him a pint. As he drunk it he noticed other people buying bar food. He was understandably annoyed, okay he was dressed for the mountains but so what. Anyhow he told me more about his bastard car: an old 'Y' registered (1982) Mercedes estate. He had bought it cheap, "A few year back", and the bastard hadn't let him down apart from the odd exhaust. He had to get the exhaust done by a garage and the part was about £170 but they said it'd last so he'd said, "Well you had better put the bastard on." He cracked me up because there was nothing crude about him it was just everything was a bastard.

177

Friday May the 22nd saw the second of what was to become a three-day attempt at what Cameron McNeish might describe as a Sunday stroll. I couldn't face the cycle up Glen Ey again so took the slightly unusual route of tackling An Socach from the Glen Shee ski area. It was very misty and there was quite a bit of rain early on so I had to use my compass skills to get me over the ridge via Loch Vrotachan and the descent to Baddoch Burn.

I'd some difficulty crossing this stream until I found a handy bridge somebody had erected. The weather started to clear at this point for the final pull up to the ridge of An Socach. From the summit I could see a distant red figure on the east end of the ridge some one and a half miles away. As I headed back along the ridge the figure got nearer and towards the end we both diverted our course so we could stop for a chat. It's quite uncanny this, you like the solitude of walking in the hills but you still want a chat with the only other person out. Walk down a high street and nobody will talk to you, on a Munro with just one other person about you have a friend.

I hurried back to the ski area as I fancied a hot drink in the café before heading back to Braemar. The café had a sign saying it closed at 16:45, I got there and at 16:25 just as they were closing early to polish the floor. With the thought of a coffee shop now in mind I headed into Braemar and found both its coffee shops had just closed. This was before 17:00 on the Friday of a bank holiday weekend and temporarily left me feeling a bit unsympathetic to those who claim it's hard to make a living out of tourism. With the thought of a hot drink still in mind I opted for a tasteless drink of tea from a Styrofoam cup outside of a roadside café, it wasn't the image I'd had in mind.

Saturday May the 23rd completed the trilogy of days tackling the Munros up Glen Ey. The remaining two were Glas Tulaichean and

Carn an Righ which I approached from the Spittal of Glenshee. I cycled up Gleann Taitneach for about an hour and a quarter and locked my bike up behind a large boulder with a handy bit of looped wire sticking out of the ground to thread the lock through. As I walked away the wind made a lonely whistling sound through the spokes of the wheels.

I climbed the south-west ridge up onto Glas Tulaichean. The wind was very harsh on top and all I could see in the distance was a massive mountain which I initially thought was Carn an Righ. It looked very far away and huge. I spoke with a father and son who thought it was Carn an Righ also. On checking the map and compass I was relieved to find Carn an Righ was a more manageable looking lump to the north-west. At this point I was desperate for food but couldn't open my pack until I got into the shelter of Mam nan Carn away from the evil north wind.

The ascent of Carn an Righ was then straightforward and I was able to follow the good path along to Loch nan Eun before dropping into Gleann Taitneach and back to my bike. The return ride was downhill with the wind behind me and took just thirty-five minutes including a stop to chat to some guys I'd spoken to as I ascended, and they descended, Carn an Righ.

Three Walks in One

Lochnagar is a famous mountain both for its height, views and surrounding inland cliffs. The reader may be familiar with the book Prince Charles wrote called *The old man of Lochnagar* as this was a striking out place during his childhood stays at Balmoral.

It is best approached from the minor road that ends near to Loch Muick. I had it in mind if I made an early start I might be able to also take in Carn a'Choire Bhoidheach and Carn an t-Sagairt Mor. If things went really well I could also take in Cairn Bannoch and Broad Cairn by walking a horse shoe type of route and descending back to my car via the south shores of Loch Muick.

The day started dull with rain in the air and a bit of a chill. The path up Lochnagar was a good one, which meant I could make a good pace. I soon took off my fleece and just had my upper body clad in a T-shirt, thin shirt and Gore-Tex jacket. Below I'd track suit trousers and a light pair of over trousers. This combination of clothing, the coolness of the day and the good path were obviously the perfect combination for me as I didn't feel the usual heaviness and managed to make a very quick pace reaching the summit of Lochnagar in just under three hours.

There are good views from the summit with a view finder plaque cast in stone. Erected by the Cairngorm Club of Aberdeen in 1924 it gave me the sense of the mountaineers of the past and how they might view the modern day Munroist. I imagined their disapproving frowns and tut tutting at the lack of purity in my approach to the mountains they were psychologically opening up for future generations.

I motored on to Carn a'Choire Bhoidheach, reflecting my good pace was perhaps due to now being off the medication for the abscess under my tooth. In addition I'd given myself a good boost of asthma drugs before I'd set out. From the summit of Carn a'Choire Bhoidheach I could see a beautiful mixture of sun and shadow on distant hills to the north-west. Moody days often give beautiful reflected colour as the sun peeps through the ever indecisive cloud.

Having reached the summit of the second Munro of the day at a shade after midday I decided all five were now a possibility. So I was off and completed the round trip in just over eight and a half hours. On the top of the fifth Munro, Broad Cairn, I thought the walk back would take me just over two and a half hours and I'd arrive at my car at about 17:00. In the event I got there at two minutes to five. I am not always that accurate but you do get a sense of how long things will take which can only come by experience. When in the mountains I always tend to think of things in time rather than distance.

The long walk back by the south side of Loch Muick starts very high above the loch (some 850 feet) and there is a view down to a wonderful isolated mansion called Glas-allt-Shiel. I later found out this is one of the royal retreats far from the gaze of the press. On the final walk to the car it started to rain which made me rather damp at the end of what was otherwise a wonderful and successful day. I had managed to take in five Munros, completing three separate single day walks from Cameron McNeish's guidebook. This resumed the status quo, which had been disrupted by taking three days to do the single day walk he recommended for the Glen Ey Munros. This just goes to underline how routes are subjective and what is given in a guidebook is often just how the author tackled it. Not right or wrong, just one of a number of ways.

This was certainly one of my best ever days of walking with regards the ease in which I could take in the terrain. I have already mentioned certain factors that contributed to this but I have since reflected my mental state was better this day. On the approach to Lochnagar I felt driven with none of the usual heaviness and mental questioning I am prone to. I became determined to do better, knowing I could. I remember being on Brighton Pier once with Gisella, David Binderman (a friend) and his girlfriend, Sarah. David and I went on the petrol driven Go-Karts and I lost hands down to David and some strangers. On getting out I asked David if he wanted another race, we got back in the karts and I started from third on the grid with David in front. Gisella could see my eyes through my crash helmet's visor. She said she'd never seen such determination. Needless to say I handsomely won the race.

Another time was when playing badminton. Taking on a

work colleague I normally lost to, the day after being stood up for the second time by the same girl, I took out all my anger and frustration. As we walked off the court at the end of the match I could tell Nigel was contemplating his five games to nil thrashing when he asked, "What got into you?"

"Woman trouble," I replied.

A Herd of Deer

The following day, May the 26th, I decided to bike out to Derry Lodge and walk Beinn Bhreac. I woke early thinking there is nothing like a good night's sleep, and that *was* nothing like a good night's sleep. With many bunks in the dormitory free the wriggler from hell had stationed himself in the bunk above mine and, if I was very much not mistaken, possibly in an attempt to settle himself, had banged one off in the early hours. It was horrendous.

As I drove through Braemar, well before 07:00, a herd of about sixteen deer, wandering through the village munching on grass, eased my irritation.

I cycled from the Linn of Dee down to Derry Lodge where I was glad to see some attempt has been made to patch the holes in the roof. It is a grand old building and it'd be a shame to see its current semi-derelict state be the first steps of it becoming a true ruin.

From Derry Lodge I decided to bike further up Glen Derry where I soon started to pass an area of forest to the east side of the glen which has been fenced in to prevent new trees from being eaten by deer. It is always sad to see as deer fencing implies an imbalance in the ecological system. I needed to cut up through the forest to reach the slopes of Beinn Bhreac but the tall fence was barring my route. I found a gate, so locked my bike nearby and headed through the trees. When I got to the fence the other side of

182

the enclosure there was no reflected gate or style. Given they have fenced off a recognised route to this mountain it must come as no surprise the fence on the east side of the enclosure is becoming damaged by people climbing over it having been fooled by the gate on the west side. Walkers don't want to cause damage but situations like this just cause friction between the walking and land management communities.

The walk up Beinn Bhreac went quite well apart from it being very windy on the top with driving snow. I took refuge behind some big boulders to eat my sandwiches. On the descent I cut to the north side of the fenced enclosure and easily re-joined the track in Glen Derry without having to climb over the fence. The walk back to my bike was quite short and I reflected if the people who'd erected the fence had put a note on the gate saying 'Please walk a half mile further north to avoid crossing this fenced enclosure' then all the damage to their fence would be avoided.

Back at the bike I did consider cycling round to Luibeg Bridge and taking in Carn a'Mhaim but decided against this as it was very windy at altitude. On the ride back I noticed some stupid campers near Derry Lodge had left a tree stump smouldering. It was raining so hard I figured it couldn't possibly spread. However, had it been dry I'd have needed to fetch help to put it out.

A bit of a Ding Dong with Avon Calling

On May the 27th I aimed to do Ben Avon and Beinn a'Bhuird. These are two remote Munros that lay at the end of Gleann an t-Slugain. I had a frustrating start from Invercauld on a maze of small tracks which no longer match the Ordnance Survey map. When I finally guided my mountain bike on to the correct route I was able to make better progress, locking up just south-east of the ruins of Slugain Lodge. Normally I thread my crash helmet through the cable of the lock to secure it with the bike. Today I didn't notice I was still wearing it until I got up and banged my head on the very tree I was attaching my bike to.

It'd rained up to this point and continued as I walked up the long and gruelling water-logged paths. I passed a couple who'd camped out and had decided to call it a day and not attempt the high ground. The wind was quite strong and I was seriously thinking this would have to be abandoned. Having to pull the hood of my jacket tight to try and protect myself from the wind and rain made me feel miserable. From the floor of the glen I could see the tops had snow on them and this added to my hesitation.

While resting by a stream, and filling my water bottle, I thought I heard voices but just assumed it was the effect of the gurgling stream and the noise of the rain and the wind. The brain tries to sort out the jumble of nature's noises into something familiar – hearing 'voices' is common as is tinny pop music. During the Second World War crews of four engine Avro-Lancaster bombers would often hear a full symphony orchestra as the engines played out their mission.

I glanced up to see three chaps, who I recognised from the youth hostel, stood looking at their map while deep in conversation. This struck home the remoteness of the place, as I couldn't properly hear people within just a few feet of me. They were heading for Ben Avon having already decided not to do Beinn a'Bhuird. I casually walked with them, sometimes getting ahead. They weren't great company from the point of view of conversation but it was a comfort to know there were fellow human beings about on this bleak and miserable wild day. I sensed a bit of friction in their group – often the case on a tough day.

When we reached the most northerly point in the path, before it descends into Slochd Mor, we went east and had a lot of trouble navigating in the mist and driving hail while crossing the snow to the summit of Ben Avon. At one stage the wind was so strong the hood tassel on my jacket kept bashing my eye. I couldn't manage to control it with my hands and didn't wish to stop and remove my gloves and risk separating from the others. So I had to suck the tassel into my mouth and hold it between my teeth to save my eye from its pummelling.

The discovery of the summit of Ben Avon was mainly due to the navigational brilliance of a chap called Brian from my trio of companions. The wind was blowing from the north, which made things relatively safe as we were being blown away from the edge of the cliffs. We ascended on all fours over the significantly exposed edges of the group of tors which make up the summit of Ben Avon.

Just Brian and I made it to the summit, the others electing to stay back. From here we descended and, at the most northerly point of the path, we split up. I had the option of going onto Beinn a'Bhuird with them but the weather was very poor and I was concerned, given there were cliffs on the south side of its summit, about the dangerous northerly wind.

I got very wet and tired on the walk back. The paths, formed by years of walkers eroding the peat down to the stone beneath, had filled with water and become streams – in general this causes people to walk either side, causing further erosion and a widening path.

All in all it was a tough day. I was out for nine hours and covered something in the order of twenty miles. I got very wet and only managed one Munro of the two when the second was only one and a half miles away from the point of giving it up. The start was frustrating because the map was out of date and the route was split across two OS sheets. Also I was using a new map case which split, causing the maps to get wet. I reflected this all while sitting in the Fife Arms hotel in Braemar viewing all the unhealthy middle-aged people flopped out in the easy chairs after a hard day of looking around gift shops. The difference between the health of people in the youth hostel and the hotel was staggering.

The following day, Thursday May the 28th, I woke with yesterday's abandoned Munro playing on my mind. Therefore I decided to go straight back and tackle Beinn a'Bhuird.

To avoid a repeat of the miserable walk in, I decided to mountain bike the very long track from Linn of Quoich. I managed to cycle in for just under two hours to a height of 1600 feet. This involved crossing the north-westerly branch of the fast flowing and deep river in Glen Quoich. I wheeled my bike up and down the bank, trying to find a place to cross. Crossing streams and rivers in Scotland is a common occurrence for the walker and there's always a dilemma whether to choose a narrow section (and therefore deep) or a wide section where the water is spread out, and therefore shallower. With the latter you have to survey the crossing, ensuring that you can make it all the way. Narrow sections are only suitable if you can jump the gap – not an option with a mountain bike. Sometimes the water splits around a small island, but these can leave no opportunity to make a run up for the far bank. Fortunately, this time I found a wider section to wade across.

After locking my bike up, just short of the last trees before the summit, I realised that once again I'd forgotten to remove my helmet. This was another trivial annoyance, as I had to undo my bike cable from around the tree, which I'd just struggled to secure.

From the top of the track, with nothing else to navigate by, I followed a compass bearing. Here I discovered I'd a strange problem with my eyes that caused confusion. In the mist uphill looked like downhill such I'd be going on my merry way and be faced with a downhill stretch not shown on the map. Therefore utter confusion. I had a similar problem in April when I was driving on the A93 with Barbara. To me it looked as if we were going downhill but the car was struggling. To Barbara we were clearly going uphill and she thought I was 'weird'. Only by looking in my rear view mirror could I confirm we were climbing. I adopted the same technique here and by looking back, managed to keep my confidence I was going up hill.

For the final one and a half hours I had snow under foot and was shrouded in complete mist. However, it was better weather than the previous day. At 13:20, three and a half hours since leaving the bike, I reached the summit, relieved. At 3924 feet it was the tenth highest Munro.

On the way back I managed, from time to time, to track my own footprints in the snow. Therefore I could follow these instead of walking on a bearing. As I descended I met three other people, otherwise it was quite a lonely day.

Friday May the 29th was a rest day. It was five years to the day since I'd watched those children burn to death, my dad was having a heart defibrillation operation and the youth hostel snoring gene had evolved to such an extent it could outperform wax ear plugs.

On waking, the snorer, having kept me awake most the night, bemoaned the bad weather. My mood was so poor I told a blatant fib that there was excellent weather on the West Coast. He didn't fall for it, on the following night he was still there.

The Devil's Point and the Angel's Peak

Having double bunged my earplugs, to shut the snorer out, I still woke early on May the 30th. But the sleep had been good so I made an early start, pleasing the hostel cat as I was able to let him in far earlier than he could normally anticipate. In typical cat fashion he then demanded breakfast and was quite put out when none was forthcoming.

Because of the early start I departed from the Linn of Dee at just after 07:00 and cycled for just over an hour to the Luibeg Bridge, passing Derry Lodge on the way. After locking up my bike I walked on for over two hours to Corrour Bothy, stopping to rest before starting the real climb.

The first part of the climb was through the cloudy Coire Odhar to a saddle offering a good access point to the ridge to take in the Munros of the day. At the saddle I climbed out of the cloud and got open views of the mountains, with some cloud still high above. This is called a temperature inversion – i.e. it gets warmer as you ascend.

I was then treated to a phenomena where the cloud, I'd just walked out of, made the occasional scamper up to me like a dog forever running to its owner, then backing off and catching up again.

The Devil's Point was easily 'bagged' by turning left onto the ridge followed by a short rough walk to its summit. The name Devil's Point is a prudish Victorian anglicised translation of the true Gaelic name of Bod an Deamhain which means Devil's Penis.

While sitting on The Devil's Point (I figure the context of using Point here is better than Penis) the cloud repeatedly rolled up from both sides of the saddle, shook hands then retreated. I marvelled on this small wonder of nature while munching on some food prior to my return to the saddle and the onward ridge walk towards Cairn Toul.

The ascent of Cairn Toul looked extremely difficult and hazardous from a distance but got easier as I approached. From there I took in Sgor an Lochain Uaine (The Angel's Peak – a newly promoted Munro).

I now had a decision to make: it was about 14:30, three Munros bagged and Braeriach was tempting me at the far end of the ridge – leaving me, late in the day, at the furthest point from the start. The alternatives were to backtrack and call it a day or to backtrack and take in the separate mountain of Carn a'Mhaim. I really wanted to get Braeriach because it is fairly remote, requiring a very long day to bag as a single mountain from a different route. My dilemma hinged on whether I could return from Braeriach by a route other than backtracking to where I'd joined the ridge at the saddle.

In the glen below was the Lairig Ghru, a famous Cairngorm path, which runs approximately parallel with the ridge I was on. If I could get down to it from Braeriach then I'd be able to make the return without the hard work of retracing the ridge.

On the top of The Devil's Point, the first Munro of the day, I'd talked with a chap who said you could descend down to the Lairig Ghru by cutting south from Braeriach. I was unsure whether the advice was sound as the map showed no hint of a let-up in the steepness on the south side of Braeriach – even if the advice was sound there was still the possibility of being unable to locate the path.

Foolishly I pressed on and at the lowest point before the ridge rose to Braeriach I happened upon a middle-aged party who'd a rather haughty disposition and in consequence I took an instant dislike to them. I spoke with them for a while and, desperately seeking reassurance, asked if they knew of the route into the Lairig Ghru from Braeriach. They didn't and I found their manner condescending. Walking on the entire incident played on my mind. Was it just their manner awakening the memories of other incidents in my life when I felt people had talked down to me? Then it struck me. They were the self-same BMW and Citroen Xantia party I felt behaved so inconsiderately with their parking arrangements at Glen Coe Youth Hostel the previous year.

The route continued, over steep ground then a moonscape-like plateau, via a horseshoe circumnavigating very steep cliffs. I reached Braeriach at 16:00 – being 4252 feet it is the third highest of all the Munros.

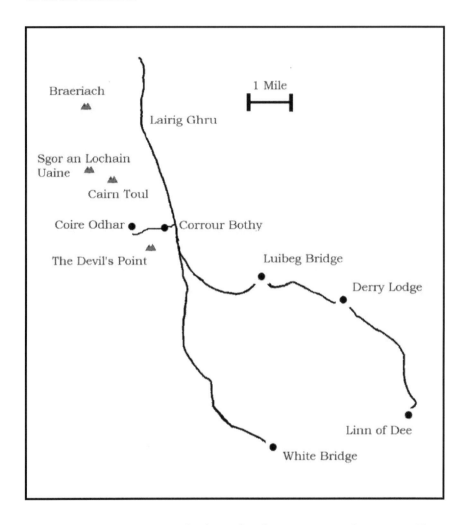

I spent some time looking for the route into the Lairig Ghru but I couldn't spot it, the glacier had taken no prisoners in this area. Now nine hours into my walk and at the furthest point, the reality started to hit home. At this rate I'd get back to the hostel at about 01:00 and it shuts at 23:30. There was nothing for it other than to hack it back on the route I took in. I did so but managed to circumnavigate Sgor an Lochain Uaine (The Angel's Peak) and Cairn Toul and I avoided The Devil's Point altogether because it was south of the point at which I got on the ridge.

At one point I stopped for some food and sat by a rusty knife plunged into the ground. It was just a simple knife, somebody must but have left it there many years before. I left it there to RIP (Rust In Pieces).

I got back to Corrour Bothy at just after 19:00. It looked a bit crowded and as I continued on I passed a series of small groups, thirteen people in all, heading for it – that must have made for a tight squeeze.

I spoke with one of the groups and a chap said they'd walked in via White Bridge and the group, in the distance, behind them had done the same. After saying goodbye I drifted towards this approaching group and said, "Hello" in passing. I carried on for a few minutes then a nagging doubt turned into hard fact and I stopped dead in my tracks. The guy in the first group said they'd walked in from White Bridge with the group behind. I had just said hello to that group, therefore I was now on the path to White Bridge and *not* Luibeg Bridge where my bike was. I quickly backtracked and put this right but it was a near thing. If I'd carried on engrossed in my thoughts then I could easily have made a very bad mistake, leaving me tired, exhausted and sleeping rough.

The rest of the walk back to my bike took about two hours accompanied by rain, whistling wind and, despite knee socks and trekking poles, my old complaint of a painful left knee.

At my bike I checked my watch and noted it was about 21:00, it felt eerie as I was beginning to sense the approaching dusk and the close of the day. I reached the welcome familiar comfort of my car at a quarter to ten giving a day of about fifteen hours.

191

On May the 31st Dave, the assistant warden at Braemar Youth Hostel, had the day off. We decided to do some walking together and found we both hadn't done Mount Keen, the most easterly of all the Munros. Dave lived down in the village so we agreed we'd meet at the hostel at just after 08:00. He met me in the entrance area and I expected him to have come by car with his mountain bike either on the roof or inside. As we exited the hostel there was his bike propped against the wall. Suddenly I was struck with alarm. Surely he didn't mean we were going to cycle all the way from the hostel? It was twenty-five miles just to the starting point. We quickly resolved it and emptied the contents of my car into his garage and squeezed his bike in.

We parked at the end of Glen Tanar and negotiated the confusing tracks through the forest and then followed the lengthy one along the Water of Tanar, leaving our mountain bikes at the point where the final stretch of the path breaks away from the stream. From here it was a one and a half hour walk through the mist to the summit. It looked closer on the map and as we were approaching what we thought might be the top we met three guys who told us we were at least forty-five minutes away.

On the way back down a group were approaching me and I said hello. One of the chaps turned to a girl in their party and said, referring to me, "So do you know him?"

I was a bit confused by this but they explained the girl, who was French, had that day bumped into two different people she knew. So we all had a quick chat on the theories of chains of knowing people. It never ceases to amaze me that when you really start to get to know somebody you can find some form of link. There is one theory there are no more than six levels between any two people in the world. That's to say if you were to put person A and person F in a room then the worst case would be A knows B who knows C who knows D who knows E who knows F. But now A knows F so bringing the entire thing closer. Of course doing things such as walking brings the circle closer than six levels due to common interest. Also this theory isn't so obvious when it is greater than one level of indirection, which is to say if you happen to meet somebody who you share a mutual friend with how do you know until you start to chat? Initially Barbara and I found a common link in she used to room share with somebody my friend Graham went to school with, so we managed the link by four people. Later we discovered I was in the same canoe club at Brighton Polytechnic as one of her best friends, thus reducing this path of association between Barbara and I to three.

Goodbye to Braemar

My final Munro to complete everything in the Braemar area was Carn a'Mhaim which involved another bike ride to Derry Lodge and beyond to the Luibeg Bridge. Before setting off I read a sign in the car park at the Linn of Dee saying they are going to 'Phase cycling out' in the area. At first I thought it is a good job I am getting my cycling in before the ban. Then I thought the Mar Lodge estate might be shooting themselves in the foot because if you ban cycling then people are more likely to go and rough camp to avoid more than one trip in.

It was a dull day and it started to rain as I reached the steepest section of the climb up. I managed to haul myself on despite the heaviness in my legs and ever frequent stops to catch my breath. The top was in mist and I had to walk along the entire ridge to convince myself I was at the summit.

On the way down I either made a navigational error, or there was iron in the rock which may have affected the compass.

Either way I ended up on the Coire na Poite which is a very steep section comprising of rock and wet ground overlooking the Luibeg Burn. From a distance it looks like a steep set of cliffs with no way up or down. I realised I'd the choice of backtracking or picking my way through the rocks and steep slopes, squelching through the water-logged peat and moss-ridden terrain. I decided to make my way down the steep face – at about the angle of a steep staircase without the steps.

I managed about a third of the way, clinging to rocks or digging my trekking pole in to gain security, before I slipped. Things whizzed past me, or so it felt, as in fact I whizzed past them. I accelerated on my bottom and spun through 180 degrees, my arms yearned for a hold, grasping for anything. Suddenly I stopped on a moss-covered ledge, oozing with water. Water soaked into the join between my glove and my arm, giving me rapid composure. I realised I was okay and got up, shaken and unsure. I gingerly looked over the edge of the ledge and pulled back in horror – if I hadn't stopped I'd have shot off the edge of a massive slab of rock and fallen fifty foot onto rocks below. I have had numerous minor tumbles on the mountains before, but this was by far the scariest. I had learnt a very important lesson which is don't take risks just to save time. From this point on I kept it in mind to listen to those deep inner voices saying, 'This doesn't feel right'.

I enjoyed my stay at Braemar. The length of time I spent there allowed me to feel a bit more part of a community, more so than the sometimes false image of a hotel or the excessive tweeness of a B&B – put together by middle-aged people with a target market of middle-aged people. Getting to know Dave the assistant warden was good, visiting him at his digs in the village. I also made friends with two other hostellers: Tony Wood who I have already mentioned and Mary Spurr a Canadian lady who spent a few nights there.

Normally I feel very shy in hostels and find myself skulking about or reading the label on my marmalade jar to avoid catching people's eye. It takes me time, I am not a born traveller – I need time to bond with people, to feel comfortable, accepted, part of it. I can't just invent that for myself in a few nights' stay, it has to be longer, stronger. The length of time I spent at Braemar gave me that and I enjoyed it.

Sometimes I can have too much of being sociable – during my later teenage years there was a pub we used to meet at on the occasional summer evening, in Chippenham, called the Rose and Crown. In the pub was a fish tank and one of the fish was christened 'Steve' because it'd spend ages hiding behind a plant or ornament, suddenly appear, enjoy itself and disappear again. This was likened, by my friends, to my personality as I wouldn't appear in the pub for weeks on end, then suddenly I'd be there, enjoying myself before scuttling off home again.

Goodbye to the East of the A9

I phoned Willy, describing my plan to move on from Braemar to Glenn Feshie to complete the final two Munros, Sgor Gaoith and Mullach Clach a'Bhlair, to the east of the A9.

"It sounds like a military campaign, Steve."

"Yeah," I replied, "but with my ageing Toyota and living in the South of England, it feels it has to be that way."

He then paused and asked, "Have you had any accidents then, Steve?"

He'd never asked that kind of thing before, how could he sense I'd had a fall on Carn a'Mhaim? Some people have a knack, an extra sense perhaps, where they raise a subject that's closely relevant to you with no verbal provocation. Willy is one such person. When we worked on the Strathclyde Police Command and Control Project he'd have a knack of coming and discussing a topic with us shortly after we'd been discussing it amongst ourselves. It became uncanny and we believed he must have an extra sense, or our office bugged.

I tackled Sgor Gaoith and Mullach Clach a'Bhlair on Tuesday June the 2nd and struggled all day. I took the good path up from Auchlean and, after passing a few people bird watching, wondered if a rare bird had been spotted in the area. However, I didn't dwell on this for too long as I'd more pressing matters to deal with, there were Munros to be bagged.

After the long haul up a well-defined path I broke out on to the broad plateau that makes up this area. It now hit me just how cold it was. I managed to survive until the top of Carn Ban Mor where I got down below the cairn and temporarily removed my jacket to put my fleece and thick gloves on. This really helped and I could focus on Sgor Gaoith which snouts up from the ridge above the remote Loch Einich.

I reached Sgor Gaoith after a total of about three hours walking. I looked south-west towards Mullach Clach a'Bhlair and it appeared very far off. I took the very boggy direct route, not reaching the longer tracks until the last half hour of the two and a half hour crossing. From the summit I descended by the track which brought me back into Glen Feshie some two miles south of my starting point. The walk back up Glen Feshie was nice, taking in a route by water and through forest.

Is It a Hawk? Is It a Buzzard? Is It an Eagle? No It Is a Helicopter!

Having stayed at Loch Morlich Youth Hostel for the nights of June 2nd and 3rd, I made the 3rd a rest day. I drove down to Kingussie and visited the same hairdressers as the previous year and was

196

surprised the lady remembered me. I did reflect perhaps the, "Have you been on your holidays yet this year?" question should have been replaced with, "Have you been on your work break yet this year?"

I then found an outdoors shop and purchased clips so I could attach my map case and compass to my jacket and rucksack to try and prevent them flapping in my face during high winds.

I drove into Glen Banchor, behind Newtonmore, on Thursday June 4th. This was to walk Carn Dearg and Carn Sgulain, Munros Barbara and I had to abandon back in April. This time there was no snow so therefore a high chance of success. I took the route along the path to Glenballoch then struck north-west up the track along the Allt Fionndrigh stream before heading west through a window in the hillside to emerge in front of the massif of Carn Dearg. From here the going was hard over rough terrain before the pull up on to the ridge and the summit itself.

I did find another use for the trekking poles: when crossing water they give you an extra few feet of clearance because you can use them to land where your feet would normally land then swing yourself forward on them thus avoiding wet feet. I am such a fan of trekking poles now.

For quite a long part of the walk there was a guy some ten minutes behind me. As he caught me at the top I realised I'd spoken to him in Glen Feshie on the approach to Sgor Gaoith. I suppose you could say it is a small world, but not really, it was still the same week and we were both Munro bagging. We had a good chat and he was asking me how the Scottish Mountaineering Club validates you before adding you to the lists of Munroists. I explained they don't and just take your word for it.

"But I could have just got to the end of the road," he replied, "and ticked these three off and turned back."

"You'd be only cheating yourself," I added.

It is difficult to fully define cheating in the Munro-bagging sense, obviously having never stood at a summit your claim would be cheating but what about taking the cable cars to do Munros where the mountains are on ski ranges? It is always tempting to take this 'helping hand' to get nearer to the summit but I regard this as cheating whereas other walkers regard this as perfectly acceptable. It is all a case of degree I guess, I am perfectly happy to park my car at the most convenient point. A true purist would start from sea level for each walk and where the Munro was bang on 3000 feet they'd presumably wait for the tide to be out.

Before setting off I took in the superb views across to the distant Geal-Charn which I climbed the previous year. The walk to Carn Sgulain took about two and a half hours, following a line of fence posts and covering a distance of five miles. I was drained and realised I was still suffering, both mentally and physically, from my fifteen hour epic walk of the previous Saturday – the first of four days of continuous walking. The last six hours of that walk were against the clock, having to spend much of the time watching my pace and working out alternative plans to bed down for the night.

My mind wandered to matters of philosophy, the solitude of the mountains allowing me to decipher the common denominators that sit behind happiness and unhappiness concluding a happy and contented life requires:

- Always having something to look forward to
- Feeling valued
- Fulfilling one's potential

Having sorted out my philosophy on life I returned my attention to the walk. From Carn Ballach, a minor bump in the ridge between Carn Dearg and Carn Sgulain, I could see a strange shape on top of Meall a'Bhothain (another minor bump on the

198

walk). As I got nearer I made out the shape of a helicopter. Unfortunately it took off before I could reach it. From the summit I returned back to my car via the Allt na Beinne stream.

This day brought the final and successful attempt at solving the swinging compass problem. It is so annoying because the compass is essential but in wind it just swings about and is very irritating. To get over this I bought a draw tassel and threaded both pieces of my compass string through it. Then I threaded the loop through the waistband of my rucksack and used the tassel to pull the compass tight against the waistband. Bingo it did the trick.

Killin Again

Once I'd completed this walk I set off back to Killin where I'd decided to stay for three nights to take in An Stuc (the new Munro Barbara and I failed to bag on two occasions in April). Also I wanted to do a repeat walk of Beinn Heasgarnich which I felt I may well have failed to reach the summit of when I climbed it the previous year.

As I drove down I passed through Aberfeldy and couldn't resist buying a veggie burger and chips, pure fatness food as opposed to fitness food. As I approached Killin it was a beautiful evening with the sun picking out Ben More at the end of Loch Tay. I stopped, took photos and began to feel An Stuc should be left for another day. Firstly, as Barbara and I had already failed to do it twice then perhaps we should do it together. And secondly Killin might be a good place to do my last Munro from, because the town has a nice atmosphere and there is plenty of accommodation if anybody wanted to join me on the walk. In the event I never did An Stuc with Barbara and neither was it to be my last Munro. However, at the time, it was for those reasons I decided to just do Beinn Heasgarnich on Friday June 5th and one of the newly promoted Munros in Glen Coe on the Saturday.

My heart sank when I was allocated a bunk in the main youth hostel dormitory. With fourteen beds I knew this would be pushing it for a good night's sleep. However, given my experience at Braemar Youth Hostel, I prevented anybody from taking the bunk above mine by spreading my things out to such an extent I created a personal exclusion zone.

To bag Beinn Heasgarnich I decided to do it from the highest point in the hydroelectric road, not marked on the maps, connecting Glen Lochay and Glen Lyon. The highest point is just north of where the pylons cross and is marked by a small cairn on the west side of the road.

I delayed the start because it was raining so hard. This proved a good decision because the weather lifted and gave me five hours rain free for a straightforward three hours there and two hours back. So had I missed the true summit of Beinn Heasgarnich the first time round? Indeed I had.

On Saturday, June the 6th, I returned to Glen Coe to do Stob na Broige which is at the south-westerly end of Buachaille Etive Mor. I took the same route up as the previous year, which is via the scree-filled corrie of Coire na Tulaich. It was tough going and very misty.

A charity was aiming to put a group of people on the top of each Munro at about the same time. Consequently Glen Coe, and the mountains, were crawling with people. As I passed beyond the mist line things felt very surreal – I could hear voices and the clanks of sliding scree but couldn't see anybody. It was like workers in a fog-bound dockyard. Some novice walkers were descending and a girl asked to borrow one of my poles, I declined because I was going up and she was going down it was unlikely I'd see it again.

Once on the ridge of Buachaille Etive Mor things got a bit

tricky as I made a small navigational error and ended up traversing the steep scree slopes of the south side. I went wrong because of the mist, or was it Scots mist, cloud, hill fog or just bad visibility! Certainly bad navigation and when I realised my mistake I headed north to regain the ridge. This detour meant I now had another navigational problem as I'd lost count of the intermediate summits on the ridge, which I was relying on to position myself against the map. Therefore I had to keep walking and work it out for myself.

I spoke with one old chap to get an exact fix of where I was. He had his map upside down and started to talk about peaks on another ridge. I left him to it and pressed on. At the final summit of Stob na Broige I spoke with two other groups of people who'd met the old chap and confirmed he didn't have a clue where he was. As I descended I found him sitting on his own. I checked up with him and he said he was now waiting for another group who'd said they'd guide him off. He shouldn't have been out on the mountains. From the way he spoke I think he had the early stages of dementia. Either that or he was a decoy weapon employed by the Scottish Mountaineering Club to put people off this newly promoted Munro.

One of the people I'd met near the top was part of a group positioning themselves for the charity event. As the mist momentarily lifted, revealing the long drop into the glen below, he was overcome by vertigo. As we were both descending I offered him one of my poles but he declined, so I set off on my own. By this time it was raining heavily but, with this being my last day of walking, I couldn't be bothered to extract my over trousers from my rucksack.

I descended off the ridge into Lairig Gartain in the company of a chap I'd met a couple of times during the day. We walked back to our cars together so it was nice to have the company and discuss the forthcoming football World Cup. Back at my car I felt very wet and, as I slowly removed my sodden things, I chatted to a guy who was concerned about his party who were now over three hours late. I offered him a lift to a phone but he turned it down. I changed into dry things and was attacked by midges, obviously the season had just begun so I was glad to be setting off home the following day.

The Canadian Rockies

As planned I spent June watching the World Cup and July working before setting off for Canada. Barbara took me out to the Rockies and we did some great hikes. Initially I was worried about tackling such higher mountains but the setup is very different. It is rare to visit the summits, some being technically difficult to reach, others difficult due to woodland. Therefore most hikes are well signposted trails cut through the trees, maybe taking in a ridge. In all a much different experience to Scotland where the unpredictable weather and the lack of trees and trails thrusts you into more wild and lonely territory. Barbara told me height is irrelevant and the Munros are far harder than walking in the Canadian Rockies.

Apparently Scotland has the greatest change of climate per 1000 feet than anywhere else in the world – Scotland is untamed. The other great difference between these mountains is the names, the Scottish mountains are all Gaelic in origin and very unphonetic to the anglicised ear whereas the Canadian Rockies were largely opened up by Anglophones and consequently have easier to pronounce names, such as 'Mount Stephen'.

Hobnobbing With the Rich and Famous

Later in the year I was browsing through a bookshop in Swindon when I saw a lecture advertising the polar explorer, David

Hempleman-Adams was giving a talk on his recent trip to the North Pole. I duly put my name down and attended the lecture held at the Railway Museum in Swindon. I was very interested in the slide show, of the expedition to the North Pole, and bought a copy of his book *Walking On Thin Ice.* I asked him to sign it and he enquired if I'd any special message.

"To Steve, good luck with the Munros," I replied.

"They are hard," he said.

What an intelligent man I thought, he has climbed the highest mountain on each continent, including Everest of course, and been to every point on the globe that has the word 'Pole' in its title and still thinks the Munros are hard. I then looked at what he'd written: 'To Steve, good luck with the Monroes.' Hmmm.

Munro Count: 167

1999

Goalkeeper at Last

One of my unfulfilled childhood dreams was to become a goalkeeper. As an asthmatic I was no good at any sport requiring rapid movement. I was also slight in build, making such things as the shotput and javelin just as humiliating as the sadistic regimes of team selection leaving me and a rather tubby boy always the last to be chosen.

In football I'd be put in goal where paradoxically I had some talent. Quick reflexes enabled me to pull off the odd good save but shattered confidence would, at other times, see the ball to trickle between my legs. To the sounds of my jeering classmates the games teachers wrote me off as a 'no hoper'.

Over the winter of 1998–1999 I continued to work for Unisys (the bit of my life between Munro bagging and visiting Canada) and the opportunity to play in a five aside mini league came up. Growing in confidence I said I was only prepared to participate if I could play the entire game in goal. Often in five aside the goal keeping position is used as a place for an outfield player to have a rest, but this time I was determined to make it a position of my own. I started in my very average style of the odd reasonable save with a few fluffs along the way. In one match my donkey-like style hit a new low when I dived for a save and my left foot trod on my undone right shoelace. I fell to the ground in a heap a yard away from the point the ball had entered the net. Fortunately my team mates didn't notice.

Then something switched in my brain, nobody had the right to score anymore. Previously I always held some strange belief that anybody coming at the goal with the ball possessed more right to score than I had to save it. But then a revelation hit me:

nobody had the right to put the ball in *my* net. Now when a player came at me with the ball I'd say to myself 'You have no right to put that ball past me'. And it worked! After one game I was sitting in the dressing room recovering, feeling exhausted. We had won by something like 13-6 and I was just contemplating gathering the energy to strip for the shower when I overheard two guys, from the opposing team, chatting.

"Shame about that game, we'd have been okay if we'd had a specialist goalkeeper like they did."

Sitting there, in my half-drugged state of mind, it took a while to register the full impact of probably the best compliment I have ever been paid – best because it was totally unintended.

So, a childhood ghost partially laid to rest – there *was* a sport I was good at.

Waking Barbara

Another thing that happened during the winter was my friend Steve Hampton contacted me to ask if I'd be interested in climbing Ben More on Mull with him during the Easter break. I was quite keen on the idea and mentioned it to Barbara who said she'd like to come along. Via some three-way email conversation, with me as the central broker, we agreed to do it on Good Friday.

I was working in Newcastle the week before so Barbara flew from Ottawa to Heathrow then on to Newcastle where I collected her. We spent a night in a hotel followed by a long, touch and go, drive to catch the 16:00 ferry from Oban across to Mull.

Once on Mull we drove up to Tobermory where, having left the arrangements a bit loose, we were lucky to bump into Steve on the main street. The walk was then planned over a meal.

The following day was April the 2nd, Good Friday, and we started walking just after 10:00 from where the B8035 meets the

Abhainn na h-Uamha stream – the best route according to the guidebooks. The weather was good, apparently the best place to be in the British Isles that day. I managed the climb well as the goalkeeping and some endurance walking over the previous weeks (including walking from Great Bedwyn to Newbury one Sunday), had got me fit.

However, Barbara was jet lagged and struggled a bit, dropping out when we reached the col on the main ridge. Steve and I set off together leaving Barbara to walk back to the car.

The continuation of the walk was over quite rocky ground with some exposure and I'd describe it as difficult walking terrain. We finally got ourselves to the top at 14:35 for a few photographs to celebrate Steve's first Munro – a rarity as, given it involves a ferry crossing, it is the most frequent one to be left to last.

The summit trig point, as indicated on the map, was no more with just a hint of concrete to indicate its once existence. I reflected I was glad I hadn't done this in mist as trig points are useful indicators to show one has indeed reached the summit. Without it I'd have been looking for higher ground.

Steve and I set off a different way down as we didn't fancy the return along our ascent route. We made a slight navigational error and hit some cliffs but managed to negotiate them slowly. At about this time we spotted a group of cars parked further west than ours marking what appeared to be a lot simpler route up than the one we'd taken.

We returned to the cars just after 17:00 whereupon Steve had to set straight off to get the ferry so I was left to myself wondering where on earth Barbara had got to. There was no evidence she'd got back to the car and I was left to ponder the dilemma for quite some time.

A middle-aged couple walked by and I asked if they'd seen a Canadian lady on their travels. Just by luck they'd spoken with

Barbara about three hours before and she'd been resting, still high up the mountain. With that I turned to look at the hills again and I could just make out a figure far in the distance and with binoculars, hastily loaned by the helpful couple, I was able to make out Barbara. I thanked them for their help and put on my bright yellow Gore-Tex jacket to go up and meet Barbara to check she was okay. When I reached her she was fine and had just been sleeping.

We spent the next day driving around Mull and decided to take the ferry to Ulva, about a two minute crossing. We followed the signs and got to the quayside and there was a boat and a sign saying ferry to Ulva, £2.50. So we got on and the boat set off. When they started talking about safety equipment and the location of the toilets our suspicions arose. Barbara immediately started asking other passengers where we were going as I inspected the dirt on my shoes. It turned out we'd strayed onto a four and a half hour sailing around the Treshnish Isles then on down to Staffa. This turned out to be a lucky accident as the trip was wonderful with a walk into Fingal's Cave on Staffa. The following day we visited Iona and its abbey before catching the ferry back to the mainland.

We then went to stay at the Ben Lawers hotel before having a lazy day prior to another attempt at An Stuc on April the 6th. An Stuc is the mountain we failed to do on two attempts the previous year.

We set off late, just before 11:00, and decided to take in the far end of the Ben Lawers ridge, involving the Munros of Meall Greigh and Meall Garbh, before reaching An Stuc. Barbara hadn't done these two before and, as it was a suitable route, I was happy to repeat them.

We started by heading straight up the south side of Meall Greigh, reaching it after about two and a half hours of walking. The weather was good until about a half hour from the summit when the wind and rain really picked up.

Unusually Barbara lagged me most of the way and when we reached the summit I became suspicious when she barely acknowledged her new Munro or perform her ritual of placing a rock on the cairn while saying, "Ohm Mani Padme Hum." I asked her if she was okay to go on and she said she was. The wind was by now very strong and it was cold and wet. When we reached the col between Meall Greigh and Meall Garbh we were able to take some shelter from the wind and rain. Barbara still said she was okay but I was unsure – she was unable to take the wrapper off a cake bar and was very quiet. I suggested we should call it a day but she replied she was fine. I added we'd have at least two to three hours of this to go and I hadn't failed to notice the difficulty she'd had taking the wrapper off the cake bar. This jolted her into a rapid reassessment of her condition and finally conceded she should pull out. Her Raynaud's disease had kicked in which has various symptoms such as the loss of motor coordination, a reduction in core temperature and the inability to think straight. It also has the effect of being unable to remove the wrapper from a cake bar.

Barbara wanted me to continue so I could bag An Stuc, normally I'd have been okay but I felt uneasy leaving her. So we returned back to the Ben Lawers hotel having let An Stuc get away for a third time.

The Cuillin Ridge Becomes the Ring of Steal

The Isle of Skye is home to the Cuillins – linked together by a dramatic and narrow ridge they are the most dangerous of all the Munros. To be safe you require a rope and some basic rock-climbing ability, neither of which I felt comfortable with. Reading the guidebooks filled me with terror and panic with such phrases as, 'this is no place to have a slip'. Therefore I decided to employ the services of a guide to make it as safe as possible.

I contacted a guide via email and we arranged four days from July the 4th in which we'd tackle the ridge together. Unfortunately, about six weeks prior to the walk, the guide dropped contact. Then, with five days to go he emailed me from America saying he could still try and find an alternative guide for me in Scotland. I thought about it for a day or so but got back to him and said I'd decided to give it a miss. I still really wanted to do it but as he'd been out of contact I hadn't put myself in the right frame of mind or fitness for it. I had also been very busy at work and was under a lot of pressure. I wasn't physically or mentally prepared.

I still finished work at the end of June and pondered what to do with the time I now had spare before flying out to see Barbara on July the 10th. It passed through my mind to still go to Scotland and take in some Munros on my own. At this stage my Munro tally stood at 168 (116 left to do) and I thought it'd be a nice idea to get it down to the round 100.

Gisella called me on the evening of July the 1st and I mused over this idea with her. She knows me too well and said, "Steve, why can't you just go to Scotland and do some Munros and not worry about getting your total left down to a hundred. You put yourself under too much pressure, just go and enjoy it."

I harrumphed a bit and while getting ready for bed that night concluded she was absolutely right. When I woke on July the 2nd I decided to drive to Scotland. I printed off my list of things to take, always handy for packing in a hurry, and bundled everything into my car in under an hour. Previously I've packed over a four day period.

It was a tiring drive on the motorway and, with frequent rests at service stations, I became convinced of an increase commercialism. Just to go to the loo I had to turn down the kind invitation to take out another credit card and to join the AA. Presumably you could take out the credit card and three steps later use it to purchase full AA membership. Having both an AA card and a credit card already I felt totally justified in barely acknowledging either opportunity to radically improve my life by such a purchase. And why is it always some middle-aged bloke selling the AA membership and some gorgeous looking female selling the credit card? Perhaps the marketers think the AA man offers reassurance and the gorgeous looking female is like a credit card – there for hopes and dreams?

It reminded me of my first week in halls of residence as an undergraduate – just eighteen living in Brighton and away from home for the first time. Lazing on my bed one evening during fresher's week a young woman knocked on my propped open door and asked to come in. I said okay and in she came and shut the door behind her. Wey-Hey I thought it is all true, women just come knocking on your door begging you to have sex with them in halls. After twenty minutes of hard sell I finally got rid of her narrowly avoiding taking out the once in a lifetime insurance policy guaranteed to buy me a house when I graduated for the price of a jar of coffee a week.

In just under ten hours I reached Crianlarich and, figuring the youth hostel would be full, planned on camping in Glen Etive. On the off chance I called in at the hostel and, to my surprise, they had room. I booked in and enquired if they could do a fax ahead booking for Glen Nevis for the next two nights. I was behind the times, the Scottish Youth Hostel Association no longer did fax ahead and instead had their own system from which you could book ahead from any one hostel to another instantly and electronically. The old days of making phone calls and begging them to hold the bed for you are long gone.

I recognised the male warden at Crianlarich as Paul Ridley who'd managed Killin Youth Hostel in 1996. I introduced myself and he remembered my stay and our attempts to fix the plumbing system there.

That evening I went for a beer at a pub in Crianlarich. I was just finishing my pint when a middle-aged chap, who I'd previously assumed was just a drunk at the bar, started his music act. He fiddled with his knobs and buttons and strummed his guitar for a bit then started to ask where people were from. There were some Irish and some Swedes.

When he asked me I replied, "Marlborough in Wiltshire."

"Ah English," he replied. "We'll let you stay for one song before we kick you out."

Hilarious I thought. The day before was the opening of the new Scottish Parliament and this guy wasn't taking the opportunity to put old grievances behind him. I stayed for one song and left. He was trying to be funny but there was the undertone of the hatred there. I once asked my friend Graham, a Scot, if he was brought up on his milk to hate the English. He confirmed he had been and gave me a look as if I was asking a rather rhetorical question.

Within the Scottish nation there are massive divisions, for example: Glasgow v Edinburgh, Rangers v Celtic, Protestant v Catholic, Highlander v Lowlander, MacDonald v Campbell. I don't think Scotland can love its neighbour until it learns to love itself.

On Saturday July the 3rd I pulled my kit on and, after breakfasting on a packet of crisps, set off for the four Munros known as the Ring of Steall. My head was a buzz as I headed off down the path towards Steall (a ruin far up Glen Nevis that lends its name to the horseshoe of Munros in whose shadow it lies). The air was perfectly fresh and the sounds of nature replaced the mechanical noises I'd become accustomed to in modern life. It took me a few minutes to adjust.

After about a mile I reached a bridge by which I'd planned to cross the Water of Nevis before beginning the ascent. As I looked at it a sense of doom swept over me – it was a three wire affair in which you walk on one wire while holding on to the other two. I didn't feel comfortable taking this on because if I'd slipped the water was deep enough to drown in.

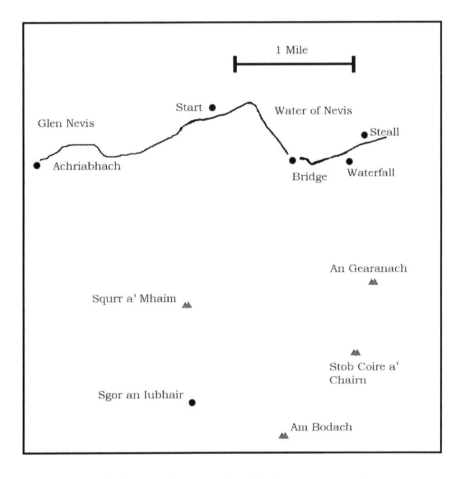

I strolled on and managed to find a crossing point near to a beautiful waterfall. This involved leaping from rock to rock and paddling through some shallow bits. Once navigated I found a path up onto the ridge of the Ring of Steall and reached An Gearanach at noon. By this time it was raining and I was surrounded by cloud. I pressed on round to Stob Coire a'Chairn then reached the third Munro of the day, Am Bodach, about six hours into the walk. Here my camera failed on me and thus began my first sequence of Munros without photographs of the summits. This turned out to be a blessing in disguise as photographing each summit was an obsession which, often in severe conditions, necessitated extracting my camera from the rucksack to take a picture of a pile mist shrouded rocks for my friends and family to ask, "So why do you put in all that effort to get *there*?"

After a further hour the weather improved and I reached Sgor an Iubhair which used to be a Munro but has now been relegated to a subsidiary top of Am Bodach. I was aware a ridge existed between this and the final Munro of the day. My guidebook had mentioned it was narrow and another walker said a book he'd read described it as 'entertainingly narrow'. Entertainingly for whom I thought, the walker or the observer?

Initially the ridge felt fine, no more difficult than many other ridges. Then it opened up in front of me. A ridge about two to three feet wide kerbed each side by instant death. 'Well I'm here now,' I thought and set off with my heart thumping and my mind trying to keep the lid on the boiling pot of panic, determined to not cut short my clock tick of existence.

It took some twenty minutes of trying to concentrate on the few feet ahead while ignoring the large drops either side. Most ridges just have instant death on one side and are therefore very safe because you just keep to one side – there wasn't much margin for error on this beast.

At the end of the most difficult section there was a rock face to lower myself down, only the height of a room but a bit daunting with the exposure. My rucksack became a liability as it kept snagging as I tried to lower myself so I took it off and tied it to one of my trekking poles and lowered it to a ledge and collected it once I'd negotiated the descent myself.

I reached the final Munro of Sgurr a'Mhaim in thick cloud and opted to play it safe by heading north-west to join the Glen Nevis road at Achriabhach, some forty-five minute walk from my car.

I was very slow on this descent as my knees were both complaining bitterly about the day of abuse they'd just gone through. I got talking to a couple of chaps who'd done the same walk as me and had caught me up having done it in seven hours (the upper book time) whereas I'd taken eleven hours. They were surprised at my time and I just casually said I was a dawdler. After I'd parted from them it struck me that two years ago I'd have been embarrassed by my time and made excuses about taking long breaks, one year ago I'd have played the asthma card to silence any criticism whereas now I was comfortable enough to cast it all off with a, "Yeah, I'm a dawdler."

Settling an Injustice or Two

I found the following day easier going, shorter at just nine and a half hours. I started through the Nevis Forest at the hamlet of Achriabhach on the Glen Nevis road and first took in Mullach nan Coirean then, in mist which required detailed map and compass work, Stob Ban.

From there I had to search out the east ridge, the most convenient, down the mountain. I descended a hundred metres on the west ridge looking for a turn off point but couldn't find it. I re-ascended and could clearly make out the east ridge but on the descent couldn't pick up the access point. I thought about taking the west ridge all the way down and pick up a path bending back round to Glen Nevis, but this would have made it a very long day. I gave it one more attempt and this time managed to spot the scar of a path heading east. I followed it for a few paces until it opened up as the route to the east ridge. I was relieved to find it and made the very slow descent on my painful knees.

The walk out took a further three and a half hours as I rested often. Here I began to dwell some more on what the Munros mean to me. I spend a lot of the time thinking and going over events in my life, settling old injustices. Stuff that'd never normally come out and is only brought to the surface by the purity of the peace from the mountains. Barbara has a metaphor for this where she likens this kind of letting go to a glacier slowly yielding what is beneath it over a great period of time.

Today an event came to mind that happened some twenty-two years previous. It had snowed and the school bus was late and while waiting we'd helped to push a teacher's car out of a snowdrift. After a further half hour we gave up on the bus and I went home and, very bravely for a twelve-year-old, phoned the school to say I couldn't get in.

The receptionist told me off and said, "Look some teachers have made it in from near where you live so you have no excuse."

I was too young to defend myself by adding, "They had a car which we helped to push." So off I set with my friend Stephen Soward and duly arrived very late for school for a serious telling off. I guess I hated school for that kind of attitude, zero tolerance and never identifying which kids were honest.

That evening I was out of food at the hostel so drove into Fort William to look for a meal. Like a magnet I was drawn to a branch of McDonald's. I don't know what it is about the McDonald's image but it certainly works. You know the food is unhealthy, fairly tasteless, all the profit is taken out of the local micro economy and

215

banked by the global market but nonetheless you find yourself drawn to its doors.

I duly ordered a veggie burger, the only menu item I could possibly consume, and ate it amongst the sterile American plastic image. With a name like McDonald's you perhaps could have expected a hint of Scottish atmosphere about the place. Perhaps the food could arrive in tartan coloured Styrofoam coffins and 'Scotland The Brave' could be played as you lift the lid followed by a round of the Stars and Stripes as the burger is consumed and the profits float across the Atlantic to be banked by descendants of people who once populated this naturally socialist country. Yeah, I regretted going to McDonald's that night, my fault, my mistake I make no excuses as I knew I'd feel that way, it was just all too convenient and I fall for it every time.

I decided I should only do one more day in the mountains before setting off home. I had hoped to stay longer but realised I'd over done it on the first walk and my knees weren't going to forgive me in the next few days.

With the final walk on The Mamores, the mountain range up Glen Nevis I'd been tackling, set to take in four Munros I decided to curtail my ambition and instead decided my final walk, July the 5th, should be to finish the Laggan and Monadhliath range of mountains which were a convenient drive away from Glen Nevis Youth Hostel.

I started the walk from the hamlet of Roughburn through forest then open ground where some heathery areas were particularly rough going. Initially it was clear and I was able to watch a RAF Tornado fly past. I soon walked into the cloud and experienced some rain.

On the ascent Beinn a'Chaorainn became obscured by a lesser rise in the foreground so, with no view of the general area to which I was aiming, I resorted to compass navigation. However, I found it difficult to keep following the compass as I had to keep diverting around impassable terrain. Therefore I sighted the compass on a large rock protruding from the immediate horizon and headed for it. When I got there I found there were so many large rocks I had trouble working out which one I'd been aiming for – my rock looked so prominent from afar but on arrival it'd taken refuge in the crowd.

As I progressed, using this method of navigation, I played games with myself as to how long it'd take to walk to each rock, timing myself between my geomorphologic waypoints. At one point I found myself in a large boulder-filled depression where when I blew my nose it echoed back. I spent a few moments enjoying my mid-face entertainment feature.

When I pulled myself onto the final ridge I turned left and headed to the highest point of the triple summits of Beinn a'Chaorainn, reaching it in under four hours from the start of the walk.

The route to Beinn Teallach required the obligatory descent and re-ascent. I went in too steep and was a bit freaked by the angle so increased my pace and reached the summit a half hour earlier than predicted. In the mountains you tend to judge distance by time rather than miles, and I've become quite accurate at estimating my time of arrival.

In the evening I sat out the front of the hostel, gazing towards the path from Ben Nevis, watching exhausted walkers returning late in the day. I began to contemplate my Munro-bagging efforts and a thought occurred to me that my Munro count was now locked in my mind as '108 to go' instead of '176 completed', a very subtle change in perspective.

My thoughts then wandered further to why I do this, what drives me, why this as a sport, a hobby, an obsession. I am very slow up the mountains, stopping every few paces on the steep bits to catch my breath, my knees often giving me pain well beyond anything that'd be described as comfortable. I constantly question why I do this on the long haul up. What am I trying to prove? Maybe to exorcise the ghosts of my childhood lack of sporting prowess? Maybe the three to four severe asthma attacks I got per year from the ages of two to fourteen? Perhaps the time when I was on a hospital bed and a consultant, with all the bedside manner of a psychopath, picked up my chest X-ray and announced to a group of eagerly attentive medical students, "See that, he'll have heart trouble in later life." Or perhaps the sadistic school games teachers who'd organise a punishment for the last one home after a cross country run? One day thwarted by me, the overweight kid and another straggler colluding to cross the finish line three abreast. Speed was their measure, not endurance, tenacity or the normalisation of physique. No games teacher saw me at my lowest point – taking ten minutes to cross a room, my father having to carry me up the stairs to use the bathroom, or chasing an ambulance to hospital. My breathing was akin to my nose being taped over and a straw stuck between my lips and taped around. Teachers only ever saw a note after a week off school explaining my absence due to an asthma attack. I would be excused the next games lesson by a further note from home, 'Please excuse Stephen from games today as he is just getting over an asthma attack' – a note I could have done without as by then I was capable of doing some light sport but that wasn't in the vocabulary of school. You had to be up there, a winner otherwise you were a skiver. Even my bad eczema (which one games teacher poked fun at) and my severe hay fever (with eyes stinging, weeping and sticking together during the summer term) cut no truck with them.

I then became aware of where this line of thought was leading. What it was trying to sort out for me, what it meant. Walking the Munros is a sport where nobody is there with a stopwatch, nobody is questioning your skill. Discussions about the time taken are brief. To have completed the Munros means you have got yourself to the top of each one, that's all – nothing else is questioned.

The following morning was my last at Glen Nevis Youth Hostel. Breakfast was supplied as part of the price and I hung on to eat it before setting off. Due to the tight budgets the hostels have to work under, it wasn't very inspiring but had been a real energy boost over the previous two days. As I ate my breakfast I couldn't help but notice a chap quietly praying before tackling his. Was this just his faith or a prayer to allow him to survive the food? I shall never know.

The Adirondacks

Shortly after this trip I flew to Canada to spend the summer with Barbara. On a couple of occasions we drove down into the USA to walk in a mountain range called the Adirondacks. I soon discovered, from Barbara, there are a series of mountains in this range known as the forty-sixers where each peak is above the 4000 foot mark. Barbara teased me about this, convinced I was going to start making a note of the ones I did. I resisted, the Munros being a challenge enough.

Munro Count: 176

2000

The Single's Club

On Sunday July the 2nd I sat on the top of Gulvain, four and a half hours and 3700 feet of ascent into my walk, contemplating the glorious views, with a sense of nervous freedom.

I had driven up over the previous two days, taking it easy for once, needing time to contemplate. Normally I'd drive up in one go and then walk the next day. However, I had two weeks off work and I only wanted to do eight Munros, reducing the target to a hundred to go.

On route I'd stopped for a while in Glen Etive and filled my water bottle from the river running along the glen. I raised the bottle to my lips and was surprised at how warm the water was. It then struck me this was late in the year for me – July and not May when the rivers carry away the snowmelt.

Gulvain is a single Munro, my 177th and only my second as a single man. Not since my first Munro, Carn Mor Dearg in 1990, had I climbed without the knowledge there was a girlfriend thinking about me – or checking my life insurance. Things hadn't worked out with Barbara – her daily lectures to me on feminism (and anything else she could think of that she deemed my responsibility), aimed at my soft underbelly, had gotten me down to the point I had, for the sake of my mental well-being, walked away. Now I was getting a succession of angry emails and answerphone messages which I'd decided to escape from.

I gazed around. It was a sunny day, a bit hazy with some high cloud and outstanding views. I could see across to the Isles of Skye, Muck, Eigg and Rum and in the foreground I could see Glen Dessarry which I have walked in twice before. To my rear was Ben Nevis sitting with its head in the clouds. All quite beautiful. The words from a Searchers song, 'Don't throw your love away, for you may need it someday' were teasing me over my recent decision. The words suddenly took on a new meaning: to stay single and wait for what feels right.

I tried to pick out Drumsallie, the point I'd started from at 08:25, followed by the long walk in on a track dwindling to a path and the subsequent 2150 feet of testing ascent over a one in three gradient.

I took a swig of water and realised I'd run low due to a miscalculation with my new, yet smaller, bottle. The old one had become discoloured to the point of appearing unhygienic. I figured it'd be a few hours before I could get to water and went through a few scenarios of when I should allow myself to drink again. Dehydration can be a real problem in the mountains as it can lead to headaches, generally feeling ill and a long recovery time. I quickly annoyed myself with the rationing dilemma, removed the top from the bottle and swigged back the entire remainder thus ending any ideas of choice.

On my way back down I caught up with Ann Robinson who I'd met on the way up. Her knowledge and memory of the Highlands was staggering. She could name just about every peak in view and when relating tales of my previous exploits she helped me out with the names where my memory failed the story.

Back at the car I returned to Loch Lochy Youth Hostel where I discovered, in the shower, I'd a bad case of pack rash. This is where the straps had caused irritation in the heat and both my shoulders were now raw with a septic rash. However, I was relieved to find what had felt like a pulled Achilles tendon was nothing more than a blister.

I also surveyed the rest of my body. Due to stress I'd recently lost eight pounds in weight, dropping to eleven stone ten – the lightest I'd been for over a decade. I certainly felt good for it so

I figured perhaps this was my optimum weight. The lightest I'd ever been at my adult height of six foot one and a quarter inches – the quarter is important – was nine and a half stone. This was when I was nineteen and studying in Brighton. Due to pressures of an engineering degree, the fear of spending too much money and the stress surrounding the death of my flatmate's brother, I'd put myself on a meagre diet. At the end of the summer term I returned home to my parents. Thinking my dad was asleep after a night shift I crept into the house and made my way to my room with a pile gear in my hands. On the landing, Dad called out, "Steve, is that you?"

I went along to his bedroom. As my silhouette appeared in the doorway he exclaimed, "Bloody hell, Steve, your mother is going to kill you."

On Monday July the 3rd I made the short car journey around to Kilfinnan and followed the forestry track. At the Allt Glas-Dhoire stream I branched onto the path which divides the separate Munros of Meall na Teanga and Sron a'Choire Ghairbh. It was a lovely warm day, the views improved with the height and opened up as I pulled myself onto the short summit ridge of Meall na Teanga.

Here I was alone, which was a good thing because I needed to do some back exercises. I had been visiting an osteopath to try and sort out the stiffness and pain I was suffering in my upper back. I underwent some serious manipulation, ranging from popping joints in my neck and back to being grasped from behind in a bear hug, told to force by buttocks into the table, and bounced up and down, and stretched, until I clicked. It was all a bit unnerving and during the bear hug manipulation it did cross my mind that if I were to turn around and the guy was fumbling with his zipper then I'd have asked for my money back.

Most of the upper back stiffness was apparently due to lack

of movement between my upper vertebrae – special stretches had been prescribed as a means to try and get things more supple.

From Meall na Teanga I descended back the way I came to the path following the stream up from the forestry track. From here, while soaking up the heat of the sun, I made the ascent of Sron a'Choire Ghairbh following a zigzag path – evidence of the many who'd suffered on the climb before me. When the gradient levelled out the zigzag path faded and I was able to turn west towards the summit.

At the top I settled with my back to the summit cairn and soaked up the heat and the views. I was then treated to an air display courtesy of the RAF. To many people the noise of Tornado's practising in the glens is disruptive and a waste of tax payers' money. I have some sympathy with this point of view, but I can't help being impressed by the technology and the skill of the pilots.

From the summit I had a choice, to either backtrack or to continue along the north-east ridge. A fellow walker warned of deep bracken on the lower slopes so I returned the way I'd ascended.

Back at the youth hostel I chatted, briefly, to the lady warden about my day. She had walked the same mountains before and had given me some route advice. While we were talking an old guy, also staying at the hostel, approached her and started to tell her about the Fort William to Mallaig steam train he'd taken that day. I didn't take a great deal of notice in the story because I was too busy making sense of his English accent, kilt, short stature, full white beard, bald on top with long white hair down the sides. He obviously wanted the attentions of the warden so I departed to the kitchen where I couldn't help but notice two stunning women cooking their dinner. I went about my food preparation whereupon 'Uncle Albert' reappeared and started to chat to the two women. They were Eastern European and I thought, 'You have no chance.' He asked where they came from and they replied "Czech Republic." On this cue Uncle Albert started to speak to them in perfect Czech. I retired to eat my pasta.

High Level Train Spotting

On Tuesday July the 4th I took the slightly longer car journey around to Fersit, just off the A86 Spean Bridge to Newtonmore road.

Having played mellow music on the car's CD player I started walking at 08:00, feeling mellow. It was a cooler day and, with my general level of fitness on this trip being high, I made good progress. I reached Stob a'Choire Mheadhoin in under four hours followed by a deep descent into the saddle between the two Munros. Here sheep casually wandered nonchalantly out of my way, dislodging rocks and making clatters as they did so. I felt warmer and removed my fleece – an option not open to the sheep.

I then climbed towards the summit of Stob Coire Easain. Far below a train rattled its way down the West Highland line towards Corrour Station, earlier a freight train had made its journey northwards.

Once on top of the second Munro I looked back to Stob a'Choire Mheadhoin and could pick out some figures, the first I'd seen all day. There was more cloud about than in previous days but there were still enjoyable views.

The events of the walk back were highlighted by spearing a sheep's turd with one of my trekking poles and having to wrestle it off with the other pole. On the final leg of the descent I spent some time sat on a large rock munching gorp, listening to the wind gently whistling around me like a familiar friend. It was good to climb these two mountains, I'd previously planned to do them on two occasions (1990 and 1996) but in both cases events prevented me from bagging them.

I spent the next day leisurely buying equipment and food in Fort William followed by a drive to Tulloch Station where I boarded the 12:32 train south – the very same train I'd watched from the mountains on the previous day. Now as a passenger I alighted at Corrour Station, a remote stop away from public roads. A lady was collecting a food parcel the ticket inspector had for her – a hint of how life was in times gone by.

I left the station to the sounds of, "Thank God it's here this time, last week my shopping ended up in Edinburgh."

I made the fifteen minute walk to Loch Ossian Youth Hostel, my home for the next two nights. The hostel didn't open until 17:00 so I was a bit worried about turning up some four hours early. Run by a German couple, Tom and Marion, I found them painting the inside of the roof of the common room. I offered to help but they said they were okay and kindly allowed me to retire to the male dormitory.

I lay on my bunk and read and listened to Tom and Marion talking to a stalker. I drifted off for a while to the smell of paint and the wood burning stove. I got up to use the outside loo. The route passed through the washroom where, on my return, I idly read the signs on the use of water: 'Bucket for fetching water from the loch only. Bowls for soapy water only. You are welcome to have a dip in the loch but without any soap or shampoo, as the loch is our drinking water supply'. Having just used the loo I realised buckets played a key role at Loch Ossian. I retired to the dormitory and shut the window, securing it with a hook over an old nail. This was my kind of place.

At 07:10 the following morning I set off and walked for an hour and a half to the end of Loch Ossian. Here a venison processing plant was being constructed, creating a deafening noise against the backdrop of nature. I then branched out for the slopes of Sgor Gaibhre, taking in the lesser summit of Sgor Choinnich, before reaching the summit after approximately four hours of walking. I enjoyed some good views as I pressed on and, in just over another hour, reached Carn Dearg. I sat for a while and again watched the 12:32 from Tulloch make its way down the line.

As other people from the hostel were planning to also do this mountain I waited at the top for about an hour and a half until somebody appeared. I had a brief chat and then set off back to the youth hostel where I was greeted by tame red deer busily munching grass.

In the male dormitory there were some new arrivals including an old chap who proudly announced this was his 148th night spent at the hostel over a period of many years.

"Have you ever considered counting them?" I enquired.

A chap called Mark, up from the New Forest with his wife Marie, touched me on the arm and gave me a smile as you would to a naughty child you know has done wrong but nonetheless has amused you.

The evening was lovely, sitting chatting. Marie had blistered badly on one of her ankles so I administered some second skin plaster.

A Danish girl was staying who I had a few chats with, although I think some of the subtleties of the English humour were lost on her. Come to think of it there aren't too many subtleties in the English humour. A young super fit German chap arrived and announced he was immediately going off to bag Beinn na Lap, my Munro for the following day. I told him about the 'Under an hour club' and tried to persuade him to have a go. This is a recorded list of all those who have run round Loch Ossian in under an hour. It requires a great deal of fitness and I was hoping to witness this guy having a go.

Later a group of us were sitting outside chatting as the German chap came down off the mountains. A few minutes later there was an almighty splash as he went for a swim in the loch. He was annoyingly fit and full of energy and I couldn't help but notice the Danish girl's eyes being impressed!

Due to the cooling evening we retired back into the common room where Mark told us about his experiences with deer that day. He had been up on the ridge and had been navigating off boulders when one of them moved and he realised it was a deer. Later he was impressed by how tame the red deer were back at the hostel.

"Well they are the bolder deer you see," I added while looking around for some acknowledgement of this pun. None was forthcoming as everybody had simultaneously lost the will to live.

A Sharing of Views

The following day, Friday July the 7th, I took in Beinn na Lap. It is one of the easiest Munros because the starting point of Loch Ossian is so high above sea level and the summit is relatively close to the hostel. However, if you follow Cameron McNeish's *Munro Almanac* guidebook things become a bit tricky as an error with the grid reference puts the summit smack in the middle of Loch Ossian. A quick confirmation with the Scottish Mountaineering Club Munro's Tables confirmed the correct position.

As I set off it became clear a fellow hostel resident, Alan Watson, was making for the same Munro so we started our walk together. He soon commented he'd not mind if I went ahead because I was clearly much younger. I explained about my asthma and the restrictions in my breathing which caused my peak flow (maximum litres of air per minute) to equate to that of a seventy-year-old man, not a thirty-five-year-old. He then told me I was in good company for he was seventy in a few months' time.

After a pull up onto the ridge leading to the summit we sat for a while and, from our high level vantage point, watched the 08:51 Caledonian Sleeper service from London Euston pull into Corrour Station, bang on time. It might sound as if I was train spotting, not really it is just seeing a manmade object in such a remote location sparks the interest.

Alan and I shared the same views on so many subjects it felt as if I was talking to myself in the future. At the end of the walk I said, "It is so nice to have somebody to talk to who shares the same views."

"Yes," he replied, "it's nice to have one's prejudices confirmed."

Back at the hostel I'd about a five hour wait for my train whereas Alan was heading south on an earlier train. He kindly cooked me lunch and we chatted some more before his departure. A couple of times there were pauses in the conversation. Old people liked to be asked about their kids. So I asked him about his kids. Alan also told me a few years back a French guy had shot himself on Ben Alder, clearly a case of going to the mountains to find the meaning of life, failing and finishing it all off there and then. It could be said he 'topped' himself, but that'd be going too far.

We also discussed why more men walk the mountains than women. I came up with a theory that what men seek in the mountains isn't typically want women need. Women form informal support networks where they can phone each other and get support and guidance. Whereas for chaps we tend to have to head for the mountains to allow things to work themselves out. As a sweeping generalisation women talk and men walk.

When the time came I was sad to leave Loch Ossian. I made my way back to the station and bought myself coffee and cake from the Corrour Station House. It is a strange place, quite elaborate for such a remote spot. As I waited for the train I reflected on a successful week, I'd aimed to get my total down to 100 to go and I had. I felt fit, I'd got good views and stayed dry. The train took me away from the remoteness and back to the modern world for another year.

Munro Count: 184

2001

The alert reader may wonder if I'd deliberately got my Munro count down to 100 left to do. Who would I be to disappoint? For a couple of years I'd been considering rounding the Munro count down to a final 100, then contacting The National Asthma Campaign to see if they'd like me to try and use the completion of the Munros in one season as a vehicle to raise money.

In the autumn of 2000 I was faced with the reality of the position I'd striven to get myself into. I now had to do something about it. I was concerned about pushing myself out there, putting myself on display and vulnerable. I started to pull back, dreading publicity, what if I failed? How embarrassing.

However, I gathered courage and contacted The National Asthma Campaign. They were keen, provided I didn't use any of the funds raised to cover the cost of the trip. This was never my intention – it sounded as though they got a lot of enquiries from people hoping to get a free trip by dipping into sponsorship money.

And so followed a period of sending begging letters to the rich and famous, to companies, a radio interview with BBC Wiltshire Sound, setting up a website, providing information for newsletters etc. I was amazed to receive sponsorship from the former Prime Minister, John Major and the explorer David Hempleman-Adams. The cheque from John Major, president of The National Asthma Campaign, was the first to arrive and, on opening the envelope, I couldn't believe somebody in his position had found the time to sponsor me. It was a real boost and I wandered from room to room in my house rereading the letter, looking at the cheque from him and Norma, while uttering, "Blimey".

As other sponsorship arrived (making a grand total of

£2,972) I began to feel the pressure of now having to do it. The only thing that could stop me was some form of physical injury. Or so I thought. Drifting off to the Radio 4 midnight news one evening in February I barely took notice of the report on the outbreak of foot and mouth disease. Even the swift closure of all the footpaths in and around Great Bedwyn didn't alert me to the possibility of my walk being in serious jeopardy.

Preparations

Slowly the reality dawned that my ambitions could be curtailed. In a sense it came as a relief, the pressure was off and I wouldn't be away from my home and friends for three months. Nor would the effects of falling over on snow and ice at Christmas be the cause of my failing: I'd done the splits while crossing the railway line near my house. I thought nothing of it until the dull ache the following morning, the mysterious lump on my lower abdomen, the visit to the doctor, the embarrassment of removing clothing (just managing to keep my underpants above my bits) and the lady doctor telling me I'd indeed ruptured myself.

At the beginning of April I went to see a surgeon, this time modesty was given no mercy. I was on my back, the trick of underpants slightly down was overlooked as the next thing I knew they were by my knees as the entire area was inspected. I was hoping for better news as by this time Scotland was just starting to re-open for walking.

"We will have to get that stitched up this year," said the surgeon.

"I'm going on a walk for three months."

I was waiting for his notice of cancellation but he replied, "That's okay I couldn't fit you in before the end of August anyhow. We will get that one stitched up and you can come and see me about the other side next year."

My heart was low as I left Savernake Hospital – I had two dodgy knees, asthma and now a double hernia. The odds were against me and I hadn't even yet set foot in the Highlands.

April became frantic, living alone there was much to prepare, ensuring all bills were covered and anything that'd need my attention, while away, was dealt with. Things to buy, and the revelation maybe I should purchase the most dreaded of items, a mobile phone. Also I fancied buying a small hand held computer for email and to write up my daily diary on. A visit to Carphone Warehouse, in Newbury, propelled me into the twenty-first century yet vowing to bury the mobile phone under the summit cairn of my final Munro.

Normally when going to Scotland I choose which Munros to do before setting off. Given I was aiming to finish them my original intention was to do no planning – I'd just start from the south and work my way up with the only diversion being a course I'd booked for the notorious Cuillin Ridge on The Isle of Skye.

However, the foot and mouth disease had me scouring the Web, on my painfully slow dialup connection, searching out Munros I could do. This was the first time I'd used the Web for route planning and it proved useful – the results throwing in to touch a mad idea I'd had of using my mountain bike instead of the car. With the Munros available being scattered, the journey would now be too dog legged. With a car the mountains can be varied daily based on factors such as weather, physical condition, state of mind and, of course, whether foot and mouth disease prevented access.

The Off

Setting off on May the 1st was difficult. I'd received a large number of good luck messages and felt homesick before I left. My next door neighbour and her six-year-old daughter banged on their window and waved as I set off at just before 07:00. Previously they'd given me Munro the sheep, a hand sized mascot for the walk.

Once on the A roads of Scotland there were a few foot and mouth disease control points to drive through. These consisted of mats designed to deposit disinfectant on the car tyres. However, the mats were mainly dry and the attendants (guys in Portakabins watching the telly) paid no attention.

I arrived in Glen Coe and decided the impersonal nature of the youth hostel didn't suit me and instead decided to try camping in Glen Etive. Driving through Glen Etive I passed two cyclists – one looked familiar. Unbeknown to me this chap was to come to my aid the next day and may even have saved my life.

On finding a suitable pitch I got out of my car to the chill air, promptly got back in again and drove back to Glen Coe Youth Hostel. Here I spent a lonely evening feeling unsure of what the following months had in store for me. Would I be home within a week or so? Or would I actually do it? My barriers were many, access restrictions, health and the natural deadline of August 12th when the grouse shooting season begins.

Troubled Start

On May the 2nd I started my 'Last 100 Munros Challenge' for real, parking in Glen Coe and setting off at 08:30 for Stob Coire Sgreamhach and Stob Coire Raineach.

Given I'd elected to 'get fit on the expedition' (another term for doing absolutely no training whatsoever) I made good progress. Passing some waterfalls I became aware of the forgotten dangers as the drops were severe. I had to tread carefully to keep safe while pulling myself up into the Hidden Valley.

I was distracted by a new piece of equipment, an ice axe, strapped to my rucksack. Previously I'd always managed to avoid serious incident on snow but with this trip something nagged at me. With an email from a friend warning of snow on the high ground I invested £60 in an ice axe. At about the 2600 feet point I was thankful as I encountered a snow field stretching into the oblivion of the mist. I swapped my trekking poles for the axe and embarked into a new experience, breaking my long-standing rule of never stepping onto snow unless I could see the other side.

Initially all went well, the gradient was forgiving and the snow soft. Gripping the axe across my chest I made progress but slowly the gradient sharpened and the snow grew colder. A small stone was sunk about eighteen inches, its own heat unmasking it. I was now digging in as I went. Away to my left I could hear the clatter of snow breaking away. I stopped dead, could this thing avalanche? I started to panic and looked down between my legs and realised just how steep the ground was. Two other walkers were ice axing their way up.

I was now climbing on all fours with the axe connecting both hands. The other two slowly reached me and the first chap asked, "Do you want me to lead for a bit?"

It then struck me they were following my footsteps, using my cutting in. They went around me and I was glad to follow but slowly I started to lose them in the distance and suddenly I was stuck. With every movement I started to slip back down the abyss of my ascent. Shakes replaced composure and I started to panic as the fall would have been very long and the snow slope ended with a good drop. I cursed myself for having broken my own rule of never stepping onto snow unless I could see the other side.

Rejecting the last remnants of male pride I called ahead, "I'm struggling."

"Dig your toes in much further," came the reply, "and sink

the shaft of your axe to the hilt before each movement."

I did and slowly I made progress just averting the panic. The pulling on my body tugged at my right hernia and the pain made me feel even more miserable.

A narrow corridor led me onto the ridge and a rendezvous with the two chaps. They introduced themselves as Keith and Ken and I recognised them as the cyclists I'd seen in Glen Etive the previous day. Keith and I looked at each other and also remembered we'd met at Loch Ossian Youth Hostel the previous year.

We continued east along the ridge and made Stob Coire Sgreamhach at 12:40. I had to push myself as Ken and Keith were very quick and I was frightened of losing them – my safe descent now depended on their good will. Any hope of Stob Coire Raineach was out and Ken and Keith said the safest route back was via Bidean nam Bian – a repeat Munro for me.

Before leaving Stob Coire Sgreamhach I considered taking the traditional summit photograph but decided it was too cold to extract the camera. Ken asked me if I was a student, I thanked him for the compliment and informed him I was thirty-five.

The walk to Bidean nam Bian was tough, my body ached through trying to keep pace with my guides. Fitting new gaiters the night before had detached the flesh from the edges of my finger nails and now each digit smarted with the cold. Keith dropped to my pace and, realising I was out of my depth, said he suffered the same on 4000m peaks in the Alps.

One stretch took us over a narrow snow-covered ridge with sharp drops either side. I held my composure and just followed Ken's footprints, focussing my eyes on no more than each step. On the summit of Bidean nam Bian I considered another photograph but realised this would merely have been to impress people with the snow-covered mountain top in a place I'd no right to be.

235

Following Ken and Keith I thought I was now home and dry but slowly the ridge narrowed until we were on a spur. With Ken now well ahead Keith took care of my every step. I was panicking, not only was the ridge narrow, pointing downwards it also cambered to my left to a sharp drop. To my right was an even sharper drop with snow cornices teasing me as I sunk my axe into snow sitting on thin air. With nervous jitters I pulled the axe closer to my body where I could sink it through snow sat on terra firma.

Now I started to really panic, with every slight movement I felt I'd slip to my death. Terrified I sat down, the worst thing I could have done as raising myself was a dangerous act as the sudden shift in my centre of gravity could have been the end.

"Reverse down," advised Keith, "and remember to sink your axe to the hilt and don't move your foot until its well dug in."

I followed the advice and slowly got to Ken who'd by this time rendezvoused with another walker, a young chap by the name of Ben. He had homemade crampons – two pieces of wood strapped to his feet with roofing bolts sunk through as grips.

"Do you want my second axe?" he enquired.

This was a wonderfully kind gesture as I could now sink both axes, something I realised was essential as I saw Ken in the distance lowering himself vertically off the ridge and descend with an axe in each hand.

"We've got to do that?" I exclaimed.

"You'll be okay," replied Keith.

First off the ridge was Keith and I followed, backwards and sinking each axe. I was terrified. This was by far an unnecessary risk.

Keith and Ben talked me through it until we hit easier slopes where I could go front ways. Ben kept my spirits up by talking of the kit he made for the mountains, his crampons were just one of a number of hand fabricated items. As the gradient dropped my spirits rose and I even managed to respond to Ben's comment that his gloves were so thick it made the handling of small delicate objects difficult with a rather predictable, "So you never go for a wee in the mountains then?"

Lowering myself down, an ice axe in each hand

At the end of the snow slope my bottle went again, each piece of exposed ground freaked me and I was glad to reach my car at around 17:00, soaked from the rain that had poured on the lower slopes and aching from a couple of tumbles I'd taken.

Keith told me this was one of the record years for snow in Scotland. Referring to it as a 'bumper year' I began to understand the difference in our emphasis. What to him was an adventure playground was to me a nightmare. Aware that these snow-covered tops could hit my Munro attempts hard, I sat in my car depressed, demoralised and missing home.

May the 3rd was an improvement taking in one of the most accessible Munros of the remaining hundred, Stob Coire Raineach. Feeling weary I didn't make good time, reaching its summit in just under three hours after a reasonably uneventful ascent. The weather was excellent and the only snowfield took no more than a few minutes to cross. From the summit I could see what I'd taken in the day before, from a great distance it looked just as hazardous.

I checked my mobile phone, there was a full strength signal so I called my mum and gave her a shock when I said I was on top of a mountain. I also collected a voice message left by my commuter friends that morning on the 07:05 from Bedwyn Station. It was lovely to hear from them and Mandy Thomas – the instigator of this act – had passed her mobile phone around the carriage and an array of people had wished me well.

During the descent my knee problems returned with vengeance, this wasn't good and I was concerned this was going to curtail my ambition to complete the Munros this year.

Snow Still With Me

I woke early on May the 4th and decided to have a crack at the four remaining Munros in the Mamores grouping, these being Sgurr

Eilde Mor, Binnein Beag, Binnein Mor and Na Gruagaichean. I let myself out of the hostel early and drove round to Kinlochleven and was walking through steep wooded ground just as the sun poked its head over the horizon. My initial progress was good, driven on by memories of the previous two days and an extra dose of asthma drugs.

The lochain on the lower slopes of Sgurr Eilde Mor was covered in sheet ice. As I made for higher ground I had a few worrying moments ice axing my way across frozen snow. Even with the ice axe tied to my wrist, fabricated from a rucksack strap, I felt out of my depth.

I knew all four Munros were a major challenge and set myself a target of reaching Sgurr Eilde Mor by noon and Binnein Beag by 14:00. In the event my timings were 11:14 and 13:46 respectively but given the amount of snow on them and my physical state, I relegated the second pair to another day and me to a long walk out along lower ground. I wasn't unduly disappointed by this as I'd managed to claim Binnein Beag which is quite a remote Munro, seven hours into the walk.

The blessing for the day was the weather, just a few snow, hail and rain moments but mainly there were clear skies and a good cool breeze. The downside was my knees and hunger. On the descents the trekking poles became crutches and the lack of energy had me, at times, feeling thoroughly miserable. I had tried to build my weight up over the last few months but I'd failed and whatever I stuck in my mouth my body refused to seek sufficient sustenance from.

Going Wild

Saturday May the 5th was a day of relative luxury – the lack of privacy in Glen Coe Youth Hostel drove me to a single room, with ensuite, in the Grand Hotel Fort William where a card in the room proudly announced Maggie and Marion had serviced it for me.

Taking a day off from walking meant my timetable was more conducive to hotel than hostel life but didn't mean the time was idly spent. I knew by now doing the last 100 was in serious doubt but I was determined I'd give it my best efforts. Looking at my maps, and checking which areas were open for walkers, I noticed the nine Munros in the vicinity of Culra Bothy were open and could be approached from a southerly angle – reducing the amount of snow to walk through.

In all I spent about twelve hours in preparation, plotting the route, buying food, checking and packing kit. Rationing is an important part of planning a wilderness trip as it is all too easy to eat all your food within the first few days with a disregard for the amount of food required for the rest of the stay. Therefore I broke each meal down into a separate sandwich bag to be opened at the relevant time. At this point I'd like to apologise to Maggie and Marion for all the bits of macaroni that missed their intended target.

With a full pack deposited in the back of my car, and my stomach full of breakfast, I drove around to Dalwhinnie for the walk into Culra Bothy.

The walk took four and a half hours on a well-made up track through the Alder Estate. The sun was out and the smell of the pine trees played a flirtation with my senses. My eyes were treated to a gorgeous day, Ben Alder in the distance, the sun glinting on Loch Ericht and a number of well-kept estate residences with turreted corners making them look like haunted castles from a Scooby Doo set.

I struggled with the weight of the pack, often stopping to catch my breath. Unable to justify the extra weight of water I carried my bottle empty, only filling it for immediate drinks. With my left hernia giving me fair notice of its mood I was glad when the bothy came into view.

Culra Bothy was set amongst a city of tents, presumably finding confidence in the vicinity of the bothy while maintaining privacy and enjoying the extra day of the bank holiday weekend.

The evening whiled away in typical bothy fashion with a group of bald men swapping stories and trying to impress the only girl amongst them. Three of them protested their follicle-challenged status was due to excessive testosterone, leaving it unsaid that in their opinion they'd be a good lay.

Feeling they hadn't convinced her that her future, well at least for this one evening, lay with any of them they embarked on a points scoring competition on high speed driving.

"Penrith to York in under an hour."

"Never, not in under an hour."

"Under an hour," nodded the claimant.

"Still wouldn't have done that before March, still had six points on my license. Never drive above eighty with six points on the license."

"It'd be rude not to break the speed limit on the M74."

"Never drive above eighty with six points on the license."

"It'd be rude not to break the speed limit on the M74."

"I did York to Walton-On-Thames in two hours forty-five."

"I did York to Walton-On-Thames in two hours forty-five."

"I did York to Walton-On-Thames in two hours forty-five."

"I don't know where Walton-On-Thames is."

I slipped off to sleep to their tales of heroism on the roads of the British Isles figuring it must be due to excessive testosterone while missing the company of my female friends but not in the sense they viewed female company.

I woke in the early hours, the fire was out and only one person remained – fast asleep. I was freezing, I'd neglected to bring my bivi bag and was now paying the price and was rapidly reassessing my last thought before sleep. A clear night sky, although welcome for walking the next day, had left the way open for a sharp drop in temperature.

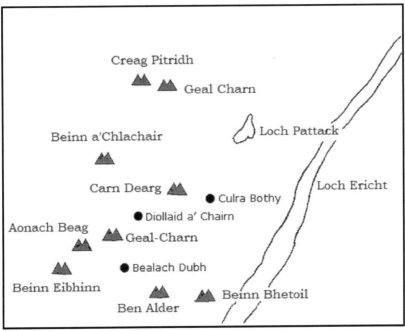

Map showing Culra Bothy and the Surrounding Nine Munros

Without much additional sleep I was up and ready to go at about a quarter to six. On emerging from the bothy I could see most of the tents were iced up and with, the wood and chain bridge across the Allt a'Chaoil-reidhe stream very slippery, I had to take great care to avoid an early dunking.

My first target was Beinn Bheoil which, after failing to locate the obvious path up, I reached at 08:25. The light was beautiful and, due to trying to keep my pack weight down, I now rued the decision to leave my camera in the car.

I looked across to my next challenge, the mighty Ben Alder,

at the same moment that an avalanche rumbled from its northerly slopes. I was relieved I was opting to walk well beyond Beinn Bheoil to tackle it from the south.

The going was slow through manageable snow with fantastic views of a winding cornice – I wish I'd brought the camera. I convinced myself Ben Alder must have been designed by committee as it has every attribute a mountain could have: sheer faces, a side with a gentle run off, multiple buttresses, a high plateau and a trig point.

The summit was gained in just under three hours from leaving Beinn Bheoil. I rested for around an hour, admiring the decrepit trig point and seeing if my mobile phone had a signal. Indeed it did and I composed an email to a group of people, saying hello from 3800 feet.

Half way through I was joined by a young chap and we had the standard conversation of, "How long are you up for? What route are you taking?" He'd taken an interesting entrance by canoeing up Loch Ericht from Dalwhinnie. I continued with the emailing and he bid me farewell. As he departed I noticed he was wearing ski boots and I wondered how difficult they'd have been to climb in. As my mobile then refused to give me a signal, and I gave up the idea of an email going as far as friends in France, Chile, USA, Canada and Australia, I glanced up to see him skiing off into the distance – now I thought I was being cool by sending an email from a mountain top!

I descended into the Bealach Dubh via easy snowfields, taking great care only to then go flying as soon as I stood on grass. This was due to the tread on my boots being full of snow, I soon learnt the technique of tapping the ice and snow off my boots each time I stepped onto grass. This reminded me of my last attempt at go-karting. On the second bend I dived up the inside of a work colleague, he shut the door and I was on the grass involving a route through a deep puddle. Back on the track I was last and hammered it into the next corner, turned and braked on the apex – nothing happened and I ploughed straight into the tyre wall. I had failed to dry the slick tyres or the brakes and had to sit, arms folded, waiting for the humiliation of the marshal to rescue me.

On the descent there were lots of dead beetles amongst the snow and, after noting they were always in the vicinity of exposed grass, I concluded the poor creatures must hatch, make their way into the big world on the snow, blink twice and promptly die.

I considered taking in the ridge to the north of the Bealach Dubh with its fours Munros. But I was glad I didn't because on the way out both of my knees locked up and I had about fifteen minutes of trying to get them moving again. In addition I sensed a sore throat was coming on, something I have periodically suffered from over the last three years.

I reached the bothy at 15:20 to find the tent city dwindled to just one and the bothy deserted.

Snow on The Hill

Determined to make use of the beautiful weather I made another early start on May the 8th, tackling the steep slopes from the bothy to Carn Dearg. From here I'd planned to descend into the Diollaid a'Chairn and then take the narrow ridge to Geal-Charn then walk on over to Aonach Beag and Beinn Eibhinn. The plan started to evaporate with the amount of snow on the obvious ridge up. The next best alternative was an ascent via a very narrow face that even the experienced writers of guidebooks saw fit to mention.

Feeling demoralised I reviewed the options and decided my best hope to complete this ridge was to abandon Geal-Charn and Aonach Beag from this approach and instead descend all the way into the path from the bothy to Bealach Dubh (the very path I exited Ben Alder from the previous day) and climb Beinn Eibhinn from its southerly flanks and then pick off Geal-Charn and Aonach Beag from that angle. This made descending from Carn Dearg a weary job as I knew a long day was about to become a very long day.

Following my route, disturbing a fox as I did so, I reached the path then the long haul up via Bealach Dubh to the high point with views ahead to Loch Ossian and Beinn Eibhinn off to my right. On the ground around me were the ancient, mangled, remains of an aircraft. It must have come down with quite a bump as the remaining pieces were scattered widely and very badly torn. I surmised it was probably a relic of the Second World War. Many such wrecks lie throughout the Highlands as testimony to that era.

The climb up Beinn Eibhinn was very slow and not helped by a succession of false summits, each teasing me into thinking I was nearly at the top. After some four and a half hours, from leaving Carn Dearg, I reached the summit ridge. Fatigue now set in and I had to concentrate on each step to prevent myself from twisting over with tiredness. I became conscious of my under-nourishment – with my day's rations already munched I eyed my emergency supply.

The ridge was covered in easy snow on a gradient that wouldn't involve a fatal slip. I followed the gentle rise towards the summit cairn by tracking the imprints of previous walkers. A good set of prints were to my right and I started to drift towards them. At the last moment I noticed the uniformity of the gash in the snow – nothing resembling a boot print. Instead it was a crack forming between the snow cornice and the solid ground. Had I stepped onto it I'd have fallen 400 feet down a sheer drop.

At the summit I rested and almost slept with my head buried into my arms. I was tempted to sit with the heat of the sun and enjoy the wonderful views and the peace and tranquillity of the day. But I knew, given I was at the furthest point from the bothy, I had to leave my eyrie and get going.

Descending towards the low point before the pull up to Aonach Beag I could see the steep narrow ridge was covered in snow. I decided to continue into the saddle and then review whether I should continue. However, I didn't even get that far as I soon discovered the ridge downwards had a sharp snow-covered point.

Finding myself still wobbly with tiredness, I abandoned Aonach Beag and Geal-Charn for the second time and instead descended via a stream towards the path which would take me back to the bothy. I needed to cross the stream to cut a corner but found I could no longer focus on picking my way through the torrent of meltwater. Instead I ended up in the glen where the gentler slope made a crossing possible.

Sat by the meeting of two streams, I pigged into my emergency rations and basked in the sun, exhausted. I sipped on my bottle of water and thought I mustn't drink it all as I needed to conserve it for the walk back. This was a wake-up call that my mind was wandering: I was sitting next to a plentiful supply of water!

I forced myself to get up and ascended north-east back towards the site of the crashed plane while ruing the missed opportunity of Aonach Beag and Geal-Charn which were now towering above me. Approaching the high point in the path I spied an alternative route up, not for today but perhaps later in the week.

I had told friends and family that I'd walk out on the Saturday and given I needed to take the following day off to rest I figured the final two days, Thursday and Friday, could be used to complete the one remaining planned walk and a return to Aonach Beag and Geal-Charn.

My mental capacity was now returning and I realised the

jeopardy my last one hundred Munros was in. Having so far done five days of bagging, abandonments had *already* created an extra three days of walking and if I failed to complete the two missed today then I'd have to add two extra days for the long walk in and out.

Descending the path back towards the bothy I came across a chap resting, I spoke with him for a while and as I set off my right knee locked up again making the final hour to the bothy a painful affair.

The following day was a day of rest spent enjoying the sun around the bothy and trying to shoo off the horses which roam wild in the glen and visit the bothy for scraps of food.

In the evening two new people, Alec and Mark, joined me in the bothy. Mark had a lovely kind and gentle manner about him and made me a drink while I lay in my sleeping bag. Alec was also a joy to meet, a train driver for EWS Railways, he was up for a few days fitting in with his shift pattern. Incredibly fit he'd managed to walk in one day what ended up taking me three days to complete.

We discussed life, the universe and everything. Alec eventually said, "I know this is going to sound very boring but marrying my wife was the best thing I ever did, we have never looked back."

The conversation paused, I think Alec was feeling he wasn't living up to some modern image of people. In almost unison Mark and I replied, "That's so refreshing to hear."

More Mobile

On Thursday May the 10th I got back on course. Starting before 06:00 I let myself out of the bothy, saying goodbye to Alec, who was moving on, and a, "See you later," to Mark.

Just as I was closing the solid wooden door the last words of

Captain Oates came to mind so I made my departing words, "I'm just going outside and may be some time."

I took in the three Munros to the north-west of the bothy: Beinn a'Chlachair, Creag Pitridh and Geal Charn, in all taking eleven and a half hours.

At the summit of Beinn a'Chlachair my mobile phone got a signal and I was able to send my email out, delayed from Ben Alder, and by the summit of Creag Pitridh I was starting to get replies from people sitting at their desks unamused by my enthusiastic account of being able to see mountains for miles and miles without a cloud in the sky. The mobile signal was probably due to being in the vicinity of the A86, and I made full use of it by calling my mum.

"Hello, Mum, it's Steve."

"Where are you, we've been worried?"

"I can't pronounce the Gaelic name, but if you look at a map I'm not too far from Dalwhinnie on the A9. I have been staying in a bothy."

"We thought about calling your mobile or sending you an email."

"Hello, hello."

"I haven't had a signal since Sunday. That's why I haven't been in touch."

"We've been worried."

"I can see for miles and miles."

"Are you walking on your own?"

"Yes. I can see right over to the Cairngorms."

"Hello, hello."

"Are there other people at the bothy?"

"One or two, it changes daily. I can see right over to Ben Nevis, it is absolutely fantastic."

"Hello, hello."

"I can see right over to Ben Nevis, it is absolutely fantastic."

"You go careful."

"Oh yeah, it's a glorious day."

Back at the bothy Mark had another go at explaining the pros of being a Jehovah Witness while I enjoyed the glory of the sun, blue skies and tranquillity of the glen while thinking whoever made this little lot did a jolly good job and I was better off sitting on the fence.

Friday, May the 11th, was my last chance to have a crack at Geal-Charn and Aonach Beag using the route I'd spied on the Tuesday. Making my earliest start yet and waking Mark and by this time a chap called Ken, I was away at about a quarter to six.

Pulling myself up through the Bealach Dubh onto the high point of the pass through to Loch Ossian I discovered further parts of the crashed plane. It felt even more unreal, all these bits of metal over a large area. I tried to make sense of it but in some strange way couldn't comprehend this obviously fatal crash. It was so unconnected to my experiences I half expected a handle-bar-moustached figure to appear in full flying gear announcing, "What ho! Ginger, went and put the kite down in a bit of a daft place."

From the crash site I climbed north-east. On the horizon stood a row of deer – they looked comical with their ears aloft against the blue sky. The sense of smell is an important part of the deer's life cycle and they obviously picked up the pong of an unwashed walker and monitored my progress until it was time for the leader to canter off with all the others in tow.

After a final sharp climb, I was on a high level plateau and, after crossing a surreal feeling snowfield to Geal-Charn, I knew these final two Munros of the nine surrounding Culra Bothy were now on.

Again the sky was faultlessly blue and no mountain was shying behind the mist. However, an icy cold wind was blowing across the tops so I made a hasty bag of Aonach Beag before retracing my steps. I arrived back at the bothy about 13:00, relieved I'd finally completed the nine Munros in the area.

Thinking my 'last one hundred Munros' was now a stronger possibility I felt a renewed enthusiasm as I packed up my things and, in blistering heat, walked the four hours back to Dalwhinnie.

Due to being unable to carry water as well as the weight of my full pack, I got heat stroke and became very dehydrated. Sat in a bar in Newtonmore I poured orange juice and lemonade after orange juice and lemonade down my throat in an attempt to re-hydrate

Double Century

Saturday became an enforced rest day which I used to take a leisurely drive to Ratagan Youth Hostel with a stop for lunch in Fort William where, by coincidence, I bumped into my old friend Willy Newlands. We had only occasionally spoken on the phone since our last meeting in 1997 so it was good to catch up with him again.

On arrival at Ratagan, I spoke with the warden about the Cuillin Ridge on Skye, the most dangerous ridge in the British Isles but once complete eleven Munros are surrendered.

"How dangerous is it?" I asked.

"It's okay if you have a good head for heights."

"Are there lots of places where if you slip you die?"

"Oh plenty."

This is what I knew anyhow, so I'd no idea why I was asking. Perhaps in hope he'd have said, "No, it's a cinch, don't know what all the fuss is about."

"Many deaths on it?"

"One or two a year."

"I'm doing it next week but I have booked a guide."

"Never been a death with a guide."

Now this was more like it. The kind of reassuring comment I was looking for.

"Who have you booked with?"

"Martin Moran."

"He's a hard man."

"How do you mean hard?" I asked, panicking again. Would this mean such situations as, "Come on Smith, it's only a 3000 foot drop and you want to be roped? You big wimp."

"Well, I don't know him well but if he soloed the ridge he wouldn't rope himself."

But I figured he wouldn't want a death on his hands, bad for business. And the booking literature did say it'd be roped. I was reassured.

"Still," continued Nick Lancaster, the warden, straightening himself after some task requiring floor level attention, "he did break his leg the other year. Fell off the roof of his house while adjusting the television aerial."

"That must have been a bit tricky for him," I said, "imagine having your leg in plaster for months on end with no telly to watch?"

On the Sunday I had a crack at the Five Sisters of Kintail, something I abandoned back in 1991. I started about 08:00 and had a long slow pull to the first Munro, Sgurr na Ciste Duibhe taking nearly two and a half hours. The skies were clear again and it was getting very hot. A narrow, yet manageable ridge, took in the newly promoted Sgurr na Carnach then Sgurr Fhuaran where, on announcing this was my 200th Munro, I was congratulated by two young chaps, doing the ridge in the opposite direction.

Psychologically, reaching my 200th Munro, was a huge

boost and, with my knees behaving, I headed towards Saileag to reduce the length of the following day's walk. Before reaching this Munro I climbed the rugged and sharp top of Sgurr nan Spainteach. I rested before dropping down and traversing the southerly face to avoid the narrow ridge. Here I experienced a minor shower but nothing worthy of Gore-Tex.

Shortly before the final ascent of Saileag I caught up with one of the chaps I'd shared my double century with. "Where is your mate?" I enquired.

"Oh he hasn't done Saileag and the next one along before, so he has left his kit with me and is running them. Here he is back now."

That put my spurt of energy in to perspective, especially as he arrived back without a bead of sweat on him.

Passage Blocked

Monday brought a runny nose and a worsening throat. Sensing it was still in its early phases I dosed myself with paracetamol and vitamin C, pored over maps and lists of Munros free of foot and mouth restrictions, put an entry in the hostel route book and set off.

A vague foot and mouth notice at the start of the walk deterred me as it didn't tie in with the information available at the hostel. Instead I drove further east to attempt Carn Ghluasaid, Sgurr nan Conbhairean and Sail Chaorainn.

A slight navigational error, at the start, put me on steep ground until the top of the first Munro where I could pick up a better route through the mist and cloud, emerging into the beauty of a temperature inversion.

On top of the third Munro I happened across a group of train spotters up from Gloucestershire. It appeared their incessant need to tick thinks off wasn't limited to just the rolling stock of the franchised railways of the South of England – more ingenious lists of items were now being ticked off.

Fortunately for me they'd a hand drawn map with them showing a route back, missing out the re-ascent of the two peaks already claimed. Armed with this information I made my descent, in one place via a path on a very steep slope, returning to my car in just over eight hours. I was satisfied with this timing as it was just over the maximum book time and meant my fitness had improved.

A worsening throat and cold laid me up for the next two days. Fortunately Ratagan Youth Hostel is a relaxed place with an excellent day room which overlooks the bay formed by the head of the loch. However, there was a limit to the amount of hostel conversation I could tolerate while munching through paracetamol and using up endless paper tissues.

A particularly odd couple frequented the day room, kitchen area, drying room. Wherever I was their peculiar tones would appear. The younger chap, probably in his late forties, evidently thought it was his role in life to give a running commentary to his older companion, white-haired, past the retirement age and called Peter. I didn't speak with him to ascertain his name, instead the younger chap felt every sentence needed a verbal full stop by the way of the word, 'Peter'.

"What shall we do tomorrow then, Peter?"

"I'm not sure, we could walk the Five Sisters."

"Yes, we could, Peter."

There was then a pause which was broken by, "Fancy a cup of tea, Peter?"

"Oh yes."

And with that he'd leap up, attend to it, returning with, "I just made it a little strong so I have diluted it down a bit. I'll just give it a stir, Peter."

A couple of chaps from Crawley, Pete and Ken, in the same dorm as me, had picked up on this also and concluded the old boy was a genius. Letting it drop there was some consideration in his will he now had a servant for life – being perfectly able to do things for himself was no longer relevant to his survival. Ken shared with me the tale of his midnight trip to the loo where he was confronted by the commentator in full flannelette pyjamas done up to the collar.

On Thursday May the 17th I felt a bit better and tackled Ciste Dhubh, Aonach Meadhoin and Sgurr a'Bhealaich Dheirg. However, I didn't escape being under the weather as the majority of the walk, made using my map and compass skills, was through constant drizzle with visibility down to just a few yards.

It was a cold and damp experience with narrow ridges adding an extra ingredient. On one occasion my boots slipped on wet rock, but not at a point where I felt unduly in danger. I shuddered with the thought of my impending trip to the Cuillin Ridge.

On the approach to the third Munro the path branched at a tricky point which I sensed it'd be difficult to locate on the way back. Using a small pile of rocks I marked the route and on the return promptly marched straight past them. Only on a patch of snow, where I could see no ascending footprints matching my own, did I realise my error. Backtracking I found my pile of rocks and reverted to the correct course and promptly bumped into Pete and Ken, the Crawley men.

"We've parked just beyond you and slashed your tyres as we walked past," said Pete.

I assumed, being from Crawley, this is a mere force of habit.

On the final descent I took a wrong path and found myself walking south-east. On checking my map, and hearing the sound of traffic on the A87, I figured this a better route and followed it, navigating by the drum of the traffic rising through the cloud.

At one stage I was worried my exit point, on to the A87, was through a foot and mouth restricted area. Knowing there were £5,000 fines for coming off in the wrong place I coaxed my way along the hillside to navigate directly to my car.

The day was cold and my knees started to grumble on the steep descent. I swallowed an Ibuprofen and, while occasionally reversing down to take the weight off my knees, finally reached my car after nearly ten hours of walking. Looking south I could make out the shrouded mountains of the South Kintail Ridge which, in 1992, was where my knee trouble began. It dawned on me I'd been carrying this problem for nine years – the majority of my Munros.

I spent a quiet evening catching up with phone calls and planning further Munros for the next day. The warden asked me to move rooms and I got the impression they needed a complete dorm free on the Friday evening and it was far easier to get the occupants of rooms to shift during the Thursday evening than the Friday morning.

Being the last to move out of the room it dawned on me if I stayed put for the one night I'd have the room to myself. Quietly shutting the door my plan appeared to work. A slight nervous sense of guilt accompanied me between the sheets. What if they truly needed this room tonight? I checked my watch – 22:15, surely no party would arrive this late? But what if that car pulling up was a mini bus? I counted the footsteps, not many. Say they are switching this dorm to a female only one and that's why they wanted me to move. And a party of women are due to arrive any minute? Knowing my luck it'd be a coach load of German Frau's on a body building weekend.

I woke at 04:00 from a dream where a former East European female shot putter was sand papering my throat. As I was still the only person in the dorm I was able to switch the light on and administer all kinds of potions, to soothe my cold, before getting a further few hours' sleep. I woke to what I knew would have to be a further rest day.

I took the day really easily and in the evening got talking to Pete and Ken, the Crawley men, again. Having now switched dorms it was apparent I was now stationed with the commentator and his older companion, Peter. Ken latched on to this and I mentioned the pressed pyjamas were now neatly laid on his bunk. I then spent many minutes trying to persuade Ken that although his idea of chopping one of the pyjama legs off stood some merit, perhaps I wasn't the best person to carry it out.

After a disturbed night's sleep, ghosted by stripy pyjama clad figures going about their business, I was sad to leave the hostel. With its comfortable and relaxed atmosphere it'd been one of the best I'd ever stayed in.

Having a number of hours to kill, before I could arrive at Martin Moran's house to check in for the Cuillin Ridge course, I decided to head into Kyle of Lochalsh in search of a thermal top – this being the only piece of equipment I was short of on Martin Moran's list of kit required for the Cuillin Ridge.

All sorts of thoughts were going through my head, one piece of equipment missing, "Right you're off the course, Smith. The heavily congested cold, the two crippled knees, asthma and the double hernia aren't a problem but you forgot your thermal top."

Driving into the Kyle I remembered what an absolute dump it was. Descending a hillside amongst shabby industrial units and drab streets I parked and looked for the optimistically signposted 'Town Centre' only to realise the collection of shops, many with the odd boarded up window, which confronted me was actually the Town Centre.

After some minutes of wandering I found what looked like

a clothes shop, only the contents of the window gave the game away as the proprietor had neglected to advertise what the shop was. Spying through the window I sensed I could see a gents' section beyond the frilly underwear and bras. Gingerly setting forth I made my way towards the rear and was duly pounced upon by the assistant who promptly tried to sell me the entire contents of the shop. I managed to just hold out for a thermal top which luckily they had. One size too big, but what the heck I was back on the course.

On leaving the shop I noticed the lower pane of glass in the door had a brick-sized hole in it, undoubtedly caused by the local youths with nothing better to do in this pit of despair. Still it keeps them out of trouble I guess.

On the amble back to my car, with a brief deviation to a chemist for further vitamin c and paracetamol, I came across signs pronouncing 'Charles Kennedy' and suddenly realised the country was in the grip of election fever. I had missed the announcement of the election and only in a telephone conversation with Gisella had I found out.

Since the death of Screaming Lord Sutch, elections have lost their appeal a bit. No longer are we treated to such joys as Margaret Thatcher making her constituency victory speech with a placard above her head announcing 'Monster Raving Loony'. It is a shame he took his own life. Perhaps it was after a visit to Kyle of Lochalsh.

The rest of the day was spent trying to make myself feel better before meeting with Martin Moran in Lochcarron. Arriving far too early I hung about the place for a few hours and started to feel more and more ill.

Being dosed up with paracetamol I had to wait until I could take a couple of Nurofen. My throat was killing me and I really needed to try and soothe it. The Strepsils weren't having much impact – they rarely work for me anyhow, possibly because I crunch them to death long before any soothing action can take place. I do, however, miss the useful little tin they once came in.

I suddenly hit on the idea of TCP. Not having used this since I was eighteen I was unsure if my memory served me correctly that it was suitable for sore throats, but it was worth a try. Tracking down a bottle to the local Spar shop confirmed it was ideal for sore throats. Well it said 'For sore throats' and I was confused if that meant it gave a sore throat or soothed one. I chanced it and bought a bottle.

Back in the car I unscrewed the cap and took a sniff. Memories flooded back of acne during my days at Brighton Polytechnic. My mum swore by the stuff, so did I but my language was a bit more colourful. She would always bundle a bottle with a food parcel so I could dab it on my facial eruptions which were optimistically called teenage spots. Then on a visit home Mum would enquire if I'd a girlfriend yet – not a chance, I always stunk of TCP. I think studying in Brighton, the gay capital of England, was playing on her mind a bit.

Stuck with a neat bottle of TCP, I had to find a means to water it down, by a ratio of five to one, then gargle on it. Digging around my car I found a half consumed bottle of Vittel natural mineral water. I used part of it to knock down a couple of Nurofen, it was almost time, and then poured in what I guessed was an extra fifth of TCP and gave it a good shake to produce a frothy green mass in a clear bottle.

I then headed into the public loos to gargle and spit. I imagined this would have given anybody a fright if they'd seen me enter with it in hand. Come to think of it would have looked more disturbing if I'd emerged from the toilets with it. A few gargles later I emerged stinking of TCP and, like when I was eighteen, single.

Cuillin Ridge – Day One

Arriving at the house I quickly discovered Martin Moran was out guiding in India and our guide for the week was a chap called Bruce Goodlad who was set to look after myself, two General Practitioners (Ali Ashton and Adrian Ogden) and an anaesthetist (Peter Stone). I figured I was in good hands if anything went wrong!

We set out at 08:00 on the Sunday for our first attempt at the Cuillins. Originally I thought this would be a training day, but what better training than the ridge itself?

After an hour's drive, over to Skye, we set off walking. Determined not to allow my asthma and cold to slow me down I tracked Bruce's speedy heels until we hit the start of the very steep ground. Here we rested and I lowered my track suit bottoms to put Deep Heat on my knees.

I caught Bruce eyeing the extent of the strapping on my legs. "Trouble with your knees, Steve?"

"Yep, but if I keep them Deep Heated they're usually okay."

Ali saved me with an, "I suppose it's all preventative."

I readily confirmed this.

As we set off Ali and I were at the back and I added, "I thought it was best not to mention the double hernia."

Due to Bruce's pace the left hernia was pulling quite a bit.

Initially Bruce wanted to take in just one Munro but after a subtle game of teasing out the closet nature of the others it emerged there was a sense Munros were important. Therefore we tackled Bruach na Frithe, an easy scramble, Sgurr nan Gillean, an exposed scramble including a roped climb up a chimney and subsequent lowering back down and finally Am Basteir which was again exposed scrambling, this time in the wet, with one short piece of rope work.

Altogether it was a successful day although I was unhappy with the exposed scrambling as the advertising literature for the course said this would be roped. We had one minor mishap when Ali dropped her helmet on the descent of Sgurr nan Gillean. It was a timely reminder of the terrain we were in as after two or three bounces it was over the edge and falling away never to be seen again.

Cuillin Ridge – Day Two

The aim of the day was to complete the Inaccessible Pinnacle, the hardest of all the Munros. Starting from Glen Brittle it took us about three hours to ascend, initially over easy ground which then became a steep scramble over rock and narrow ridges. From time to time my nerves started to get the better of me and I required Bruce, the guide, to talk me through it.

As we rose we hit the cloud base and on reaching the top of Sgurr Dearg things started to become surreal. The Inaccessible Pinnacle, the true summit, was just west and through the cloud we could barely make out this towering shape of a blade of rock. Only the clanking of loose rock told us other climbers were positioning themselves to make their ascent. The episode felt like a ship arriving at a fog-covered harbour, the blade of rock the hull and the people milling about being the dockyard workers waiting for the ship to berth.

There are two approaches to the Inn Pin, a short sharp 60 foot climb or a longer ridge climb from the rear. We elected the longer ridge as the climbing was less technical. However, this required a tricky descent on wet boulders to reach the base of the long ridge, unnerving both Ali and I.

Bruce roped us together and free climbed to the top. While waiting for the rope to tighten, the signal to start climbing, we got talking to some middle-aged chaps who were due to meet a guide. However, he hadn't materialised and they were left in the cold contemplating how to make the ascent unaided. The rope went tight and we were climbing and the men's parting words to me were, "I'll have his jacket" and "I reckon his boots would fit me."

Getting started was difficult, foot and hand holds scarce. I had two goes, it threw me off twice. On the third attempt I was climbing, beginning my long-standing imaginary ascent.

Thankfully cloud was right up to our feet, hiding the 3000 foot drop below.

I was third on the rope, Adrian was first, Ali second and taking up the rear was Peter. By this time I felt we were starting to bond well, I was deliberately playing the fool, my silly sense of humour and passion to bag the Munros was a sense of amicable amusement to the others. Bruce was way out of sight, taking the rope in as we climbed, so the bit by bit climbing was down to the four of us.

We made slow progress. Finding suitable hand and foot holds and confidence were our main problems but we all helped each other with very supportive advice and words of encouragement. Given we were all roped together on a blade of rock overlooking a 3000 foot drop, the sense of comradeship was high.

At one stage Ali was having trouble progressing up a narrow vertical ridge, she couldn't get purchase for her left foot. I stepped forward, jammed my left knee into a crack, took hold her foot and placed it on my knee. "Give that a try," I said.

"That's great, thanks," she replied, pushing herself on up.

It was then my turn and it took me ages to find suitable holds and confidence. Ali called back trying to direct me to the 'foothold' she'd used. I didn't have the heart to say it was actually my knee and being attached mid-way up my leg, was an impossibility.

It took us an hour to get to the summit, covering the ground which Bruce free climbed in a few minutes. From the top we were, one by one, lowered down the short side, to relative safety and a scramble back to the base of this Munro's long ridge to collect our rucksacks. The middle-aged chaps were still there, just giving up on their guide. We descended the tiring scree slopes back to Glenn Brittle where we duly bumped into a guide asking if we'd encountered a group of middle-aged men on the Inn Pin.

The Inaccessible Pinnacle

Cuillin Ridge – Day Three

Tuesday May the 22nd proved very successful with an initial ascent from Glen Brittle to An Dorus, an entry point to the ridge. Initially there was a good pull up a path in the heat of a faultless sky followed by a narrowing scree-filled gully. Again I elected to track Bruce's heels to maintain a pace while Adrian, Ali then Peter followed.

As there was so much scree we had to take care not to dislodge any large rocks. We were managing this, just sending the odd bit of loose scampering away for a few feet. Suddenly a yell from Adrian turned Bruce and my heads to see a large boulder tumbling into the path of Ali who just scrambled out of the way as it gathered pace. A haunting crash echoed in its wake as it headed off into oblivion. Fortunately nobody was hurt but it was a timely reminder of where we were and if somebody had been hit the consequences would have been very serious.

When we reached the ridge we headed north and, via an exposed scramble, made it to the summit of Sgurr a'Mhadaidh. Bruce realised, due to my nerves, that I was slow and from there on roped me, and occasionally Ali, to him.

We then did the classic ridge scramble over the further Munros of Sgurr a'Ghreadaidh and Sgurr na Banachdich. Given the Gaelic translation for Sgurr is point, or peak, the name gives a good indication of the terrain.

Being roped aided my confidence and speed, suddenly I could move as freely as the others. I now had the confidence to remain upright and this, by putting the weight over my feet, gave me much more grip.

Once back at the mini bus we all realised what a tremendous day it'd been, superb views, three Munros and a classic ridge traverse.

Cuillin Ridge – Day Four

Earlier in the week Bruce had mentioned the possibility of camping out. This was something I wasn't looking forward to because it'd involve carrying heavy equipment to high terrain. It also meant sharing a tent and I'd paid a single room supplement for the accommodation!

However, with the awesome weather and the daily long trip from Lochcarron to the Cuillins, the advantages of a night's camping became more obvious.

So on the Wednesday we made a more leisurely start and, with full camping kit, started our walk from Glen Brittle just before 11:00. From here we ascended the Coir' a' Ghrunnda – a geological feast of two ridge spurs forming a dry dock-like feature, rising for a couple of thousand feet, containing football pitch-sized slabs.

The area was mainly bare rock which held the heat causing us to swelter on the ascent. The gabbro rock gave good grip but was interspersed with streaks of slippery basalt rock. Overall it gave the appearance of a beautifully laid road which the Gas Board had then dug a trench through and filled with tarmac.

After some three hours of hauling ourselves and our packs we reached the loch which hangs in the gap between the Coir a Ghrunnda and the final rise to the ridge of the Cuillins. It was an awesomely beautiful location, a throwback to the ice age. Now there are only mere streams where once there was a hanging glacier.

After pitching our tents and some lunch, we set off and climbed the boulder fields to the south-east and an exposed scramble to Sgurr nan Eag – the most southerly Munro of the Cuillins. Descending into the bealach between it and Sgurr Dubh Mor I realised the ascent was going to be another exposed climb. I shared my concerns with Bruce who promised I'd be roped.

Ali elected to drop out at this stage as the heat was slowly melting her and she made the safe descent back to camp as we ascended over a rocky ridge. Watching Ali's route downhill coincided with the conversations, of the four remaining males, following a similar path.

It all started as a woman, called Elaine, ascended towards us on a rocky peak in the ridge. We had to wait for her on a wider section as the path was too narrow to proceed. Unfortunately for her, but fortunately for us, she was wearing a low cut top and not the best bra in the world. So for a few moments, as we gentlemanly monitored her ascent, we were treated to a wobbly feast, averting our eyes from the glory of the ridge.

As she reached us she confessed she was finding the ridge difficult and she was nervous. I just kept myself from saying she looked a bit wobbly, well not until she was suitably out of earshot. From here things went downhill and cued us to mercilessly take the rip out of Bruce. Mainly for his ability to send us over the most difficult terrain only to join a path which fed from an easier route.

At the summit of Sgurr Dubh Mor, with an expansive view of the ridge, we understood the true beauty of the Cuillins – the summits glowed in the evening sun as light played through the gaps in the ridge.

On the descent I had to lead on the rope and, after picking a series of fruitless descent lines, Bruce roared with laughter and shouted after me to change course. At one stage I had to re-ascend and was spread across a rock with my legs wide apart suffering agony as the harness cut in to my hernias. Bruce started to pull on the rope and I had to shout for him to stop as the pain bit into me. At this stage I came clean.

"I forgot to tell you something, Bruce."

"What's that?"

"Double hernia."

"Steve, you are a total fucking invalid."

We reached the camp at about 20:30 where another tent had appeared, it was zipped up but we could detect movement from within. We speculated why anybody would want to stay cooped up in a tent on such a fine evening. While making supper a man and woman appeared out of the tent, she went for a paddle in the loch occasionally glancing towards him while he sat gently smoking a cigarette. Not that I am suggesting something had just taken place. But you'd wonder, wouldn't you?

After supper Bruce made us all hot chocolate which we took to the edge of the drop into Coir a Ghrunnda. I was last to arrive and as I approached the other four were sat silhouetted against the fading pure sky. It felt like the scene from the ending of a Hollywood movie. I reached them, sat down and looked out over the islands of Rum and Canna and the signalling lighthouse at of Oigh-sgeir. It was a very peaceful and magical moment, bonded with nature and each other as we'd trusted our lives to one another.

Cuillin Ridge – Day Five

After a good night's sleep, with Peter electing to sleep under the stars, we set off to claim Sgurr Alasdair, our tenth Munro of our five day course and leaving just one not bagged, Sgurr Mhic Choinnich on the main Cuillin traverse. The greater traverse also includes Bla Bheinn which was never a possibility as part of the week's course.

The ascent onto the ridge, from our camp, was fairly rapid – a nice temperature and a high starting point eased our way. From here we should have ascended the ridge north-east to the summit but Bruce took us over the ridge for an approach from the rear. Leaving us alone, he went ahead and surveyed the route.

"Bruce, you have done this one before haven't you?" I asked.

"Err, not from this angle."

We collectively went quiet as he called us forward and roped us together, a few metres apart, me at the back due to a disagreement I was having with a re-hydrated meal. With him way

266

ahead, anchoring the rope round a rock, we surveyed the three hundred foot rock climb over a grade of 'vdiff'. This stands for very difficult which was about how we found it. As we started to move we dislodged boulders and scree. Minor panic attacks began to set in. Peter at the front, and me at the rear, had developed a banter which, on occasion, rendered Adrian and Ali motionless with laughter. I think the humour kept me going, being roped to three ex-medical students wasn't top of my list of how to spend a Thursday morning.

At the top I sat firm to allow my nerves to recover as Bruce said, "Fair play" to all the tongue in cheek abuse we were hurling at him.

We then returned to our camp, packed away the tents and started the long walk back to Glen Brittle.

On the descent of the slabs in the Coir a Ghrunnda Bruce roped me for one tricky section.

"I didn't notice the exposure on this bit yesterday," I said.

"I know, Steve," replied Bruce, "I kept you talking then, this time you can see it and I've had to rope you."

Cuillin Ridge – Day Six

With the departing of Bruce we were left with two Munros to complete: Sgurr Mhic Choinnich on the main ridge and Bla Bheinn which forms part of the greater traverse of the Cuillin Ridge.

On the top of the Inaccessible Pinnacle I'd got talking to another guide and taken his phone number. Both Ali and Adrian were keen to complete Sgurr Mhic Choinnich so I phoned and booked the guide, George Yeoman, for the Saturday.

This left Bla Bheinn for the Friday. Given Ali had previously climbed it, and her first husband had proposed to her at the top, Adrian and I set off together shortly after 10:30 and ascended through the cooling wind (or should that be 'Cuillin' wind), scree and rock.

I was on a roll, for once my body was totally in tune and we made 440m of ascent in the first hour. This was an incredible rate for me as I am normally lucky to make 300m per hour.

We reached the summit in just under two and a half hours and briefly stopped for food. There then followed a mad dash back to the car to beat the rain now driving in. Adrian commented he'd never come off a hill so fast and Ali was surprised when I called her on her mobile so early. We rendezvoused in a hotel bar where Ali had the drinks lined up waiting for us. This was my first ever rendezvous via the use of a mobile phone.

Cuillin Ridge – Day Seven

Due to a nocturnal plastic bag rustler practising his art, I woke early on Saturday May the 26th at the Glenbrittle Youth Hostel. Feeling tense I breakfasted then drove off to meet our guide and rendezvous with Ali and Adrian at the Glenbrittle campsite.

To try and destress I played a relaxation CD of waves crashing on a beach. Parking up, I overlooked the sea loch and enjoyed the rest of the music until the others arrived. Stepping out of the car I was hit by the sad realities of our modern era as I was treated to the sound of the sea really crashing on the shore instead of the recorded version I'd sat listening to in my car.

George warned us the wind speed was about 35mph on the summit and it could mean abandonment and the fee, £105, would still be payable. However, we had the choice of opting out now and owe nothing. I sensed Ali and Adrian were as committed as I was so I simply handed over £35, my share, and said I was on for it.

After a long pull into the coire, and an ascent close to the edge of a scree run off, we reached the ridge and then came the time to put on helmet and harness. At this point I discovered what an excellent guide George was to work with – helpful, attentive and caring.

We could hear a helicopter buzzing around and it was then George revealed his radio and said he and a number of other guides, who worked the Cuillins, were in constant radio contact reach with each other, the police, navy and RAF. So I was now walking with two doctors and a member of the local Mountain Rescue Team. Fortunately a radio communication with the helicopter informed us it was simply a training flight and George didn't have to rush off.

After close guiding across the ridge, in which it appeared George knew every rock and hand hold, we reached Sgurr Mhic Choinnich in just over three hours from the start of the walk and therefore completed all the Munros on Skye. I was a happy man as we descended and said our goodbyes.

No Forcan

On Sunday May the 27th I woke and realised I was in new territory, I'd walked for seven days without a break and I'd no plans to take a rest so drove back to the mainland and tackled The Saddle and Sgurr na Sgine in Glen Shiel.

The initial ascent was through mild drizzle over a well-made up path. My pace was good and again I exceeded 400m of ascent per hour. To reach The Saddle you can take the aptly named sharp Forcan Ridge, which is narrow and exposed. However, there is an alternative route I took, skirting the lower reaches before a long pull up an easier ridge.

By this time it was starting to rain quite hard and I sensed my knees could do with an extra dab of Deep Heat but I didn't dare reveal them as the cold and wet would do more harm than good.

Instead I swallowed an Ibuprofen and hoped for the best.

To save weight I'd started the day with an empty drinks bottle. Ironically, with all the rain falling, I now struggled to find water. I became very thirsty and it was only when I found a trickle of a stream, and used a stone to guide it into my bottle, I was able to quench my thirst.

From the top of The Saddle I followed an intricate path, requiring close navigation to locate the route. I arrived at Sgurr na Sgine in just under two hours after departing The Saddle.

In all it was a miserable wet day, the rain got harder as I approached my car and I was nothing short of drenched when I climbed inside. I reflected how I missed the company of my walking companions over the last week and the drama of the Cuillin Ridge in comparison of the more mundane Munros I'd now returned to.

Still Going Strong

With an impending brief visit home penned in for later in the week, and my body not showing any signs of major complaint, I decided on a ninth consecutive day of taking in the Munros. This was in excess of my previous best of four continuous days and lifted my spirits with regards to completing the Munros this year.

After only a bit of sleep I was out walking at just before 08:45 on the An Caorann Mor path, in Glenn Shiel, to take in the Munros of A' Chralaig and Mullach Fraoch-choire. Branching off to the north-east I climbed sharply onto the ridge to A' Chralaig in light rain – compared with the previous day the conditions were great.

The summit cairn, an impressive structure, shaped like a policeman's helmet, tested out my newly found rock-climbing abilities. It took me a few moments to ascend it and pat the top with my hand.

From here I followed an exposed ridge which narrowed to the point where I became concerned a slip would lead to serious injury. It also required an occasional bit of scrambling – again testing out my newfound skills from the Cuillin Ridge. There then followed the pull up onto Mullach Fraoch-choire to complete my thirty ninth Munro of this trip.

At the summit I decided that I didn't fancy the reverse traverse of the ridge as the exposure didn't play well with my sense of humour. Instead I descended one of the steep coires and, after the point of no return, regretted it. The steepness of the slope had me moving each foot in turn, with the other, and my trekking poles, firmly dug into the ground. I had to think through each move to prevent a tumble that, although unlikely to be fatal, would prove serious. It was like playing chess with the devil, once a move was made I could relax a moment before the fear of the next move overwhelmed any feelings of security.

Once out of the coire it began to rain and I started the squelchy trek to the An Caorann Mor path. Looking back I noticed two women, who'd done the ridge traverse a few minutes behind me, descend into the Coire Odhar. We had previously exchanged pleasantries and I fancied the company on the long walk back. Seeing they were a matter of a hundred yards behind me, I figured they'd soon catch up. The next time I looked back they were gone, a slight deviation took them from my sight.

Arriving back at our cars, only a few minutes apart we enjoyed the drying wind and exchanged our stories of the day. At any point we were no more than a few minutes from each other but only saw one another twice. I reflected how the hills can be such lonely places.

Alternatively they might have thought I was some kind of weirdo and were hiding from me.

The End of The Mamores

Day ten of my continuous stint of Munro bagging dawned with mist and rain. Initially I planned to do A' Ghlas-bheinn and Beinn Fhada. However, with a niggling doubt about them, I instead drove south to tackle Na Gruagaichean and Binnein Mor on the east end of the Mamores ridge. These two Munros being the ones I abandoned due to snow earlier in the month.

Starting from the Mamore Lodge hotel at 10:00, and making a mental note to pay the £2 parking charge on my return, I set off on the steep south-west slopes of Na Gruagaichean through wind and rain. As I rose so did the wind until on the ridge it tried its best to disconnect my feet from the ground. A lone grouse, which I set flying, was the only distraction I had from the bracing wind.

At the summit everything was obscured by the mist. Descending towards Binnein Mor the weather suddenly cleared, showing me I was on the wrong path. Backtracking, I made my way across the ridge to my second Munro of the day. I was relieved to reach its summit as on one or two occasions I'd doubted the sense of being out in such conditions.

Backtracking over the summit of Na Gruagaichean, now in clear visibility, the wind pounced on me like a bully. The descent was a miserable affair, only the reappearance of the grouse brought a smile to my face. To keep my spirits up I whistled 'Scotland The Brave' – the country was taking me over like some Orwellian plot.

An Stuc at Last

Due to a pre-operative examination for my hernia, booked for Friday June the 1st, I figured I could manage one more sortie into the hills before popping home. For this I elected the most southerly of my remaining Munros, An Stuc on the Lawers ridge, with the idea, if time permitted, I could drive home straight afterwards.

This was my fourth attempt to bag An Stuc, the previous three were all hampered by a combination of late starts, bad weather and an argumentative girlfriend. However, the information gleaned from these attempts was useful and gave me an idea it'd take around seven hours. With a starting time of just before 07:30 it gave me a good chance of bagging it and being home, in my own bed, before midnight.

My car looked lonesome as I ascended from the National Trust visitor centre, making good progress over the made up paths then the rising slopes of Beinn Ghlas. I cut onto the steep western flanks of Ben Lawers, avoiding an already claimed summit, and spent quite a bit of time picking my way along to avoid a slip on the steep wet slope. With the weather clearing I made it to the summit of An Stuc in under three hours.

The return walk was hampered by getting myself on a very steep section of the west side of Ben Lawers. Once or twice I had to backtrack and took a couple of falls, one an undignified slide on my bottom. Cutting between Beinn Ghlas and Meall Corranaich I started to make good progress again and with the better paths, shared with visitors to the Ben Lawers National Nature Reserve, I made good progress.

Passing many people walking up I was struck by how many gave me a second glance. Checking my nose, trousers, actually anything where embarrassment might lie I couldn't fathom the interest. Then a chap, in full kit and trekking poles, stopped me and asked about the conditions on the tops. I now understood – he looked as out of place as I did. The typical walkers I was encountering were just out for a stroll from an ever-filling car park. The vision of me thundering towards them with a bright Gore-Tex jacket, over trousers, full yeti gaiters, trekking poles and a rucksack must have been quite intimidating. No wonder they all got out of my way.

I completed the walk in under five hours which gave me a leisurely drive home.

NHS Stitch Up

A few fast and furious days were spent catching up at home, including the pre-operative examination. All went well save for a conversation with the hospital sister. "So you need to tick this box," she explained, "and sign to say you will accept day surgery."

"And if I don't want day surgery?"

"Well it is up to you but you will need a hospital bed. That could be eighteen months."

"Okay, day surgery it is. How long will the recovery be?"

"Four to six weeks."

"Can they not stitch both sides at the same time?"

"Not in day surgery, you'd have to stay in for both at the same time."

"And that'd be eighteen months."

"Yes."

"So I am going to have to have two lots of four to six weeks recovery time instead of one lot if I wait eighteen months?"

"Yes, just sign here, Mr Smith."

I realised I missed the purity of being away from the demands of modern life. I longed for just the car full of gear to worry about. Of course until I set off back to Scotland on the Sunday where I immediately felt very homesick.

The drive started to take its toll on my ageing Toyota, its thirst for oil continued along with a petrol leak making refuelling an art form. I have no complaints, he is remarkably well-behaved for a teenager.

I made a one-night stop in Newtonmore before the drive over to Torridon Youth Hostel taking in Am Faochagach on the way. What was meant to be a straightforward Munro was extended by my failure to cross the Abhainn a' Gharbhrain river which connects Loch a' Gharbhrain to Loch Glascarnoch. After some hour of prospecting up and down I walked to the north side of Loch a' Gharbhrain and crossed the two rivers feeding it, wading in one place.

A long pull up in a north-easterly direction took me onto a misty windswept ridge which, after some three hours of walking, led to the summit. The descent was difficult as the wind, a determined enemy, strengthened causing a vacuum effect in my nostrils reconfirming how sore they still were after my recent cold.

The drive to Torridon reminded me of how depressing the north-west of Scotland can feel, single track 'A' roads, sparse population and shops no bigger than your front room gave me an eerie sense of being alone.

Setting eyes on Torridon Youth Hostel didn't help matters, a grey complex of 1960's style purpose built in an era of stark functionality. But then we had The Beatles, The 1966 World Cup, Formula One success etc. Britain was riding high so there was no need to build nice buildings as we got our kicks elsewhere. Trouble is the buildings are the things that survive.

It reminded me of a university campus, an idea soon supported by being billeted in the same dorm as a group from Durham University. All fresh faces and a slant on original humour. I was tempted to ask if they studied with The Pink Panther but figured they'd already have heard the joke or not know who The Pink Panther was, being, like myself, another relic from the sixties.

I skulked about all evening, eavesdropping on the enlarged group of students take on the forthcoming general election. Sadly I could remember myself believing I too once had all the answers. If only they'd do it *my* way. Now I realise I am just one very small cog in a very big machine and the best anybody can hope for is a life that works for oneself. Changing the world is a bit tough. The group of experts droned on and reminded me opinions are like bottoms, everybody has one but nobody wants to listen to yours.

Tuesday June the 5th I made an early start, trying not to wake the hungover students who, given their due, had failed to wake me when they went to bed the previous evening. Making my breakfast, amongst the empty beer cans and wine bottles and avoiding knocking over the trophy of a Charles Kennedy sign, I reflected who has got it sussed. The Durham Uni group, life still all ahead of them but not yet on their true path or me, life mapped out but taking the mick out of a bunch of students.

I made the short drive west to the Coire Mhic Nobuil Bridge car park and sat for a while as the rain pattered on my car's roof and ran down the windscreen. I had the newly promoted Tom na Gruagaich and Sgurr Mor to bag which form the greater mountain of Beinn Alligin. I finally got motivated at around 08:30, donned my kit and got out the car.

I picked off the Munros after two hours twenty and three and half hours respectively. It was all in total mist, depriving me of a view of one of Scotland's best mountains. I was glad of their popularity as there were good paths to follow.

Divided Munros

Determined to make full use of my stay at Torridon I next tackled the two Munros of Liathach. Making an early exit, avoiding disturbing the hung over students by changing in the corridor, I was walking at 06:50, plodding my way up a good path to the ridge

276

and final ascent to Spidean a'Choire Leith where I experienced sunshine, rain, hail then snow in a matter of a few minutes. British weather forecasters describe this as 'changeable'.

The snow obscured the path which made navigation both slippery and less obvious and as I sat on the summit I determined I had three choices: take in the exposed ridge to the second Munro, return and drive to the other end of the ridge or return and take the rest of the day off. In the end I set myself a target that if I could reach the car by noon I'd tackle the second.

Sitting in my car at eleven minutes to midday I cursed my speed – I had to do it now. After a short drive west I was walking again, first over steep heather-clad slopes then steep scree leading to the awesome sandstone brute of Mullach an Rathain. My pace dropped as I completed my day of 6700 feet of ascent making for a slow return through the rough terrain and sporadic rain. On a few occasions tiredness had me tripping and falling to the ground.

June the 7th brought election day. Having not sorted out a postal vote I was unable to contribute and instead decided to tackle the last two remaining Munros within easy reach of Torridon Youth Hostel.

My body felt weary so it wasn't until 08:30 that I set off along the Coire Dubh Mor track. With my head down I plodded against the terrain and fatigue. Looking to my left I could see the upper reaches of Liathach, which I climbed the previous day, were now being dusted with snow. This gave me warning of what to expect on today's pair of Munros on the broader mountain of Beinn Eighe.

The route was interesting, taking a low traverse around Sail Mhor, followed by a short pull to the small loch nestling beneath a triple buttress. From here I made a scree-ridden climb to the ridge leading to Ruadh-stac Mor. On the ridge the weather deteriorated, strong wind, hail then snow, ripped into me and stung my face. Visibility was poor and frequent references to the map were accompanied by a need to wipe the snow away. Finally, after a slow four and half hours, I reached the summit – dull compared with the dramatic ascent past the loch and the buttresses.

From the summit I had a few navigational challenges to negotiate the spurred ridge round to Spidean Coire nan Clach. Only by close map and compass work, and the brief revelations provided by moving cloud, did I find my way. The final summit was a tease, a trig point marked only the first rise and a semi-scramble over a windswept ridge finally took me to the high point and my 233rd Munro. I descended by a stalkers path and reached the single track A896 about a mile and a half east of my car, wet and windswept.

Restrictions

For my fiftieth Munro of this trip, I elected to take in Maol Chean-dearg, necessitating a shift in accommodation to the independent hostel at Achnashellach. My plans were soon thrown into disarray with a foot and mouth disease 'Keep Out' sign. Given the route went very close to a farm house, I figured, despite the sign now possibly being illegal, caution was a better approach – the possibility of being faced with a shot gun tends to override any concept of right or wrong.

Instead I drove into Lochcarron, did some shopping, filled the leaky petrol tank and heaved a sigh of relief when I realised the wet forecourt hid the spilt fuel. Planning the remaining Munros now had a new factor, reducing the miles driven to keep the car going.

Returning to the start of the walk to do Maol Chean-dearg. the signs hadn't changed, nor had my hesitation. Figuring perhaps

I could tackle it from an alternative approach I altered plans and did Moruisg and Sgurr nan Ceannaichean. These were very straightforward and my fitness allowed them to be completed in five and a half hours.

Independent Munroing

I arrived at Gerry's Independent Hostel with mixed feelings. Unlike the Scottish Youth Hostel Association the independents are all owner run and, consequently, the rules differ between each hostel.

When I phoned to make the booking, Gerry had sounded very precise and I worried if he might be a man of many rules. And, to a degree, he was. Insistent on disinfecting all footwear and notes pinned up all over the place put me ill at ease. Being shy and quiet by nature, I often find I'm a magnet for picky bastards who select me as a victim to bolster up their own personality defects. Not I am complaining of course.

However, I soon warmed to Gerry as it was quite clear he just wanted to lay down the ground rules and then leave me to be. A lovely log fire warmed the funky common room. An array of old furniture, wooden floors and faded elegance relaxed me and I decided I was going to like it here. A survey of the common room walls brought in grossly out of date calendars, posters for events long passed by and a letter pinned to the wall, addressed to Gerry, dated 1980.

During the evening, fellow guests arrived and we sat chatting.

"Have you been in the loo yet?" asked a chap from Glasgow.

"No," I replied while pondering the ramifications of my answer.

"The teeth on the wall."

"I saw those too," answered another chap.

"Are they human?" I asked.

"No, look like sheep or something."

"How are they stuck to the wall?" asked another.

This gave me such a good opening. "Gum," I replied.

"It is going to be a long night," replied a Liverpudlian chap who'd earlier already fallen foul to my sense of humour.

Gerry's Independent Hostel

On inspecting the loo, I realised Gerry was quite a modern artist, making shapes, set into the wall, out of relics such as locks, bones, magnifying glasses and shells. And of course, teeth. Not that I was concerned but my eyes did fall on a phallus made from two round pebbles set either side a pistol-shaped one with a mushroom-shaped pebble tacked on the end.

On Saturday June the 9th I started from Achnashellach Station and walked through the forest then sluggishly ascended the south-east ridge of Beinn Liath Mhor. At this point the weather improved and the ridge, wide enough for enjoyment but narrow enough to spark those 'on top of the world feelings' gave me a panoramic view of the mountains, showing off the ridges of Beinn Alligin, Liathach and Beinn Eighe. These were all Munros I'd barely got a glimpse of when climbing them over the previous week.

After nearly four hours I reached the summit of Beinn Liath Mhor and the slippery scramble down to the small lochs that head the pass through from Achnashellach to Torridon. As I reached the head of the pass I met a lady, sat looking out towards the north-west.

"Hello," I called as I approached her from behind.

"Oh hi," she replied, half turning towards me.

It wasn't a good day for shy people. We stumbled out a conversation and soon decided although we both had empathy with the surroundings our most common feature, of both being introverts, was stalling the conversation a bit.

Bidding farewells I climbed the north side of Sgorr Ruadh, a scramble over rock and rubble, reaching the peak in just under six hours from the start. A long descent was then required, passing the small lochs, fording the River Lair and a return to my car where I gave away a selection of chocolate bars to a bunch of starving students who'd been out in the hills for three days and totally underestimated the amount of food they needed.

Sunday became a much needed day off which I spent cleaning kit and fabricating a repair to one of my trekking poles using the limited contents of my car's toolbox. A leisurely trip into Lochcarron took in lunch and shopping for provisions.

Back at Gerry's hostel I spent a few hours relaxing in the common room, alone until interrupted by a minor commotion outside terminated by the opening of the common room door.

"Hello, how much is it to stay in the hostel?"

The accent was distinctly German. The figure was a strapping young German man.

"Nine pounds a night," I replied.

"Nine pounds a night. But we have, how you say it, a youth

hostel discount card."

"This isn't a youth hostel," I replied in what I hoped was a helpful voice.

"But it says on the map it is a hostel."

These Germans were sticklers.

"Not a youth hostel, it is a private hostel."

With that the spokesman disappeared. I sensed, heard and saw much movement about the outside. The door then swung open again and there appeared a second appointed spokesman.

"You are Gerry?" he asked.

"No, English," I replied.

"No, are you Gerry?"

"Oh, I see. No, just a guest," I replied while attempting to maintain composure.

"I see."

And with that the door shut.

Fifteen minutes later the door opened again and the original spokesman had regained his position.

"How do we book in eight people?"

"The dormitory is through there, just grab a bed and Gerry will see you later."

With that the group of eight German students, who'd been out in the hills for three nights, piled in and took bunks. I was glad of the company; the place was feeling a bit lonely and I certainly didn't want to have to explain to Gerry I let eight Germans escape.

On Gerry's appearance, he gleefully checked them in – foot and mouth had hit his business hard. I expected some youthful resistance to his rules. But they loved it. Each rule they repeated back to him to ensure they'd got it right. I hid behind my book and enjoyed the warmth from the log fire. The Germans settled around me and began to talk. With my German being limited to 'Hände hoch' and 'schnell' I switched off and only tuned in when I made

282

out a familiar English phrase.

"Ben Nevis?"

Five hands went up.

"Whisky Distillery?"

The other three hands joined them. I started to laugh, not just from the organised approach, the preference of whisky over climbing Ben Nevis but also the comparison with the *Dad's Army* episode entitled 'The Deadly Attachment' where Private Walker, in an attempt to buy fish and chips for a captured U-Boat crew, is met by a continued show of hands for choices such as salt, vinegar and cod.

"You understand German then," said the second spokesman, directing his voice towards me. "We didn't realise."

"Well, no."

"But you laughed."

"Ben Nevis? Five hands go up, Whisky Distillery all eight of you raise your hands, it didn't take a lot of working out."

"Oh, I see," he replied and they all politely laughed.

Slipping off to sleep, with my belly containing some of their whisky they'd kindly shared with me, I reflected I was indeed now in a hostel full of Gerrys.

An early start, around 06:20, saw me off to the ridge to take in Sgurr Choinnich, Sgurr a'Chaorachain and the very remote and lonely Maoile Lunndaidh. On the first bit of climbing I reflected how much my navigation had improved. Pleased with myself, I missed the summit and promptly marched south towards Loch Monar. On realising my mistake I re-ascended then close navigated the ridge to the derelict trig point of the second Munro. Then came a further three hours of having to mark off every dip and rise in the ridge as the cloud only gave moments of visibility, teasing my eyes away from the map.

From Maoile Lunndaidh I set off north into Gleann Fhiodhaig to pick up the track back to the start. From this height I could make out a ruin and the ancient layout of fields. I detoured to visit the ruin and stood amongst what most have played host to many families until the clearances. I felt sad for the people who were probably evicted from their way of life and ended up on a boat to Canada.

I passed Glenuaig Lodge and a pair of graves where a family were buried. I then took the long walk out, resisting the temptation to make use of a parked- up mountain bike.

At the end of the walk, after nearly twelve hours and twenty miles, the mountain bike, and rider, zipped passed me. I reflected my bike would have been useful for quite a few of the last hundred Munros, but alas the hernias prevented me from lifting it on and off the roof of my car.

Tuesday June 12th brought in another epic walk covering some eighteen miles and 5200 feet of ascent. Suffering from another poor night of sleep I was walking at just after 06:15, taking the path through Achnashellach Forest I'd followed the previous day. I spent a weary three hours placing one foot in front of the other until I pulled myself up onto the Bealach Bhearnais. Only here did the walk split from that of the previous day.

An ascent of Beinn Tharsuinn (a Corbett) brought into sight the first Munro of the pair I was trying to take in today, Bidein a'Choire Sheasgaich. I had to lose a lot of height to make it to the outer reaches of its cliff walls. Not fancying these, I traversed round towards Coire Seasgach. From here I spied a way through and set off up tiring slopes reaching steep ground where I had to go on all fours, and cling to tufts of grass, to pull myself onto a plateau like area below the summit.

I now felt drained. Sitting by a stream I forced as much

food down as I could and drank ample water. Setting off again, I flirted with exhaustion. This was turning out to be two twelve-hour-days back to back and my body was screaming at me. I slowed my pace and used a technique of just concentrating on half steps – one foot forward and then bringing the other half way in front of that. It takes the weight off the body, very slow but it does work.

At the summit I feasted again before setting off towards Lurg Mhor which I reached in just over another hour – fortunately I had the foresight to ignore the grid reference in Cameron McNeish's *Munro Almanac* guidebook which is a mere 10km to the east. Here I was seven hours into the walk and at the furthest point. Descending to the lowest point between the two Munros I fancied I could pick a route back which involved a drop down to the Allt Bealach Crudhain stream that feeds Loch Monar. A painful five hours of walking out then followed only aided by the fantastically clear views I'd had all day.

Into the Wilds Once More

Thursday June 14th brought in Maol Chean-dearg, my final Munro, in the Achnashellach area and a shift in accommodation from Gerry's hostel to Glen Affric Youth Hostel.

This single Munro was the one I'd blown out a few days previously due to the foot and mouth warning signs. Having got some useful information from Gerry I approached from an alternative route a few hundred yards to the north-east of the closed farm.

Here I was greeted with a rare thing – a footbath that actually had disinfectant in it. Many footbaths were littering the Highlands, serving as no more than rain water butts. I can only assume these were put down by people who like to invent rules.

The notices that went with them sometimes went as far as suggesting the entire foot and mouth outbreak was due to the walkers and not the farmers.

There never was any evidence walkers spread the disease. The government's rapid closure of the countryside cost the tourism industry dearly. One hostel owner told me his takings had dropped from £1000 to £60 a week. He didn't get compensated whereas the farmers did.

I duly dipped my feet, and my trekking poles that strangely all signs neglected to mention.

The walk went well, a very nice path took me nearly to the top and I enjoyed my final glimpse of Torridon in the gloriously clear day while sitting at the interesting-shaped summit cairn, built like the rays of the sun that warmed me. The only downside was a nasty blister on my right heel which I administered to at the summit.

Back at my car I repacked my kit, drove to Glen Shiel and then made the two and a half hour slog of a walk into Glen Affric Youth Hostel.

Walking past another plane crash site, I turned the corner of the hill and saw, in the distance, Glen Affric Youth Hostel. A hostel since 1949, remote, no roads, and all that remains of the ancient hamlet of Alltbeithe. The second Munroist, Ronnie Burn, used to enjoy staying here with Angus Scott and his family in the very early part of the twentieth century. And this epitomised the changing of the countryside in Scotland as Ronnie Burn's diaries recount how he'd walk up remote glens and stay with families.

I hadn't booked a space at the hostel, the Liverpudlian chap who'd stayed at Gerry's had told me there was always room. Looking down I could see the place was swarming with many people heading towards it. As I slowly descended my heart sank – a sleep out would be no fun. After crossing the ornate bridge I plonked myself on the hostel steps and found the party were just passing through and not stopping. And these were the last people I was to see for twenty-four hours.

The hostel was empty, Beryl, the warden, was on a mission to Fort William and a note to a 'Mr Price' told him which dorm to take. I took the other dorm and spread my kit out. My breathing then started to change and I became short of breath. I spied dog hairs and an inspection of the kitchen revealed a food bowl on the floor. Leaving a note to Beryl explaining she'd an extra guest, I gathered my stuff and moved into an overspill annex, cold yet free of dog.

Starting at 06:45 I ascended into the mist. A right turn on the ridge took in An Socach and, after backtracking, I reached the mighty Sgurr nan Ceathreamhnan where the cold wind and rain chilled me. My blister and knees complained, which I dealt with while ruing, and minimising, the time bare flesh was exposed. With frozen hands, and the odd patch of snow still about, there followed a long walk out to Mullach na Dheiragain, a very remote spot in the British Isles, before the four-hour descent to the hostel and a lovely chat with Beryl the warden.

After a sound night's sleep I walked back to Glen Shiel, bumping into a chap who asked me, "Are you Steve?"

This surprised me and the explanation was he'd been staying at Glen Affric the night I arrived and he and Beryl had seen my note.

"Ah, you're Mr Price then," I said, smiling.

"Yes," he replied, underlining the remoteness of these hills.

Ratagan Again

From Glen Shiel I made a quick dash to Ratagan Youth Hostel to book in before the reception closed for the daytime. This allowed me use of the washing facilities I was aware I was in dire need of.

Route planning and kit checking, drying and cleaning absorbed the remainder of the day, followed by an appalling night's sleep due to a very loud snorer. Nick, the warden, had previously told me a story of how he once had to expel somebody for hitting a snorer in the night. Fair play I'd say, they should have built a statue to the guy and allowed the rest of us to come and worship it as a shrine.

Grumbling to myself, and feeling terrible about running over and killing a bird, I started the ascent of A' Ghlas-bheinn and Beinn Fhada, also known as Ben Attow, at just before 06:15. The initial path left my options open as which of the two Munros I could tackle first. I fancied Beinn Fhada but changed my mind when I realised the route to A' Ghlas-bheinn was easier, and from it I'd be able to spy the route up Beinn Fhada.

There were a few places where I had to do some minor bits of scrambling. At one point a rock slipped beneath my feet causing me to nose dive. I stuck my left hand out to break my fall, puncturing my palm on a sharp rock. Blood began to ooze out so I sat quietly until the pain eased and the blood clotted.

I reached the summit at 09:00 where it promptly started to snow. But I managed to enjoy this minor milestone: my 63rd Munro of 2001 beating my 1997 record by one.

I descended in my full Gore-Tex gear then took the route up Beinn Fhada, reaching it in just over a further three hours. Now there was glorious sunshine and my rucksack bulged as I shed outer garments.

I switched dorms at the youth hostel in the hope of getting a better night's sleep. All was going well until 23:15 when I was thrust into consciousness by the door being flung open, the light turned on and three bullish men determined to talk, sort out their kit as noisily as they could and get on and off the bunks at least six times each.

My mood wasn't good and at 01:00, with their snoring adding to my anger-driven insomnia, I removed myself to the common room and camped out, spread over a series of adjoining chairs. Grabbing a few hours of sleep, I woke at 04:30 and laid in waiting for the warden to open up at 07:00 so I could recover my membership card and then make the planned trip to Loch a'Bhraoin where I planned to take in three Munros: Meall a'Chrasgaidh, Sgurr nan Clach Geala and Sgurr nan Each.

Starting off in glorious sun, my mood improved and my tension was converted into pace. Passing an unusual two-storeyed ruin, with a perfectly intact boat house, I made the summit of Meall a'Chrasgaidh in two hours, after having at first mistaken a large rock for the summit cairn. To my left I could see how easily Sgurr Mor could be claimed but, although tempted, it'd have been pointless as its top can be claimed as part of another walk involving four Munros – or so I thought…

Progressing on, I claimed the second and third Munros in another hour then thirty-nine minutes respectively. I really had the bit between my teeth and decided to extend the walk to claim a total of five Munros, the additional two being Sgurr Breac and A' Chailleach.

The weather, although clouding, held and I took in some marvellous views towards Torridon. On the summit of Sgurr Breac I chatted with a chap doing what I was doing in reverse but intending to bivi out. He pointed out a path over ridge spur which meant I could later descend by a quicker route. Taking in the final Munro, at about six and a half hours from the start, I backtracked to the ridge spur and, feeling exhausted, took the easy path back to Loch a'Bhraoin where quite a collection of cars had amassed.

Without any accommodation booked I decided to camp – it looked like a nice night and I was desperate for my own company. I get this from time to time, the bullish men in the dorm had thrown me out of sorts. Despite shyness I can be sociable but all my life I have had the need for my own peace and space. My secondary school institutionally condoned bullying – being shy, a bit socially awkward, physically impaired due to the asthma and unwilling to fight was seen as a weakness. In turn this has driven me to periods of just wanting to tuck myself away and be alone. Being confronted by bullish men wasn't a good reminder and drove me to my tent where I spent a happy and peaceful evening, exhausted, yet delighted with the five Munros.

In the early hours rain lashed down hard, buffeting my waterproof tent. A few hours later I was aware of a car starting. On retiring only two cars remained, mine and a modern Skoda (the sort that starts in the rain). I can only assume bivi man, who'd directed me to the path off, had been defeated by the weather and made his way back to the preferable sanctuary of his Skoda.

Finally waking some hours later, I stuck my head out of the tent to ensure that indeed it was the Skoda that had gone and not some thief making off with my Toyota. The cloud was low, covering the four Munros which lay ahead of me to complete the Munros of the Fannich Forest: Beinn Liath Mhor Fannaich, Sgurr Mor, Meall Gorm and An Coileachan.

I made the short drive to Loch Glascarnoch and got walking just before 08:00 taking in paths along the rivers Abhainn an Torrain and Allt an Loch Sgeirich. I then branched onto the north-east slopes of the minor summit of Creag Dhubh Fannaich where rain and ferocious winds rapidly altered the priority of the day.

Gusts became so strong I frequently had to lean backwards into the southerly wind and dig my trekking poles in front of me just to remain on my feet. Between the hardest of the gusts I made slow progress, often being blown sideways, just managing to regain my footing before the next onslaught of wind and rain.

I started to look for quick exit routes, twice sheltering below piles of rock and using my trekking poles, held aloft, to test the continued ferocity of the weather. I quickly resigned myself to not completing the four Munros, but I had resolve to gain the first, Beinn Liath Mhor Fannaich. The need to revisit the ridge on another day made its gathering academic but I was determined to get something out of the day.

I forced my way on through an exposed boulder field, the wind tossing me sideways at every opportunity. I resorted to jamming my feet between rocks as I took each step, ensuring I always had one foot anchored.

I made the summit in three and a half hours from the start and took sanctuary in the north side of the cairn. Feeding myself was an effort, it took me ages to remove and undo my pack, peeling wrappers required concentration and lifting the food to my mouth was an effort.

My gaiters had been troubling me for this entire trip: the toe covers kept peeling back and required brute force from thumb and fingers to hook them back over the toe of the boot. I couldn't manage it, my energy was sapped.

Re-sealing my map case, normally a very simple operation, required a slow methodical approach. My mental capacity and coordination were slipping away. A voice from within slowly fought through until I heard its chant. At first it tried to gently wake me with a whisper, 'hypothermia'. I heard but it didn't register, it tried again, 'You are becoming hypothermic'. And again, 'Remember the posters you've seen in every youth hostel describing the symptoms'. The voice repeated itself until I lifted my head from my knees. I forced myself to think: fleece and thick gloves. I extracted them from my pack, removed my Gore-Tex jacket and then a hailstorm struck. Stinging my exposed neck I forced myself into the fleece, fumbled back into my jacket and put on the gloves. I wanted off this mountain very quickly, and the wind was only too willing to help me. The mountains shoulder no responsibility.

Forcing down more food, I figured an emergency route north would drop my height and perhaps then I'd find a path back. Each step was painful as it had been too cold to add Deep Heat to my knees. However, as I dropped height my condition improved and the weather abated.

In the distance I could see two walkers emerge on to the ridge. I headed for them, firstly to explain the situation above and secondly because it implied they'd ascended on a path. Approaching them I asked, "What route are you taking?"

"Doing the four," replied a middle-aged man dismissively. Actually I could only make out a moustache protruding from his hood. But he sounded middle-aged.

"Err, it is very windy up there," I replied. "I've turned back. Couldn't even stand up."

"We've been out in all sorts," explained his female companion intent on putting me right. "This is okay."

"It's some of the worst conditions I've experienced," I added.

There was no convincing them. They continued on, probably resolving to defy me beyond the point they'd have normally turned back.

It took another three hours to get back to my car where I sat wet, bedraggled and unhappy the mountains had, so quickly, reclaimed the bonus day they'd handed me the day before – I now rued missing out Sgurr Mor, if I'd claimed it then the remaining two, lost today, could have been claimed in a much shorter walk.

Strath Faraway

The Strathfarrar hills had been bothering me for some time. Mainly because the ridge of four Munros requires access from the private glen road which, on a good day, is only open for nine hours.

Thinking laterally, and casting my eye northwards on my map, I worked out a route in from Strathconon – twice as long but with no time restrictions. So I headed up the long Strathconon road with a view to a second night of camping. I parked up and sat in my car hoping the driving rain, pummelling the roof and smacking the windscreen, would abate. After three hours, and with the evening drawing in, I erected as much of the tent as I could within the confines of the car then threw caution to the wind (and rain), dived out and put the damned thing up. I got thoroughly soaked in the process. As it was impossible to cook, I lay in my sleeping bag and munched my way through a fruitcake.

At around 05:00 I became aware of a break in the weather – I think the silence woke me. I heated up last night's pot noodle for my breakfast and surveyed the scene: dark heavy clouds looking on. I just managed to take the tent down and sit in the car before the rains came again. A long drawn-out decision then followed but I eventually set off for the Strathfarrar hills – having driven the sixteen miles up the single track glen road the night before was a factor in the decision to give it a go.

I first passed through Inverchoran, waking every dog as I did so, before branching onto the hill tracks. I made steady progress on a tortuous route with beautiful streams and Scots pines. On exiting the forest below Creag a' Ghlastail, I was on the banks of the lovely River Orrin. Here I began to check my map – according to the Ordnance Survey there should be a bridge to my right. My heart sank. So would I if I'd tried to cross the river, wide and deep. All my efforts so far were now in jeopardy. I then looked to my left and like some old friend yelling 'Cooee' there it was, within just a few feet of where I stood! Either the Ordnance Survey got it wrong or the forest has grown. I doubt they moved the bridge.

Once safely across, I took the path alongside a tributary stream, picking my way along its eroded bank until the stream forked and I took an easterly route to try and gain Carn nan Gobhar, the first Munro of the day. I found it quite easily, after four hours from the start, and questioned whether I was indeed at the summit. Heavy cloud, rain and wind thwarted any attempt to confirm it by a view. Taking the bearing for Sgurr na Ruaidhe the terrain didn't make sense, a brief view didn't help either. Backtracking to the summit I decided to continue south and confirm if I'd indeed reached the top of Carn nan Gobhar. Finding myself descending, which didn't tally with the map, I considered if perhaps I was lost. Given the definition of lost is you don't know where you are then yes perhaps I was lost.

My plan was to bag Carn nan Gobhar, go east and get Sgurr na Ruaidhe, backtrack and retake Carn nan Gobhar then walk west and take in Sgurr a'Choire Ghlais and Sgurr Fhuar-thuill. A tortuous itinerary but the route up from Strathconon hit mid-ridge, forcing the need to backtrack.

There was another break in the cloud where I was able to make out Sgurr a'Choire Ghlais. From this I confirmed I had indeed just bagged Carn nan Gobhar. I now backtracked and worked my way towards Sgurr na Ruaidhe. Now the wind and rain hit hard and when I arrived at Sgurr na Ruaidhe, some two hours after making the ridge, I knew the third and fourth Munros, higher than the two just bagged, were for another day. This was confirmed when I turned towards them and my face was pummelled by the hail that had just been beating the back of my head. I was just able to make out the cloud whizzing around their summits.

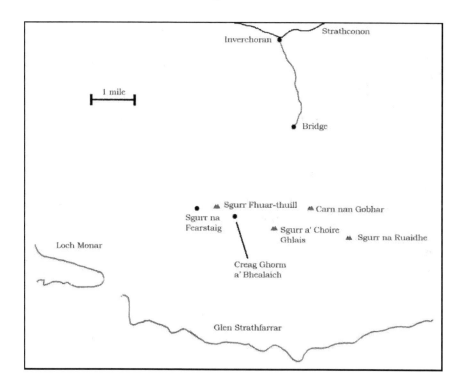

Fully realising the odds do apply to me I headed back down, taking a further three and a half hours with tired and very wet feet. Looking back towards the mountains I could see the ridge had cleared, offering a truce in their day of anger. But I made the right decision at the time and that is always the best approach in the mountains – staying put, hoping for a break, has its own risks.

When I was sitting in my car at the start of the walk I couldn't face the soggy leather boots and gaiters of the previous day and instead used clean socks and my nice dry Gore-Tex boots. Through the day I was left rueing this decision as they let water, had less grip on wet rock, and the lack of gaiters meant water flowed in over the tops. Now sat in my car at the end of the day my boots were sodden and my socks were dripping wet. I closed the socks in my car window and used the breeze from the drive back down the glen to attempt to dry them. I got some strange looks.

Now demoralised and exhausted, I drove from Strathconon to Cannich with the view to attempting the final two Munros of the ridge the next day in the nine hour window Strathfarrar is open.

Arriving at the locked gate at 08:45, fifteen minutes before it was due to open, the gatekeeper appeared and, after I'd sprayed the underside of my car with disinfectant, I was allowed through.

After a thirteen mile drive up the glen I was walking before 09:45, determined to make good progress through the cloud and rain to avoid any problems with the nine hour time slot. After just over two hours of following a good path, I was on the ridge and navigated myself through Sgurr Fhuar-thuill, the minor top of Creag Ghorm a'Bhealaich and over to the second Munro of the day, Sgurr a'Choire Ghlais where a double summit cairn and a trig point left me in no doubt of my location.

Returning the same route, over the minor top I met a late middle-aged couple who, though clearly experienced walkers, were a bit uncertain of their location.

"Where do you think we are?" they asked.

I pointed to the map. "Just west of Creag Ghorm a'Bhealaich."

Then followed a few moments of them trying to convince me I was still west of the first Munro. I was cautious in being forthright about my location, of course I could have been wrong myself.

"Well it took me an hour between the two Munros on my way east, and I have only been walking forty-two minutes back."

"You've probably covered more ground than you think," added the lady while the guy nodded sagely and asked, "We are going east aren't we? We've left the compass in the car."

As I continued west I re-encountered Sgurr Fhuar-thuill,

thus proving me correct about my whereabouts. I then descended further west and, after a bit of confusion about the route through the socked in cloud, reached the original entry point of the ridge. For the hell of it I continued east and took in the minor top of Sgurr na Fearstaig. Tops are always optional when Munro bagging, just outlying rises of the same mountain and I do them if they are close by and there is time, they aren't part of being a Munroist.

Heading back east, to the ridge entry point, I had a thought: without a compass that couple may have made a mistake when coming off Sgurr Fhuar-thuill as I'd required mine to keep me on track. Re-ascending I encountered them, clearly having navigated it successfully. I could see they were split between a certain level of gratitude for my concern and a certain level of embarrassment for their original mistake of their whereabouts. As I said goodbye they hung back until I'd got some distance away from them.

Back at my car in a total of six hours I was pleased to be well within time but reflected the entire ridge and the drive in and out would have been a bit tight for nine hours.

A one-night stay at Loch Lochy Youth Hostel was followed by a day of preparation for the arrival of my old work colleague and friend, John Pennifold, on the overnight Caledonian Sleeper from London Euston to Fort William. The preparations involved bagging up food for an intended seven days in the wilds of The Fisherfields and Knoydart.

I also made a decision my last Munro would be on July the 21st. I had been aiming for the 14th but I was starting to realise people needed to know an exact date to enable them to make plans to come and join me.

At 09:43 on Saturday June 23rd the sleeper arrived bang on time at Fort William. A drive north, with a stop for lunch, brought us to

Dundonnell. A good hour then followed of distributing kit between our two packs in the blazing heat.

I'd been worried about John's arrival, having completed all the Munros and three of the seven highest continental mountains in the world, I was concerned he might take over a bit. But all was fine as kit and plans were amicably spread around.

The three-hour walk into Shenavall bothy was long, hot and very arduous. John informed me he'd been training by carrying his pack, full of National Geographic, around the streets near his house.

"You bastard," I whispered as he left me standing.

A good track became a path and I struggled with the ascents in the heat and was relieved when the bothy finally came into view, set back and nestled into the mountains with a loch some mile or so before it. I was glad to shed the pack as my left hernia was very uncomfortable and I feared I'd perhaps made it worse.

The bothy had the traditional crop of stinging nettles alongside it. Stinging nettles and bothies are synonymous, urine has a high degree of nitrate – nettles favourite nutrient. But I assume some equilibrium is achieved when the nettles grow too high, catching out anybody answering a night-time call of nature.

John wanted to camp in preference to sleeping in the bothy. As it was a nice night and he offered to put the tent up and confirmed he didn't snore, I readily accepted.

My mind was in neutral when John called, "I'll just show you how to assemble and light the stove."

My heart sank. I had managed to get away without erecting the tent and was hoping a lit stove would duly follow. Twenty minutes later, with John having forgotten how it fitted together, I finally managed to assemble it after digging deep in the recesses of my memory of how Barbara's stove, a similar model, went together.

John then showed me how to use his digital video camera, which was interesting and I was able to put the newfound skill to use when he went off for a number two. Zooming in from a distance I gave a running commentary as I recorded him going from rock to rock looking for a suitable pitch, only stopping the camera when decency required.

We enjoyed the late evening as walkers emerged from the mountains, some as late as 21:30, and headed for their tents or the bothy. John and I reflected on how long through the day this was and whether it was sensible. We didn't know that twenty-five and a half hours later two wet and very tired figures would emerge from the gloom and the rain, making their way back to their own tent.

The morning started with breakfast, a couple of comments about my choice of food, and a departure shortly before 07:30. A river crossing took us to the foot of Beinn a'Chlaidheimh and a three-hour slog up a very steep hillside in blistering heat. John commented on my use of walking poles, evidently he hated them with vengeance. My style of taking steps was also spared no mercy.

A further two hours of a broad ridge took us to Sgurr Ban and the views just got better and better. The trekking poles continued to take a hammering to a point where I fancied wrapping them around John's neck. At the summit a third walker joined us with poles.

"Poles useful?" I enquired.

"Ah yes," replied the holder and then gave a long list of their pluses – much the same list as I'd spent the last five hours repeating to John, but from a new mouth some silence was bought.

It only took another hour to gain Mullach Coire Mhic Fhearchair and then a change of direction to the west took in Beinn Tarsuinn after a further one and a half hours. By this time my speed had improved and John was beginning to tire. A return to the tent was possible but we both agreed to go on and take in the final two Munros of the Fisherfield's horseshoe: A' Mhaighdean and Ruadh Stac Mor. By this time I was flying and I left John, and his constantly exploding bottom, behind me making the summit just before 18:30 and the final summit, after some navigation I wouldn't have cared for in the mist, at about 19:30.

Here we picked the fastest descent route we could but, with John now faster again, it still took us a further three and a half hours of route marching, with rain for the last hour, to get back to the tent. Too wet to cook outside we made use of the bothy to make our supper.

After a long lie-in, and drying and packing our kit in the sun, we set off at 11:00 walking back towards the car. I struggled with the weight of my pack and I was grateful when, after two hours, we reached the high point of the path. Here I shed half my pack's contents into my plastic bivi bag, dumped it by a small loch and set forth for Sgurr Fiona, the first Munro of the greater mountain known as An Teallach.

The weather was good to us. John tried again to humiliate me with my use of trekking poles but was starting to get the hint he was needling me when I suggested, "John I have an excellent idea for a cure for your rotten backside."

"What is that?"

"Well I have two ideas, one I plug it with a trekking pole, or two we claim a government grant to connect it up as a renewable energy resource."

Sgurr Fiona yielded at 16:00 and there then followed a walk traversing the magnificent pinnacles which loop around Loch Toll an Lochain with its magnificent chutes, sandstone and quartz buttresses and repeating triangular effects.

As John broke for another video stop, breaking wind at the

same time, I walked on and met a woman. We got chatting and enthused about the beauty of the mountain and I couldn't help but notice how beautiful she was. I explained I'd been walking for seven weeks and she said some nice words about my project. In awe of the mountain we fell silent. When John reappeared she made to leave.

"Nice to meet you," I said.

"You too," she quietly replied.

As she departed John raised his eyebrows and revealed his sensitive side. "Would you have given her one then, Steve?"

"Don't," I replied.

Carrying on the ascent we made Bidein a'Ghlas Thuill and then a sharp descent to Loch Toll an Lochain, disturbing a herd of wild mountain goats as we did so. We then returned to our kit then back to the car.

Knoydart

We had a meal in a hotel in Dundonnell but elected, at £60 each per night, to give the bed and breakfast a miss. Instead we drove to the Aultguish Inn, arriving at 22:30, where bed and breakfast was just £16 each.

John, being quite pale skinned, had been viciously attacked by biting insects and consequently spent ages in the bathroom removing ticks. Being dark skinned I tend to be spared their quest for blood. Finally exiting from the ensuite he announced, "Think I've got them all, can you just check I got them all out of my arse?"

"Oh no," I replied.

"Won't take a second."

And indeed when he dropped his pyjama trousers my glance was so brief it didn't take a second. "None there," I announced.

"One of the bastards got the end of my penis."

"No way, John, no way."

After a night where John's ability to fart found new levels, we drove to Kinloch Hourn and the four-hour slog of a walk to Barrisdale, a remote, road-free hamlet of a few houses on the Knoydart peninsula and the best bothy I have ever visited – it had a flushing loo.

Starting just after 07:15, on what was my 36th birthday, we followed the path then the north-east ridge to the summit of Ladhar Bheinn. It took just over four hours and I found the going tough with the ground feeling like glue on the soles of my boots.

John, testing me with many questions to which I didn't know the answer, was also a dent to my morale. I can only assume the pile of National Geographic he'd previously carried in his rucksack were well thumbed.

Having already completed the Munros this was a repeat for John. "I am not sure what path me and Peter took last time," he said.

"All we have to do is look for the bits of paper with 'help me I am stuck in a quiz show' written on them," I replied.

"Oh, I thought you were enjoying it," he replied, sounding hurt.

I regretted my remark. Although John, over the week, made many critical comments (on my walking style, how I blew my nose, my driving style, the height of my car head restraints, my use of trekking poles, how I buckled my rucksack, my diet, how I put food into my mouth) he is a very kind, interesting, knowledgeable and considerate man with infinite patience. We got over it and I was spared any further questions.

Also I have John to thank for getting me into the Munros. He was the work colleague, mentioned in the preface to this book, who first told me about them.

At the summit of Ladhar Bheinn we rested and John's prediction of a thunderstorm materialised.

The following day, June 28th, was a miserable and wet affair. Again starting at just after 07:15 we ascended the stalkers path to Mam Barrisdale and followed the ridge, in wind and rain, to Luinne Bheinn then the intricate ridge around to Meall Buidhe arriving some five and a half hours after the start.

Unable to see, we descended further south to the safety of a long path back to Mam Barrisdale and then the bothy. The entire walk took eleven hours and we appreciated a drying wind in the evening but not the downpour on the walk back to the car the following day.

The extended dangers of Munro bagging became apparent on the drive out along the narrow roads. It all nearly came to a sharp end when the Post Bus hurled itself at us at high speed. Pulling my car to a halt, John and I had a few moments of terror as the bus skidded across the road and parked itself nose first in a ditch. We got out to help but it soon became obvious we weren't going to be able to help push it out. It also became obvious my left hernia wasn't prepared to allow extracting vehicles from ditches to be part of this trip – I was made to pay for it with a deep ache in my lower abdomen over the next few hours.

Homing In

Having dropped John at Fort William Station on the Friday evening I made my way to Glen Nevis Youth Hostel for a three night stay to take in the Grey Corries and Aonach Beag, leaving its neighbour, Aonach Mor, for July the 21st as my final Munro.

I elected to make Aonach Mor my final Munro because it's over 4000 feet but has a gondola cable car to a half-way restaurant, reducing the climb for anybody wanting to accompany me. I, of course, would have to start from the bottom.

My activities of the evening included (i) trying to persuade a sixteen-year-old lad, who'd just climbed Ben Nevis, that lager wasn't the best way to re-hydrate while making excursions to refill his water bottle and purchase a Mars bar to up his sugar levels, and (ii) miserably trying to explain to a Polish mathematician why we have separate hot and cold taps in the UK and not a simple mixer like the rest of the world. I think I struggled when trying to justify it was okay for one tap to give first degree burns while the other dished out a dose of hypothermia.

Sat in my car on the last day of June at the head of Glen Nevis I surveyed the scene: just after 08:00 and a huge downpour with rain hammering on the roof of the car. With just fifteen Munros to go and twenty-two days to do them in I didn't feel the need to get out and get going.

This was my second turn at being under motivated this morning: at breakfast I'd been happily engaged in conversation with my Polish friend until he asked, "Please can you explain Armitage Shanks business one more time?"

Shortly before 09:30 there was a gap in the weather and I made a start with the aim of doing Aonach Beag and the two Munros, of the four, on the west of the Grey Corries. Quickly I reviewed my plans and decided to miss out Aonach Beag and instead do all four Munros on the Grey Corries.

I started slowly, reaching Sgurr Choinnich Mor in just over three and a half hours with a body not in full agreement with my mental plans. Through the mist the only thing of interest was a flattened patch of grass where I assumed a deer had slept the previous night.

After a further hour, l I reached Stob Coire an Laoigh where I ate and took paracetamol for my throat and Ibuprofen for my knees. Clearing weather saw me flying across the longest section of the ridge. At one stage I found myself running, barely able to take note of the quartz lines in the rock which looked like the markings on a badminton court.

With the weather clear and views all around, I took my eyes off the map and made what I thought was the summit in exactly an hour. But then I became concerned, in the last few minutes the mist had come down and I was now unsure if I was truly at the summit or some top on the approach. I tried the GPS but, with low batteries, it gave me an inconclusive reference. I carried on along the ridge and, by referring to the map, it became clear I'd reached the summit of Stob Choire Claurigh.

Backtracking, I descended the southerly route and the sharp rise to Stob Ban, arriving at just after 17:00. It now dawned on me I was a long away from the car. Increasing my pace I dropped into the glen and started to power walk it back. Power walking? What on earth is that? Well I didn't know myself until this evening but essentially it means you use the brain to move the legs far faster than the subconscious, and the body, would deem sensible.

This higher use of my brain set my chatterbox off, something that had been going from time to time on this last one hundred Munros stint. The chatterbox is a kind of affectionate term for that bit of the brain which mulls things over and has all those pretend arguments with people. The arguments you originally lost outright but when nobody is around you win. The case was put across coherently and the other party sat there, nodding and agreeing with every point and conceded you had been right all along.

The wind clipped my face and brought me back to the reality of the world I'd decided to spend my summer in. Pushing myself on up the lonely glen, I past the ruin of Steall and the waterfalls. I got back to the car, three and a half hours since the last summit, a damp and bedraggled figure.

The following day I took in Aonach Beag. Being worried about accidentally bagging Aonach Mor, planned for my final Munro, I hit the ridge to its south-east and ascended the two minor tops (Sgurr a'Bhuic Stob and Choire Bhealach) before approaching, in mist and rain, what I hoped was Aonach Beag. Still concerned of wandering too far and ruining my final Munro plans, I switched on my GPS. After many minutes it asked me to 'Select Country'. Well pardon me, this little beast cost me the best part of £200 – even with my navigation I know what bloody country I am in. I selected UK, Scotland (I was in a helpful mood) and, with a bit more ascent to the ridge, it finally conceded my location, safely saying Aonach Beag was just in front of me.

From the top I descended back towards the ruin of Steall, at the head of Glen Nevis, neglecting Deep Heat and Ibuprofen for my knees. I was soon made to pay for it with pain and stiffening forcing a stop for medication.

Everything Abandoned

Monday July the 2nd brought another rest day and a move in location to the Aultguish Inn to tackle the remainder of the Fannichs and Ullapool hills. Blue skies and warm weather tempted my Beach Boys CD from its cover for the sticky three-hour drive with every mountain showing off its summit. This was only the second perfect day for a month and both of them on enforced logistical rest days – I think I'm destined to be a loser where the weather is concerned.

I had a frightening moment on the drive as I witnessed the seemingly traditional sight of a Post Bus mounting the pavement while trying to enter a petrol station. A second glance revealed the driver was the self-same chap who'd nearly taken John and I out the previous Friday. I made a mental note never to use a Post Bus and to buy a car with air bags before I head anywhere north of Fort William again.

On Tuesday July the 3rd I had another go at Seana Bhraigh, a Munro Ady Glover and I'd abandoned in 1997 during a sixteen-hour epic adventure. Back then, with a lack of features and constant ascents and descents through peat bogs, we'd found it difficult to follow the map.

In my log I'd put 'Sunny day only' against Seana Bhraigh as I realised my best chance of the summit was to be able to see it. Letting myself out of the hotel at just after 06:00 I was walking at about 06:45, grateful for the cloud being high. All was going well as I ascended via Inverlael Forest then the long gentle slopes until the path petered out just beyond the Coire an Lochain Sgeirich whereupon I was in thick mist.

Taking an easterly bearing, I paced myself until I hit the stream joining Loch a'Chadha Dheirg. From here things got very boggy with constant backtracking to find a route that didn't require sinking up to my knees in filthy peat-ridden water. Actually sinking to my knees was likely, but this time out of tiredness – with only ten Munros left I'd passed through a psychological barrier and I was all for slowing my pace.

In this boggy area I disturbed numerous frogs – like the deer it is an animal I take great pleasure from seeing. With each footstep carefully placed, frogs leapt in all directions – big ones, small ones and medium sized ones. I made a point of apologising to each one for my intrusion. Like the male deer (who role in their own urine) the male frog has a curious mating habit which you kind of wonder about. After selecting a partner he jumps on her and hangs on for all his worth, sometimes for days. Now, not wishing to downplay his passion to reproduce, there have been recorded instances of the female expiring and the male still hanging on to her decaying corpse. Personally I'd have noticed.

On reaching the loch I continued east, following a feeder stream from a higher loch where I took a compass bearing direct for Seana Bhraigh. After walking for some time I got an eerie feeling I didn't know where I was. The GPS proved inconclusive – it had me over the edge of one of the cliffs protecting Seana Bhraigh, and I simply couldn't recall making a fatal fall.

Munching some lunch I pondered the situation and decided I'd head south-east as the ground looked as if it rose that way. And indeed it did and I reached a cairn at 12:00. But I wasn't convinced, with visibility down to just a few feet I reckoned this was the 906m spot height on the map and not the 927m (3041 feet) of Seana Bhraigh. A close study of the map showed if I went east and there was a cliff it'd be the Munro, otherwise the 906m top. I soon was descending over easy ground so I turned back and regained the cairn knowing it now to be the 906m point. Knowing my exact location allowed me to take a bearing directly for Seana Bhraigh.

After about twenty minutes I was nowhere again, the ground began to drop in front of me and to my left. I guessed I must have hit its south-west flank so went north-east and found the ground rising and with relief made the summit at just after 12:30.

The slog of a walk back to the car took over four hours, but I was glad Seana Bhraigh was now bagged, it'd been playing on my mind for a while. I know a bad workman blames his tools but I wondered if there was some inaccuracy in the Ordnance Survey map. I do make navigational errors but to mess this mountain up in 1997 to the point of being on the wrong summit and then to have so many troubles today left me wondering. An alternative piece of equipment to blame, other than myself, was my compass. But normally compasses are accurate but I did think, given I had three with me, I should have checked them all to see if one was right, one was wrong and the third would tell me which was which.

I woke at 04:30 on July the 4th to a throbbing right toe, a long term ingrowing nail problem had re-materialised and it was swollen and puffy. With just about enough space to spare in my boots I was walking just after 06:15 to take in the three Munros left in the Fannichs I'd previously abandoned due to the severe wind. The shortest route was from the Loch Glascarnoch side but I fancied the good stalkers path from the Loch a'Bhraoin side.

In thick cloud I made slow progress along the track, branching at a stream to ascend to the low point between the previously two bagged Munros of Meall a'Chrasgaidh and Sgurr nan Clach Geala. I was hoping to navigate to the small lochain there and then take in the minor top of Carn na Criche before the final ascent to the days first Munro, Sgurr Mor.

Navigating to high lochains is always difficult due to being unable to see them until you're above them – anything else would defy the laws of physics. I duly made a mess of things and after some back and forth, I suddenly found myself ascending eastwards. This turned out to be a stroke of luck as a check with the map indicated this could only be in the direction of Carn na Criche. Thankful a navigational error had, for once, actually helped me, I took in this top then Sgurr Mor at just under four hours from the start.

Descending I made another navigational error and found myself drifting towards the east ridge, soon correcting I dropped down the south ridge and navigated the final two Munros, Meall Gorm and An Coileachan in a total of just over six hours.

The route back was identical to the route in and just half an hour shorter – it's often the case that descents are only slightly less than ascents.

Wearily I opened the car up and slumped in. Except for a brief few moments there was mist all day, my left hernia was killing me, my big toe nail was mercilessly macheting its way down to the bone and to add insult to injury my right shoulder was also having a grumbling day with muscular discomfort. However, this walk did complete all the Munros I'd ever abandoned and all those remaining were new territory.

The Last Few

Another bad night's sleep had me awake at 04:30 with light pouring in through the thin curtains of my hotel room at the Aultguish Inn. Aching all over, and unable to get my body motivated, I lay in the bath for an hour, then read for a bit and was first down for breakfast at 08:00.

Feeling better for hot food, I packed up my car and drove across to Incheril (near Kinlochewe) for the ascent of Slioch. I got walking before 09:30, initially losing my way through the marshy ground on the approach to Loch Maree. Once back on course I made quick progress, following paths. I crossed the Abhainn an Fhasaigh then north followed by the north-west ascent, in total mist.

The path helped my navigation which had become a bit rusty over the last few days. But I couldn't explain my pace, why this much faster? Then I thought about all the other times I'd been quick and realised a pattern – all were after drives of at least an hour. Perhaps the delay allowed the energy from breakfast to kick in or night allergies to abate. My legendary early starts, due to poor sleep, may not actually suit me.

It took me just over four hours to reach the trig point summit of Slioch. With the guidebook stating the north top afforded a better view I crossed to it. However, it was covered in the same level of mist shrouding the trig point. Heading east I took in the minor top of Sgurr an Tuill Bhain before the southerly descent and the laborious walk back to the car, completing the walk in just under eight hours.

Now with just the four most northerly Munros to do, before Aonach Mor near Fort William, I surveyed the map and realised I might as well return to the Aultguish Inn. Finding a signal on my mobile, I called and they stalled about room availability.

"What about room thirty-two?" I asked.

"I suppose we could, but it isn't serviced yet."

"Well I checked out of it this morning, just pop a new towel in and I'll be over in an hour."

A rest day followed with a sweltering drive, and a beautiful blue sky, to Inchnadamph. Again I rued my day off being so fine.

I pitched the tent for a night's camping next to a wooded area. With midges swarming everywhere I zipped up the tent and settled down for the night.

I'm never that comfortable with rough camping and, as I snuggled in my sleeping bag, I feared somebody might come along and complain about my presence. My nerves weren't helped by an almighty crash, in the late evening, from the direction of the wood. It made me jump wildly and, with my heart thumping against my chest all sorts of thoughts went through my mind: A gang of bandits? A berserk axe murderer? Finally plucking up courage I went outside to explore and witnessed the beauty of the late evening light. Assuming it was a tree falling I retired back to bed.

I woke at 05:30 on Saturday the 7th with rain pouring on the tent and ruing my luck of yet another day of walking in poor weather. I lay in for a couple of hours, until the rain stopped. Dismantling the tent was a rapid affair amidst an attack by a multitude of midges.

I finally started walking, from Inchnadamph, for an attempt on Ben More Assynt and Conival, at just after 09:15. I soon hit thick cloud, making the indeterminate approach to Conival problematic. Again I was unhappy with my navigation and wasted a good hour backtracking, getting myself into a pickle. Seeing a couple of middle-aged walkers approach me I thought I'd see if they knew the exact location.

"Do you know where we are?" asked the chap.

They were as lost as I was – his Second World War compass was swinging about a bit. However, after a while we fathomed it out between us and I made the summit of Conival in four and a half hours with my newfound companions Jim and Sarah.

A further hour saw Ben More Assynt added to the list of climbed Munros and here we departed as I fancied going to look for a the wreckage of a Second World War Wellington bomber I had the grid reference for.

While re-ascending Conival, the most convenient path back, I hopped up onto a square boulder the size of a washing machine. Under my weight it tipped towards me and I had to leap in the air and forward to prevent it crushing me. Fortunately it only did the one roll, I wouldn't have wished to have been responsible for setting that off down the mountain. Unfortunately it jarred my body and set my left hernia into serious grumble mode and made the muscular discomfort in my right shoulder scream out under the weight of my pack.

Demoralised, I took a compass bearing to the Wellington Bomber. After a long march I hit water – any one of a number of lochs marked on the map. As the mist was so thick I couldn't make out its shape to determine which it was. For safety sake I took a west bearing to drop back towards Inchnadamph, completing the round trip in ten hours. I never did find the Wellington Bomber, I probably got as lost as its crew did all those years ago.

I spent the night at the Inchnadamph Field Studies Centre and, with only three Munros left to do, I had a bit of a lie-in before the drive round to take in Ben Klibreck.

What was supposed to be a straightforward Munro turned into another navigational nightmare. I could blame this on another day of thick mist, but in truth somewhere along the way I took my eye off the ball and ended up making a series of blunders.

The ascent went well, navigating to Loch na Glas-choille, then following the line of a fence rising to Loch nan Uan before the long pull to the summit, depicted by a standing trig point and the remains of a toppled derelict one. Trig points often get vandalised for keepsakes and one of the metal bits from this fallen trig point was lying free on the ground. I picked it up and contemplated, then decided it belonged to the mountain, so quietly hid it from view in its rightful place.

After food, Ibuprofen and Deep Heat I was ready for the off but was delayed by a sudden congregation – five people and a dog, in two separate parties, ascended on me and we had a good chat for about twenty minutes before I set off.

My navigation all went wrong on a piece of ridge half way down the steepest slope. Going too far south I dropped west onto wet peat-covered ground where I promptly slipped and slid on my bum for about twenty feet. Picking myself up, very wet and dirty, I continued but unsure of my location. After much marching west, in the hope of hitting Loch nan Uan, I hit water but, by its shape, I determined was Loch na Glas-choille. Somehow I missed Loch nan Uan. I then kept west until I reached my car followed by a drive around to Tongue Youth Hostel.

For many years I fancied Ben Hope as my final Munro, mainly because it is the most northerly and I liked the name – hope is part of the meaning of life.

However, hope was something I almost gave up on when the day started with a hiccup. Waking early I had a lie in and, after breakfasting, I was ready to go at the standard youth hostel 'getting your membership card back' time of 07:00. Unfortunately I'd failed to read a small notice saying the reception at Tongue Youth Hostel didn't open until 08:00 – different to the hostel handbook and every other Scottish Youth Hostel I have ever stayed in. This set me in a grumpy mood. I had plans to do Ben Hope and then make the long drive across to John O'Groats. My grumbling mind also reflected the night before; the warden had taken the trouble to point out the sign advertising their own 'Soup and Roll' but had failed to point out the one saying he likes a lie-in.

The walk up Ben Hope went well, starting alone the weather was good for the climb along a stream and then the long pull up the main slopes to the summit cairn and trig point where I was promptly deposited in cloud and cheated of a view. I hadn't had a proper view from a Munro since June 25th.

I was soon joined by a young couple who I lunched with and we jointly rued the lack of anything to look at but each other and cloud. They were impressed I only had one Munro left and were happy to take a photograph of me. Before leaving they asked, "Was that your car parked at the bottom?"

"The battered old Toyota?" I replied.

"Yes, we parked next to it at Ben More Assynt, Ben Klibreck and now Ben Hope."

"I suppose these most northerly ones have a certain order" I replied. "But I guess you were surprised to see it at Ben Klibreck?"

"Why?" replied the girl.

"Because it actually goes," I quipped.

On the descent the weather cleared – if only that damned warden had slept in until 09:00 I'd have had a view!

Bumping into a chap I'd seen the day before, at the summit of Ben Klibreck, I was greeted with, "Just one left now?"

Then I came across three other guys I'd also seen the day before and received the same greeting. The 'news' appeared to have got up and down the mountain and, as I descended, I bumped into a number of people who I'd never met before, asking, "Are you the guy with just one to go?"

It was quite touching I'd generated an interest.

The drive along the north coast of Scotland was nice – a mix of single track 'A' roads and beautiful coves. Noticing I was low on fuel I stopped at a roadside pump – the type that reminded me of my childhood where you could simply pull off the road and an attendant would come and fill your car. Well I kept this attendant talking, distracting him from the hole in my filler pipe busily depositing petrol on the bit of tarmac at the side of the road he optimistically referred to as his 'forecourt'.

As he was finishing up he told me some garages charge extortionate prices, far greater than his 91.9p per litre – already 14p per litre higher than the prices in Fort William. Still this wasn't Fort William and I needed to keep him distracted. I quickly paid by cash, something I'd started to do to make quick getaways. Setting off I checked my rear view mirror as he surveyed the puddle on his 'forecourt'.

Arriving in John O'Groats I booked a coach tour for the Orkneys for the next day then went in search of accommodation. Looking for John O'Groats Youth Hostel, I was just about on terms with them again, proved fruitless until I discovered it was three miles away at a place called Canisbay. Now call me Mr Picky but if you're advertising a youth hostel in the most north-easterly part of mainland Britain then wouldn't it be a good idea to actually put it there and not some few miles inland?

Parking, at the edge of the road, opposite the hostel, I crossed and entered.

"Was that you that just parked opposite?"

The middle-aged female warden was trying her charm.

"Yes," I replied.

"Well there is parking around the back."

"I'm sure but first I wanted to check you had a bed free for tonight."

"Yes I do, but please move your car right away."

Wandering out I realised I was already on a wrong footing, I find this with certain people. I don't know if I go around with a big sign above my head saying 'please take out all your pathetic frustrations on me' but it certainly feels like it at times. Knowing I wasn't going to enjoy the stay I moved my car, back to John O'Groats.

Trying one B&B that advertised 'from £14.50' which normally refers to one family room where the baby is charged at £14.50 I was informed there was no single room available but if I paid a surcharge I could have a double for £25. Not an extortionate price but with the foot and mouth disease Scotland was fairly empty and if I'd been the proprietor I'd have filled the rooms any old way and forgot about penalising people for remaining single.

Crossing the road I was greeted with a nice smile and a triple room for £20 and no supplement. I spent the remainder of the afternoon double checking I'd indeed climbed 283 Munros while noticing, rather wryly, the B&B opposite had its 'Vacancies' board up all evening.

Later in the evening I sat in the B&B's lounge. A fearsome

looking middle-aged Scottish woman, on hearing my English accent and raising the subject of tolls on the Skye Bridge, looked at me angrily and said, "I don't suppose there are any tolls in England."

Fortunately I was able to straighten that one out.

So followed some twelve days of pleasing myself, a genuine tourist in Scotland for once perhaps, taking a day trip to Orkney, a two day canoeing course and visiting various sites pending July the 21st.

It soon became apparent that, via Gisella's father, Mike Storm, the press were taking some interest in my Munroing. I was copied articles from the *Newbury Weekly News* and an inaccurate article from the *Wiltshire Gazette and Herald* overplaying my need for medical attention. However, the short fame was fun.

Holidaying with ones parents at the age of thirty-six could be seen as uncool, not since the age of sixteen had a family holiday been had so it was interesting when my mum and dad visited and we spent the two days together before the 21st. We had fun, walking to a bothy to make lunch, visiting Glen Roy and taking the train across Rannoch Mor. I found it strange having so much company, after two and a half months largely on my own having lengthy conversations was odd.

Walking on Air

Waking on July 21st, in the Spean Bridge Hotel, felt strange. I'd had weird dreams all night – my mind racing ahead for a conclusion of my twelve-year adventure.

At the foot of Aonach Mor I met with Willy Newlands who'd set off from Glasgow in the small hours; Ali Ashton and Adrian Ogden, both of who I met on the Cuillin Ridge course and their friend Kate Wilson who, as a threesome, humbled me by having driven up from Rotherham overnight.

Just after 08:15 Gisella, who'd driven up from Exeter the day before, waved us off.

We made good progress and it initially felt like any other walk, my mind not adjusting to what this was all about. At the top of the Gondola we rendezvoused with Gisella's parents and her aunty who'd come to wish me well and my mum and dad who were determined to walk the remaining 2000 feet with me.

I'd raised the subject of hernias with the others and how I'd be so grateful if they didn't get mentioned. My mum wouldn't have been too happy to discover I'd just climbed ninety-nine Munros with a double rupture. They duly promised not to mention them!

We made steady progress, my parents, unused to hill walking, needed a slower pace but I was touched they wanted to do this with me even though it was clearly a struggle for them at times. The last major walk I did with them was as a youngster when they were a lot stronger than me. Now age and having spent the best part of three months walking has made a difference. But they were determined and made a consistent pace.

Willy went on ahead and took in Aonach Beag and returned across Aonach Mor just as we were arriving. I could see the cairn through the thick cloud and I started to feel very strange and slightly emotional. Every time I stopped the others stopped behind me and, after a few further moments, I went forward and to the bemused looks of a chap sat quietly, eating his sandwiches, I touched the cairn, became a Munroist, turned to the others and celebrated with hugs, champagne and photographs.

On the descent Willy shot ahead. Worrying he'd decided to go on back, having an appointment in Glasgow that evening, I ran after him and caught him at the Gondola Restaurant. We soon found Gisella's family who'd waited there for us.

On the final leg from the Gondola Restaurant to the car

318

park I again walked with Willy. With my parents now out of earshot on the cable car he asked, "So how did you get the hernia, Steve?"

Back row: Kate, Ali & Adrian. Front row: Willy, Mum, me & Dad

"I did the splits on ice at Christmas, as simple as that. I didn't know until the next day when I had a dull ache and a lump."

"What kind of lump?"

"You can see it through my track suit trousers," I replied, tilting myself backwards and pointing to the lump on my lower abdomen. At this precise moment we passed under a gondola car with my mum banging on the glass and waving.

"How are you going to explain that one, Steve?"

"I have no idea, Willy, no idea."

Back at the car park we stood chatting until one by one people drifted off to go and get ready for the evening celebrations. With just me, Mum and Dad left a guy approached us. "I'm having a problem with the sliding door of my camper van."

"Oh," I replied in a 'please ask somebody else' kind of way.

"It won't take a moment, it just needs holding while I guide it back into the runner."

If alone I'd have explained a hernia and lifting aren't always a good combination but with my mum there I'd no choice but to suffer ten minutes of discomfort.

The Spean Bridge Hotel did us proud for an evening meal. With a separate room, we were all mellow and it was a lovely gentle occasion. I didn't want to over celebrate and enjoyed the peaceful company.

I was then asked me to make a speech and I simply read a piece of Hamish Brown's introduction to 'The Munros':

Completing the Munros is apt to be a humbling experience, a poignant time with a layer of sadness below the icing on the celebratory cake. It has meant so much for so long. Only a succession of hills, but so much of life lies suddenly behind. Golden memories of brassy expectations, but it was worth every mile and every smile of the way.

And that was exactly how I felt.

Munro Count: 284

Can You Spare Some Time to Give a Review?

Your honest opinion matters. You can rate this book on www.amazon.co.uk (under 'Your Orders' then the 'Write a product review' button) or www.goodreads.com

Many thanks.
Stephen P. Smith

About the Author

Along with the Munros Steve (as he prefers to be known) has also completed the Nuttalls, seven coast to coast crossings of Scotland and numerous other walks. These are also due to be published as books. He is currently working his way through the Donalds, Grahams and Corbetts.

Steve has also written two novels, The Unsound Convictions of Judge Stephen Mentall and The Veteran and The Boy. He has also had books published on computer programming and Charlie Chaplin, (a biography entitled 'The Charlie Chaplin Walk"). He has also written for TGO Magazine, Viz, The Oldie, NewsThump.com and also authors the Facebook page UKNewsFake.

Steve has a first class honours degree in Computing and Electronics, a field he then worked in for thirty years.

Steve is also a seasoned rail campaigner and in 2013 he received Rail Future's Clara Zilahi Award for Best Campaigner.

He is married with one child.

Glossary

Abhainn	River
Allt	Stream
Alt	Stream
An	The
Aonach	Ridge
Ban	White / fair
Beag	Little
Bealach	Pass
Beinn	Hill
Ben	Hill
Bheinn	Hill
Bidean	Hill – pointed or craggy peak
Breac	Speckled, spotted
Buidhe	Yellow
Buachaille	Shepherd
Caisteal	Castle
Carn	Stony hill
Ceann	Head
Clach	Rock
Coire	A steep-sided hollow at the head of a valley or on a mountain side
Corrie	A steep-sided hollow at the head of a valley or on a mountain side
Creag	Rock / cliff
Cruach	Round hill or stack
Damh	Stag
Dearg	Red
Doire	Copse
Druim	Ridge
Eag	Narrow gap

Eun	Bird
Fhada	Long
Fhuar	Cold
Fionn	Blond
Gaoith	Wind
Geal	White
Glas	Grey
Gleann	Glen
Gobhar	Goat
Gorm	Blue or Green
Inver	Confluence of waters, mouth of river
Iolaire	Eagle
Leathad	Broad Ridge
Liath	Grey
Linn	Waterfall / rushing water
Maol	Bare head
Meadhoin	Middle in size or position
Meall	Hill – lumpy or round hill
Mor	Big
Mullach	Indicates the top of something
Odhar	Brown
Ruadh	Red
Sail	Heel
Sgurr	Hill – pointed or craggy peak
Socach	Hill – snout shaped
Sron	Hill – nose shaped
Stac	Stack
Stob	Hill – lumpy or protruding
Stuc	Hill – Pinnacle or peak shaped
Tarsuinn	Transverse

Appendix 1: Brief note about my breathing

My Breathing Rate Compared With The Average

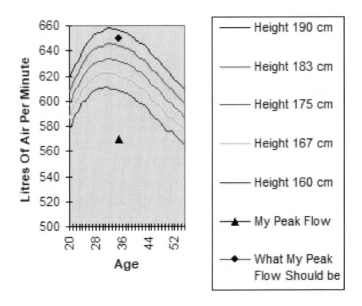

Peak flow is a measure of litres of air one can breathe per minute. The best I could achieve, when I was doing the Munros, was a reading of 570 litres per minute (depicted by the triangle in the above chart). This is below what it should be (about 650 – depicted by the circle in the above chart) and explains why I struggled so much during my mountain ascents.

Appendix 2: My Certificate

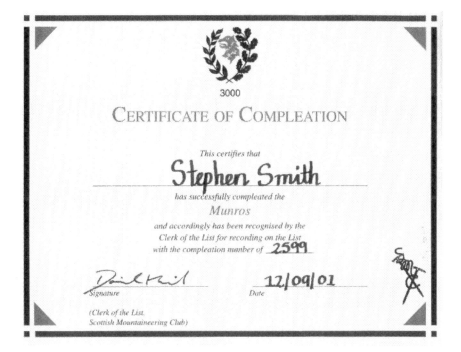

3000

CERTIFICATE OF COMPLEATION

This certifies that

Stephen Smith

has successfully compleated the

Munros

*and accordingly has been recognised by the
Clerk of the List for recording on the List
with the compleation number of* 2599

Signature   *Date* 12/09/01

*(Clerk of the List,
Scottish Mountaineering Club)*

Appendix 3: The Walks & Munros

The following table depicts all the Munros and tops I have climbed along with dates and, where recorded, time. Where I did not note the time I have used n/r (not recorded).

Munro names are emboldened, with the height in feet in brackets, and given a number in the right hand column – 'My Munro Number'. This number depicts the sequence in which I did the Munros. Munros I repeated are given the same number. This, in some places, makes the 'My Munro Column' appear out of sequence. You'll note this for the first entry where Cairn Gorm was 'bagged', at the age of 13, on a family holiday, and {9}/8/1978 is a best guess – I have a letter I wrote to a friend on 8/8/1978 where I did not mention the mountain, therefore I climbed it on the 9th, 10th or the 11th. However, the cable car was used so I don't count it until I climbed it properly on 26/8/1995 and made it my 39th Munro.

Some Munros took a few goes: for example An Stuc only yielded on the fourth attempt. For completeness I have included all abandoned attempts.

Occasionally I recorded the departure time from a summit. I have denoted these by 'Departed summit'. Where 'Departed summit' isn't shown no assumption can be made I left immediately. If it was a nice day I might have sat for some time, if poor weather I might only have stood on the summit, or crawled in high wind, for a matter of a second or so. Some of the memories have faded but the experience will be forever in my soul.

Date	Time	Location	My Munro Number
{9}/8/1978	n/r	Cairn Gorm Via cable car	39
14/5/1989	n/r	Mullardoch Cottage	
	n/r	NH218341. 861m peak above Loch Mullardoch. This was a Munro recce to see how I did with my asthma.	
	n/r	Mullardoch Cottage	
18/5/1989	n/r	Mullardoch Cottage	
	n/r	Abandoned Toll Creagach and Tom a'Choinich	
	n/r	Mullardoch Cottage	
7/5/1990	n/r	Glen Nevis	
	n/r	Abandoned Ben Nevis	
	1400	Carn Beag Dearg	
	n/r	Carn Dearg Meadhonach (a deleted top)	
	n/r	Carn Mor Dearg (4012)	1
	n/r	Glen Nevis	
6/5/1991	0915	NS360983	
	1145	Ben Lomond (3195)	2
	n/r	NS360983	
7/7/1991	n/r	The A87 (road)	
	n/r	Abandoned Sgurr na Ciste Duibhe and Sgurr Fhuaran	
	n/r	The A87 (road)	
10/7/1991	0850	Killilan	
	1630	An Socach (Mullardoch) (3507)	3
	n/r	An Riabhachan – West Top	
	n/r	An Riabhachan – Southwest Top	

Date	Time	Location	My Munro Number
	1845	An Riabhachan (3704)	4
	n/r	Abandoned Sgurr na Lapaich and Carn nan Gobhar	
	0000	Loch Mullardoch	
10/8/1991	1100	Tyndrum	
	1500	**Beinn Dubhchraig (3205)**	5
	1600	**Ben Oss (3373)**	6
	n/r	Tyndrum	
25/8/1991	1015	The A85 (road)	
	1250	**Ben More (Crianlarich) (3852)**	7
	1340	**Stob Binnein (3822)**	8
	n/r	The A85 (road)	
22/9/1991	1015	The A82 (road)	
	1230	**An Caisteal (3264)**	9
	1410	**Beinn a'Chroin (3084)**	10
	1615	The A82 (road)	
1/2/1992	1000	Garbat	
	n/r	An Cabar	
	1240	**Ben Wyvis – Glas Leathad Mor (3432)**	11
	n/r	Garbat	
24/5/1992	1045	NH217243	
	1350	**Toll Creagach (3458)**	12
	n/r	Toll Creagach – West Top	
	1535	**Tom a'Choinich (3645)**	13
	1745	NH217243	
25/5/1992	1130	South Ballachulish	
	1520	**Sgorr Dhearg – Beinn a'Bheithir (3360)**	14
	1650	**Sgorr Dhonuill – Beinn a'Bheithir (3284)**	15

Date	Time	Location	My Munro Number
	n/r	South Ballachulish	
28/5/1992	0810	Cluanie Inn	
	1105	Creag a'Mhaim (3107)	16
	1155	Druim Shionnach (3238)	17
	n/r	Druim Shionnach – West Top	
	1252	Aonach Air Chrith (3350)	18
	1419	Maol Chinn-dearg (3218)	19
	1525	Sgurr an Doire Leathain (3314)	20
	1610	Sgurr an Lochain (3294)	21
	1755	Creag nan Damh (3012)	22
	2000	West end of ridge	
29/8/1992	1025	Arrochar (Succoth)	
	1320	Beinn Narnain (3038)	23
	1532	Beinn Ime (3316)	24
	1835	Ben Vane (3002)	25
	2130	Inveruglas	
1/6/1993	1200	Ben Lawers visitor centre	
	n/r	Meall nan Tarmachan – South Top	
	1300	Meall nan Tarmachan (3422)	26
	n/r	Meall nan Tarmachan – Meall Garbh	
	n/r	Meall nan Tarmachan – Beinn nan Eachan	
	1800	Ben Lawers visitor centre	
3/6/1993	n/r	The A85 (road)	
	n/r	Abandoned Meall Glas and Sgiath Chuil	
	n/r	The A85 (road)	
4/6/1993	1105	Bridge of Orchy	
	1335	Beinn Dorain (3530)	27

Date	Time	Location	My Munro Number
	1520	Beinn an Dothaidh (3287)	28
	n/r	Bridge of Orchy	
1/5/1994	1030	Linn of Dee	
	1515	Beinn Bhrotain (3816)	29
	1640	Monadh Mor (3651)	30
	2230	Linn of Dee	
3/5/1994	1205	Glenn Shee Ski area	
	1325	The Cairnwell (3061)	31
	1545	Carn a'Gheoidh (3199)	32
	1810	Carn Aosda (3008)	33
	n/r	Glenn Shee Ski area	
5/5/1994	n/r	Inverey	
	1620	Derry Cairngorm (3789)	34
	n/r	Linn of Dee	
27/8/1994	1210	The A82 (road)	
	1700	Beinn Tulaichean (3104)	35
	1805	Cruach Ardrain (3431)	36
	n/r	The A82 (road)	
28/8/1994	1045	Ardlui	
	1505	Ben Vorlich (Loch Lomond) (3094)	37
	n/r	Ardlui	
30/6/1995	0742	Glen Nevis Youth Hostel	
	1200	Ben Nevis (4409)	38
	1255	Departed summit	
	1525	Glen Nevis Youth Hostel	
	1625	Fort William	
26/8/1995	0805	Camp at NH987072	
	1015	Ski Lift Restaurant	
	1130	Cairn Gorm (4085)	39

Date	Time	Location	My Munro Number
	n/r	Cairn Gorm – Stob Coire an t-Sneachda	
	1500	Ben Macdui (4295)	40
	1710	Camp at NJ010003	
27/8/1995	0830	Camp at NJ010003	
	0946	Beinn Mheadhoin (3878)	41
	1044	Camp at NJ010003	
	1330	Camp at NJ010003	
	n/r	Camp at Fords of Avon Refuge Hut NJ043032	
28/8/1995	0920	Camp at Fords of Avon Refuge Hut NJ043032	
	1051	Beinn a'Chaorainn (Cairngorms) (3550)	42
	1205	Camp at Fords of Avon Refuge Hut NJ043032	
	1330	Camp at Fords of Avon Refuge Hut NJ043032	
	1630	Foot of Bynack More (hid kit)	
	1750	Bynack More (3576)	43
	1925	Near Bynack Stable	
3/5/1996	1200	Inverarnan	
	1400	Start of main ascent.	
	1540	Beinn Chabhair (3061)	44
	1745	Inverarnan	
4/5/1996	0825	Ardvorlich	
	1230	Ben Vorlich (Loch Earn) (3232)	45
	1450	Stuc a'Chroin (3199)	46
	1750	Ardvorlich	
6/5/1996	0900	Invergeldie	
	1150	Ben Chonzie (3054)	47

Date	Time	Location	My Munro Number
	1220	Ben Chonzie	
	1400	Invergeldie	
7/5/1996	0840	Opposite viaduct on West Highland Railway line.	
	1140	Start of ascent	
	1350	**Beinn Mhanach (3130)**	48
	1720	Opposite viaduct on West Highland Railway line.	
9/5/1996	0920	The A83 (road)	
	1410	**Beinn Bhuidhe (3110)**	49
	1710	The A83 (road)	
10/5/1996	0820	Achallader Farm	
	1230	**Beinn Achaladair (3409)**	50
	n/r	Meall Buidhe	
	1430	**Beinn a'Chreachain (3547)**	51
	1810	Achallader Farm	
12/5/1996	1000	Mullardoch Cottage	
	1325	**Carn nan Gobhar (Mullardoch) (3255)**	52
	1545	**Sgurr na Lapaich (3772)**	53
	1915	Mullardoch Cottage	
14/5/1996	0934	East shore of Loch Mullardoch	
	1050	West shore of Loch Mullardoch	
	1345	**Beinn Fhionnlaidh (Carn Eige) (3297)**	54
	n/r	Stob Coire Lochan	
	1515	**Carn Eige (3881)**	55
	1625	**Mam Sodhail (3871)**	56
	1945	West shore of Loch Mullardoch	
	2050	East shore of Loch Mullardoch	
16/5/1996	1136	Achnasheen	

Date	Time	Location	My Munro Number
	1427	Fionn Bheinn (3061)	57
	1535	Achnasheen	
19/5/1996	0940	The A85 (road)	
	1155	Beinn a'Chleibh (3005)	58
	1326	Ben Lui (3707)	59
	1525	The A85 (road)	
20/5/1996	0820	Glen Lochay	
	1100	Meall Ghaordaidh (3409)	60
	1240	Glen Lochay	
8/9/1996	1200	Strathan	
	1800	Sourlies bothy	
9/9/1996	0800	Sourlies bothy	
	1335	Sgurr na Ciche (3415)	61
	1533	Garbh Chioch Mhor (3323)	62
	n/r	Abandoned Sgurr nan Coireachan and Sgurr Mor	
	2000	A' Chuil Bothy	
10/9/1996	n/r	A' Chuil Bothy	
	n/r	Strathan	
11/9/1996	1030	The A9 (road)	
	1335	Meall Chuaich (3120)	63
	1610	The A9 (road)	
12/9/1996	0930	The quarry track by the A9 (road).	
	1201	Carn na Caim (3087)	64
	n/r	Carn na Caim – South Top	
	1409	A' Bhuidheanach Bheag (3071)	65
	1619	The quarry track by the A9 (road).	
15/9/1996	0800	Glen Nevis Youth Hostel	
	1300	Ben Nevis (4409)	38
	1530	Glen Nevis Youth Hostel	
4/5/1997	1043	The A82 (road)	

Date	Time	Location	My Munro Number
	1503	Ben Challum (3363)	66
	1800	The A82 (road)	
5/5/1997	1000	Glen Lochay	
	n/r	Meall a' Churain	
	1400	Sgiath Chuil (3067)	67
	n/r	Beinn Cheathaich	
	1720	Meall Glas (3150)	68
	2000	Glen Lochay	
7/5/1997	0820	Glen Lochay	
	1210	Beinn Heasgarnich (3530) (I failed to find the summit cairn and went back on 5/6/1998 and properly bagged this one).	69
	1510	Creag Mhor (Glen Lochay) (3438)	70
	1710	Glen Lochay	
9/5/1997	0815	National Trust visitor's centre	
	1025	Beinn Ghlas (3619)	71
	1130	Ben Lawers (3983)	72
	1345	Meall Corranaich (3507)	73
	1520	Meall a'Choire Leith (3038)	74
	1805	National Trust visitor's centre	
10/5/1997	0830	Tombreck	
	1320	Meall Greigh (3284)	75
	1515	Meall Garbh (Ben Lawers) (3668)	76
	1710	Lawers	
12/5/1997	1002	Braes of Foss	
	1307	Schiehallion (3553)	77
	1527	Braes of Foss	
13/5/1997	0836	Invervar	
	1136	Carn Gorm (3373)	78
	n/r	An Sgorr	

Date	Time	Location	My Munro Number
	1250	Meall Garbh (Carn Mairg) (3176)	79
	n/r	Meall a' Bharr	
	1455	Carn Mairg (3415)	80
	1613	Creag Mhor (Meall na Aighean) (3218)	81
	1734	Invervar	
14/5/1997	0840	Glen Lyon	
	1058	Meall Buidhe (Glen Lyon) (3058)	82
	1211	My car in Glen Lyon	
	1235	My car in Glen Lyon	
	n/r	Sron Chona Chorein	
	1505	Stuchd an Lochain (3150)	83
	1657	Glen Lyon	
16/5/1997	0830	Falls of Cruachan	
	n/r	Stob Garbh	
	1201	Stob Daimh (3274)	84
	n/r	Drochaid Ghlas	
	1457	Ben Cruachan (3694)	85
	1743	Falls of Cruachan	
17/5/1997	0830	The B8077 (road)	
	1233	Beinn Eunaich (3245)	86
	1401	Beinn a'Chochuill (3215)	87
	1559	The B8077 (road)	
19/5/1997	0843	Glen Etive	
	1224	Ben Starav (3537)	88
	n/r	Stob Coire Dheirg	
	1459	Beinn nan Aighenan (3150)	89
	1709	Glas Bheinn Mhor (3271)	90
	1928	Glen Etive	
20/5/1997	0925	Elleric	
	1302	Beinn Sgulaird (3074)	91

Date	Time	Location	My Munro Number
	1546	Elleric	
22/5/1997	0840	Glen Coe	
	n/r	Stob Coire nam Beith	
	1206	**Bidean nam Bian (3773)**	92
	1553	Glen Coe	
23/5/1997	0831	Ski centre at the east end of Glen Coe	
	1100	**Meall a'Bhuiridh (3635)**	93
	1224	**Creise (3609)**	94
	1602	Ski centre at the east end of Glen Coe	
24/5/1997	n/r	Inverlael	
	n/r	NH214848	
25/5/1997	0740	NH214848	
	1111	**Beinn Dearg (Ullapool) (3556)**	95
	1252	**Cona' Mheall (3215)**	96
	1415	**Meall nan Ceapraichean (3205)**	97
	n/r	Ceann Garbh	
	1557	**Eididh nan Clach Geala (3045)**	98
	n/r	Abandoned Seana Bhraigh	
	2310	NH214848	
26/5/1997	n/r	NH214848	
	n/r	Inverlael	
29/5/1997	1052	Arnisdale	
	1401	**Beinn Sgritheall (3195)**	99
	1612	Arnisdale	
30/5/1997	1051	Glen Coe	
	1303	**Stob Dearg (Buachaille Etive Mor) (3353)**	100
	1516	Glen Coe	
31/5/1997	0809	Caolasnacon	

Date	Time	Location	My Munro Number
	1140	Meall Dearg (3127)	101
	n/r	Stob Coire Leith	
	1408	Sgorr nam Fiannaidh (3173)	102
	1608	Caolasnacon	
2/6/1997	0834	Glen Etive	
	1131	Stob coir an Albannaich (3425)	103
	1324	Meall nan Eun (3045)	104
	1549	Glen Etive	
3/6/1997	0850	Victoria Bridge (Forest Lodge)	
	1132	Stob a'Choire Odhair (3094)	105
	1335	Stob Ghabhar (3556)	106
	1716	Victoria Bridge (Forest Lodge)	
4/6/1997	0850	Glen Coe	
	1119	Buachaille Etive Beag (Stob Dubh) (3143)	107
	1333	Glen Coe	
6/6/1997	0947	Achnacon	
	1320	Sgor na h-Ulaidh (3261)	108
	1549	Achnacon	
7/6/1997	0920	Glen Etive	
	1302	Beinn Fhionnlaidh (Glen Etive) (3146)	109
	1531	Glen Etive	
8/6/1997	0920	Fersit	
	1148	Stob Coire Sgriodain (3202)	110
		Stob Coire Sgriodain – South Top	
	1310	Chno Dearg (3453)	111
	1448	Fersit	
9/6/1997	n/r	Strathan	
	n/r	A'Chuil Bothy	
10/6/1997	0550	A'Chuil Bothy	

Date	Time	Location	My Munro Number
	0851	Sgurr nan Coireachan (Glen Dessarry) (3127)	112
	1307	Sgurr Mor (Glen Dessarry) (3290)	113
	1622	A'Chuil Bothy	
11/6/1997	n/r	A'Chuil Bothy	
	n/r	Glen Pean Bothy	
12/6/1997	0840	Glen Pean Bothy	
	1134	Sgurr Thuilm (3159)	114
	1422	Sgurr nan Coireachan (Glen Pean) (3136)	115
	1638	Glen Pean Bothy	
13/6/1997	n/r	Glen Pean Bothy	
	n/r	Strathan	
14/6/1997	0932	North shore of Loch Quoich	
	1158	Gleouraich (3396)	116
	n/r	Craig Coire na Fiar Bhealaich	
	1438	Spidean Mialach (3268)	117
	1650	North shore of Loch Quoich	
15/6/1997	0816	Loch Quoich dam	
	1211	Gairich (3015)	118
	1519	Loch Quoich dam	
16/6/1997	0937	Quoich Bridge	
	1237	Sgurr a'Mhaoraich (3369)	119
	1534	Quoich Bridge	
18/6/1997	0725	Lay-by 84 on the A9 (road)	
	0922	Geal-Charn (Drumochter) (3008)	120
	1101	A' Mharconaich (3199)	121
	1216	Beinn Udlamain (3314)	122
	1344	Sgairneach Mhor (3251)	123
	1550	Lay-by 84 on the A9 (road)	
19/6/1997	1054	Garva Bridge	

Date	Time	Location	My Munro Number
	1338	Geal Charn (3038)	124
	1538	Garva Bridge	
20/6/1997	0825	Aberarder	
	1110	Carn Liath (Creag Meagaidh) (3300)	125
	n/r	Meall an t-Snaim	
	n/r	Sron Coire a' Chriochairein	
	1248	Stob Poite Coire Ardair (3455)	126
	1345	Creag Meagaidh (3707)	127
	1658	Aberarder	
9/4/1998	1304	Braedownie	
	1610	Driesh (3107)	128
	1714	Mayar (3045)	129
	1952	Braedownie	
13/4/1998	1101	Glen Banchor	
	1401	A' Chailleach (Monadhliath) (3051)	130
	n/r	Abandoned Carn Sgulain and Carn Dearg	
	1720	Glen Banchor	
18/4/1998	1422	Ben Lawers Visitor centre	
	1655	Beinn Ghlas (3619)	71
	1818	Foot of An Stuc	
	1822	Turned back, abandoned An Stuc	
	1934	Beinn Ghlas (3619)	71
	2046	Ben Lawers Visitor centre	
20/4/1998	1322	Lawers	
	n/r	Abandoned An Stuc	
	2105	Lawers	
23/4/1998	1005	The A93 (road)	
	n/r	Meall Odhar	

Date	Time	Location	My Munro Number
	1139	Glas Maol (3504)	131
	1233	Creag Leacach (3238)	132
	n/r	Creag Leacach – Southwest	
	1502	The A93 (road)	
14/5/1998	0845	Old Blair	
	1447	Beinn Dearg (Blair Atholl) (3307)	133
	1735	Old Blair	
16/5/1998	0810	Blair Atholl	
	1354	Carn a'Chlamain (3159)	134
	1537	Blair Atholl	
17/5/1998	0745	Loch Moraig	
	1012	Carn Liath (Beinn a'Ghlo) (3199)	135
	1209	Braigh Coire Chruinn-bhalgain (3510)	136
	1354	Carn nan Gabhar (3704)	137
	1732	Loch Moraig	
18/5/1998	0926	North of Glen Shee ski area	
	1132	Carn an Tuirc (3343)	138
	1225	Cairn of Claise (3491)	139
	1337	Tolmount (3143)	140
	1425	Tom Buidhe (3140)	141
	1725	North of Glen Shee ski area	
20/5/1998	0835	Linn of Dee	
	1242	Carn an Fhidhleir (3261)	142
	1431	An Sgarsoch (3300)	143
	1711	Linn of Dee	
21/5/1998	0750	Inverey	
	1154	Beinn Iutharn Mhor (3428)	144
	n/r	Carn Bhac – Southwest Summit	
	1437	Carn Bhac (3104)	145
	1709	Inverey	

Date	Time	Location	My Munro Number
22/5/1998	0905	Glen Shee Ski Area	
	1307	An Socach (Braemar) (3097)	146
	1618	Glen Shee Ski Area	
23/5/1998	0733	Spittal of Glenshee	
	1057	Glas Tulaichean (3448)	147
	1303	Carn an Righ (3376)	148
	1606	Spittal of Glenshee	
25/5/1998	0820	Loch Muick	
	1110	Lochnagar (3789)	149
	1207	Carn a'Choire Bhoidheach (3668)	150
	1307	Carn an t-Sagairt Mor (3435)	151
	1344	Cairn Bannoch (3320)	152
	n/r	Cairn of Gowal	
	1420	Broad Cairn (3274)	153
	1658	Loch Muick	
26/5/1998	0720	Linn of Dee	
	1025	Beinn Bhreac (3054)	154
	1227	Linn of Dee	
27/5/1998	0830	Invercauld	
	1410	Ben Avon (3842)	155
	n/r	Abandoned Beinn a'Bhuird	
	1731	Invercauld	
28/5/1998	0803	Linn of Quoich	
	1318	Beinn a'Bhuird (3924)	156
	1610	Linn of Quoich	
30/5/1998	0703	Linn of Dee	
	1147	The Devil's Point (3294)	157
	n/r	Stob Coire an t-Saighdeir	
	1338	Cairn Toul (4242)	158
	1433	Sgor an Lochain Uaine (4127)	159
	n/r	Carn na Criche	

Date	Time	Location	My Munro Number
	1600	Braeriach (4252)	160
	2142	Linn of Dee	
31/5/1998	1017	Glen Tanar	
	1333	Mount Keen (3081)	161
	1527	Glen Tanar	
1/6/1998	0912	Linn of Dee	
	1228	Carn a'Mhaim (3402)	162
	1514	Linn of Dee	
2/6/1998	0939	Auchlean	
	n/r	Carn Ban Mor	
	1249	Sgor Gaoith (3668)	163
	1509	Mullach Clach a'Bhlair (3343)	164
	1752	Auchlean	
4/6/1998	0832	Glen Banchor	
	1203	Carn Dearg (Monadhliath) (3100)	165
	n/r	Carn Ban	
	n/r	Carn Ballach	
	1450	Carn Sgulain (3018)	166
	1712	Glen Banchor	
5/6/1998	0910	High point in the road connecting Glen Lochay and Glen Lyon	
	1151	Beinn Heasgarnich (3530)	69
	1348	High point in the road connecting Glen Lochay and Glen Lyon	
6/6/1998	0911	Glen Coe	
	n/r	Stob Coire Altruim	
	1255	Stob na Broige (Buachaille Etive Mor) (3136)	167
	1515	Glen Coe	
2/4/1999	1003	NM507368	
	1435	Ben More (Mull) (3169)	168

342

Date	Time	Location	My Munro Number
	1705	NM507368	
6/4/1999	1055	Lawers Hotel	
	1320	**Meall Greigh (3284)**	75
	n/r	Abandoned An Stuc	
	1555	Lawers Hotel	
3/7/1999	0835	Glen Nevis	
	1200	**An Gearanach (3222)**	169
	n/r	An Garbhanach	
	1304	**Stob Coire a'Chairn (3218)**	170
	1423	**Am Bodach (3386)**	171
	1532	Sgor an Iubhair (3286)	
	n/r	Stob Choire a' Mhail	
	1649	**Sgurr a'Mhaim (3606)**	172
	1947	Glen Nevis	
4/7/1999	0825	Glen Nevis	
	1220	**Mullach nan Coirean (3081)**	173
	n/r	Mullach nan Coirean – Southeast Top	
	1420	**Stob Ban (The Mamores) (3277)**	174
	1759	Glen Nevis	
5/7/1999	0847	Roughburn	
	1213	Beinn a'Chaorainn – South Top	
	1230	**Beinn a'Chaorainn (Glen Spean) (3451)**	175
	1301	Beinn a'Chaorainn – North Top	
	1536	**Beinn Teallach (3002)**	176
	1739	Roughburn	
2/7/2000	0825	Drumsallie	
	n/r	Gulvain – South Top	
	1310	**Gulvain (3238)**	177
	1410	Departed summit	

343

Date	Time	Location	My Munro Number
	1805	Drumsallie	
3/7/2000	0800	Kilfinnan	
	1210	Meall na Teanga (3008)	178
	1235	Departed summit	
	1415	Sron a'Choire Ghairbh (3067)	179
	1445	Departed summit	
	1710	Kilfinnan	
4/7/2000	0800	Fersit	
	1140	Stob a'Choire Mheadhoin (3629)	180
	1150	Departed summit	
	1254	Stob Coire Easain (3661)	181
	1335	Departed summit	
	1715	Fersit	
6/7/2000	0710	Loch Ossian Youth Hostel	
	1037	Sgor Choinnich	
	1037	Departed summit	
	1117	Sgor Gaibhre (3133)	182
	1130	Departed summit	
	1234	Carn Dearg (Corrour) (3087)	183
	1405	Departed summit	
	1530	Loch Ossian Youth Hostel	
7/7/2000	0655	Loch Ossian Youth Hostel	
	0905	Beinn na Lap (3074)	184
	0915	Departed summit	
	1030	Loch Ossian Youth Hostel	
2/5/2001	0832	Glen Coe	
	1240	Stob Coire Sgreamhach (3517)	185
	n/r	Abandoned Stob Coire Raineach	
	n/r	Bidean nam Bian (3773)	92
	1705	Glen Coe	
3/5/2001	0848	Glen Coe	

Date	Time	Location	My Munro Number
	1137	Stob Coire Raineach (3035)	186
	1417	Glen Coe	
4/5/2001	0655	Kinlochleven	
	1114	Sgurr Eilde Mor (3307)	187
	1346	Binnein Beag (3084)	188
	n/r	Abandoned Binnein Mor and Na Gruagaichean	
	1757	Kinlochleven	
6/5/2001	n/r	Dalwhinnie	
	n/r	Culra Bothy	
7/5/2001	0547	Culra Bothy	
	0825	Beinn Bheoil (3343)	189
	n/r	Sron Coire na h-Iolaire	
	1110	Ben Alder (3766)	190
	1520	Culra Bothy	
8/5/2001	0636	Culra Bothy	
	0838	Carn Dearg (Loch Pattack) (3392)	191
	n/r	Abandoned Geal-Charn and Aonach Beag	
	1309	Beinn Eibhinn (3609)	192
	n/r	Abandoned Aonach Beag and Geal-Charn	
	1800	Culra Bothy	
10/5/2001	0555	Culra Bothy	
	0917	Beinn a'Chlachair (3569)	193
	1151	Creag Pitridh (3031)	194
	1321	Geal Charn (3442)	195
	1732	Culra Bothy	
11/5/2001	0546	Culra Bothy	
	0902	Geal-Charn (Alder) (3714)	196
	0934	Aonach Beag (Alder) (3655)	197

Date	Time	Location	My Munro Number
	1258	Culra Bothy	
	n/r	Culra Bothy	
	n/r	Dalwhinnie	
13/5/2001	0759	The A87 (road)	
	1028	**Sgurr na Ciste Duibhe (3369)**	198
	1135	**Sgurr na Carnach (3287)**	199
	1222	**Sgurr Fhuaran (3504)**	200
	n/r	Sgurr nan Spainteach	
	1639	**Saileag (3146)**	201
	1757	The A87 (road)	
14/5/2001	0848	The A87 (road)	
	1121	**Carn Ghluasaid (3140)**	202
	n/r	Creag a' Chaorainn	
	1234	**Sgurr nan Conbhairean (3642)**	203
	1329	**Sail Chaorainn (3287)**	204
	1650	The A87 (road)	
17/5/2001	0753	The A87 (road)	
	1038	**Ciste Dhubh (3222)**	205
	n/r	Sgurr an Fhuarail	
	1308	**Aonach Meadhoin (3291)**	206
	1410	**Sgurr a'Bhealaich Dheirg (3405)**	207
	1744	The A87 (road)	
20/5/2001	0918	Southeast of Sligachan Inn	
	1230	**Bruach na Frithe (3143)**	208
	1421	**Sgurr nan Gillean (3166)**	209
	n/r	Basteir Tooth	
	1603	**Am Basteir (3068)**	210
	1803	Southeast of Sligachan Inn	
21/5/2001	0936	Glenbrittle House	
	1302	Base of the Inaccessible Pinnacle	
	1404	**Inaccessible Pinnacle (Sgurr**	211

Date	Time	Location	My Munro Number
		Dearg) (3235)	
	1739	Glenbrittle House	
22/5/2001	0938	Glenbrittle Youth Hostel	
	1227	Sgurr a'Mhadaidh (3012)	212
	1326	Sgurr a'Ghreadaidh (3192)	213
	1533	Sgurr na Banachdich (3166)	214
	n/r	Sgurr na Banachdich Central Top	
	1723	Glenbrittle Youth Hostel	
23/5/2001	1052	Glen Brittle	
	1409	Loch Coir a Ghrunnda (camp)	
	1533	Loch Coir a Ghrunnda (camp)	
	1641	Sgurr nan Eag (3037)	215
	n/r	Sgurr Dubh an Da Bheinn	
	1901	Sgurr Dubh Mor (3097)	216
	2033	Loch Coir a Ghrunnda (camp)	
24/5/2001	0838	Loch Coir a Ghrunnda (camp)	
	n/r	Sgurr Thearlaich	
	1047	Sgurr Alasdair (3258)	217
	1229	Loch Coir a Ghrunnda (camp)	
	1328	Loch Coir a Ghrunnda (camp)	
	1607	Glen Brittle	
25/5/2001	1034	Loch Slapin	
	1300	Bla Bheinn (3045)	218
	1447	Loch Slapin	
26/5/2001	0916	Glen Brittle	
	1236	Sgurr Mhic Choinnich (3110)	219
	1541	Glen Brittle	
27/5/2001	0916	The A87 (road)	
	1228	The Saddle (3314)	220
	n/r	Sgurr na Sgine – Northwest Top	
	1421	Sgurr na Sgine (3100)	221

Date	Time	Location	My Munro Number
	1650	The A87 (road)	
28/5/2001	0842	The A87 (road)	
	1116	A' Chralaig (3674)	222
	n/r	Stob Coire na Cralaig	
	1231	Mullach Fraoch-choire (3615)	223
	1603	The A87 (road)	
29/5/2001	1000	Mamore Lodge hotel	
	1230	Na Gruagaichean (3461)	224
	n/r	Binnein Mor – South Top	
	1336	Binnein Mor (3701)	225
	1613	Mamore Lodge hotel	
30/5/2001	0728	National Trust visitor centre	
	n/r	Creag an Fhithich	
	1014	An Stuc (3668)	226
	1224	National Trust visitor centre	
4/6/2001	1026	Northwest end of Loch Glascarnoch	
	1317	Am Faochagach (3130)	227
	1531	Northwest end of Loch Glascarnoch	
5/6/2001	0831	Core Mhic Nobuil bridge car park	
	1050	Tom na Gruagaich (3025)	228
	1159	Sgurr Mor (Beinn Alligin) (3232)	229
	1444	Core Mhic Nobuil bridge car park	
6/6/2001	0650	The A896 (road)	
	n/r	Stob a'Coire Liath Mhor	
	0948	Spidean a'Choire Leith (Liathach) (3458)	230
	1149	The A896 (road)	
	1217	The A896 (road)	
	1516	Mullach an Rathain (Liathach)	231

348

Date	Time	Location	My Munro Number
		(3356)	
	1722	The A896 (road)	
7/6/2001	0830	The A896 (road)	
	1253	Ruadh-stac Mor (Beinn Eighe) (3314)	232
	1444	Spidean Coire nan Clach (Beinn Eighe) (3258)	233
	1652	The A896 (road)	
8/6/2001	0950	The A890 (road)	
	1155	Moruisg (3045)	234
	1320	Sgurr nan Ceannaichean (3002) This Munro was later demoted to a Corbett	235
	1517	The A890 (road)	
9/6/2001	0741	Achnashellach Station	
	1122	Beinn Liath Mhor (3035)	236
	1317	Sgorr Ruadh (3150)	237
	1632	Achnashellach Station	
11/6/2001	0621	Gerry's Hostel	
	1024	Sgurr Choinnich (3277)	238
	1111	Sgurr a'Chaorachain (3455)	239
	n/r	Carn Nam Fiaclan	
	1405	Maoile Lunndaidh (3304)	240
	1808	Gerry's Hostel	
12/6/2001	0617	Gerry's Hostel	
	n/r	Beinn Tharsuinn (Corbett)	
	1229	Bidein a'Choire Sheasgaich (3100)	241
	1336	Lurg Mhor (3235)	242
	1845	Gerry's Hostel	
14/6/2001	0657	Coulags	
	0953	Maol Chean-dearg (3061)	243

Date	Time	Location	My Munro Number
	1225	Coulags	
	n/r	The A87 (road)	
	n/r	Glen Affric Youth Hostel	
15/6/2001	0645	Glen Affric Youth Hostel	
	0839	An Socach (Affric) (3018)	244
	n/r	Stob Coire na Cloiche	
	1028	Sgurr nan Ceathreamhnan (3776)	245
	n/r	Carn na Con Dhu	
	1230	Mullach na Dheiragain (3222)	246
	1622	Glen Affric Youth Hostel	
16/6/2001	n/r	Glen Affric Youth Hostel	
	n/r	The A87 (road)	
17/6/2001	0613	Strath Croe	
	0900	A' Ghlas-bheinn (3012)	247
	1215	Beinn Fhada (Ben Attow) (3386)	248
	1445	Strath Croe	
18/6/2001	0909	The A832 (road) near Loch a'Bhraoin	
	1111	Meall a'Chrasgaidh (3064)	249
	1210	Sgurr nan Clach Geala (3586)	250
	1249	Sgurr nan Each (3028)	251
	1438	Sgurr Breac (3281)	252
	1542	A' Chailleach (Fannich) (3277)	253
	1756	The A832 (road) near Loch a'Bhraoin	
19/6/2001	0752	Loch Glascarnoch	
	1120	Beinn Liath Mhor Fannaich (3130)	254
	n/r	Abandoned Sgurr Mor, Meall Gorm and An Coileachan	
	1448	Loch Glascarnoch	

Date	Time	Location	My Munro Number
20/6/2001	0708	Strathconon	
	1050	Carn nan Gobhar (Strathfarrar) (3255)	255
	1245	Sgurr na Ruaidhe (3258)	256
	1623	Strathconon	
21/6/2001	0937	Strathfarrar	
	1151	Sgurr Fhuar-thuill (3441)	257
	n/r	Creag Ghorm a'Bhealaich	
	1248	Sgurr a'Choire Ghlais (3553)	258
	n/r	Sgurr na Fearstaig	
	1540	Strathfarrar	
23/6/2001	n/r	The A832 (road) Corrie Hallie	
	n/r	Shenavall	
24/6/2001	0728	Shenavall	
	1041	Beinn a'Chlaidheimh (3000) This Munro was later demoted to a Corbett	259
	1238	Sgurr Ban (3245)	260
	1344	Mullach Coire Mhic Fhearchair (3343)	261
	1513	Beinn Tarsuinn (3071)	262
	1822	A' Mhaighdean (3173)	263
	1929	Ruadh Stac Mor (3012)	264
	2257	Shenavall	
25/6/2001	1100	Shenavall	
	1300	Dumped kit	
	n/r	Sail Liath	
	1600	Sgurr Fiona (3474)	265
	1707	Bidein a'Ghlas Thuill (An Teallach) (3484)	266
	1909	Collected kit	

Date	Time	Location	My Munro Number
	2030	The A832 (road) Corrie Hallie	
26/6/2001	n/r	Kinloch Hourn	
	n/r	Barrisdale	
27/6/2001	0717	Barrisdale	
	1136	**Ladhar Bheinn (3346)**	267
	1503	Barrisdale	
28/6/2001	0719	Barrisdale	
	1012	**Luinne Bheinn (3080)**	268
	n/r	Luinne Bheinn – East Top	
	n/r	Meall Buidhe – East Top	
	1247	**Meall Buidhe (Knoydart) (3104)**	269
	1822	Barrisdale	
29/6/2001	n/r	Barrisdale	
	n/r	Kinloch Hourn	
30/6/2001	0924	Glen Nevis	
	n/r	Sgurr Choinnich Beag	
	1309	**Sgurr Choinnich Mor (3592)**	270
	n/r	Stob Coire Easain	
	1417	**Stob Coire an Laoigh (3658)**	271
	1438	Departed summit	
	n/r	Caisteal (Caisteil)	
	n/r	Stob Coire Cath na Sine	
	n/r	Stob a' Choire Leith	
	1538	**Stob Choire Claurigh (3861)**	272
	1707	**Stob Ban (Grey Corries) (3205)**	273
	2028	Glen Nevis	
1/7/2001	0912	Glen Nevis	
	n/r	Sgurr a'Bhuic	
	n/r	Stob Choire Bhealach	
	1333	**Aonach Beag (Nevis Range) (4048)**	274

Date	Time	Location	My Munro Number
	1625	Glen Nevis	
3/7/2001	0642	Inverlael	
	1232	**Seana Bhraigh (3041)**	275
	1649	Inverlael	
4/7/2001	0617	The A832 (road)	
	n/r	Carn na Criche	
	1010	**Sgurr Mor (Fannich) (3645)**	276
	n/r	Meall nam Peithirean	
	1122	**Meall Gorm (3113)**	277
	n/r	Meall Gorm – Southeast Top	
	1222	**An Coileachan (3028)**	278
	1752	The A832 (road)	
5/7/2001	0922	Incheril	
	1323	**Slioch (3215)**	279
	n/r	Sgurr an Tuill Bhain	
	1705	Incheril	
7/7/2001	0916	Inchnadamph	
	1345	**Conival (3238)**	280
	1454	**Ben More Assynt (3274)**	281
	1913	Inchnadamph	
8/7/2001	1045	The A836 (road)	
	1325	**Ben Klibreck (3153)**	282
	1645	The A836 (road)	
9/7/2001	0836	Minor road to west of Ben Hope	
	1054	**Ben Hope (3041)**	283
	1248	Minor road to west of Ben Hope	
21/7/2001	0817	Foot of the gondola	
	1341	**Aonach Mor (4006)**	284 ☺
	1641	Foot of the gondola	
17/5/2002	n/r	**Mullach Clach a'Bhlair (3343)**	164

Date	Time	Location	My Munro Number
23/5/2006	n/r	Cairn Bannoch – Crow Craigies	
6/2/2009	n/r	**Cairn Gorm (4085)**	39
11/7/2009	n/r	**Schiehallion (3553)**	77

Index

A

B

M

N

R

S

Printed in Great Britain
by Amazon